THE NORTH CAROLINA ROOTS OF
AFRICAN AMERICAN LITERATURE

© 2006
The University of North Carolina Press
All rights reserved
Manufactured in the United States of America
Designed and typeset in Monticello
by Eric M. Brooks

The paper in this book meets the guidelines
for permanence and durability of the Committee on
Production Guidelines for Book Longevity of
the Council on Library Resources.

A gift from the Paul Green Foundation
provided copies of this book to a number of
public school libraries in North Carolina.

Library of Congress
Cataloging-in-Publication Data
The North Carolina roots of African American literature:
an anthology / William L. Andrews, general editor.
p. cm.   Includes bibliographical references.
ISBN-13: 978-0-8078-2994-3 (alk. paper)
ISBN-10: 0-8078-2994-3 (alk. paper)
ISBN-13: 978-0-8078-5665-9 (pbk.: alk. paper)
ISBN-10: 0-8078-5665-7 (pbk.: alk. paper)
1. American literature—North Carolina. 2. American
literature—African American authors. 3. African
Americans—North Carolina—Intellectual life. 4. African
Americans—Literary collections. 5. North Carolina—
Literary collections. 6. African Americans—North
Carolina. I. Andrews, William L., 1946–
PS558.N8N625   2006
810.8'08960730756—dc22   2005016883

cloth   10 09 08 07 06   5 4 3 2 1
paper   10 09 08 07 06   5 4 3 2 1

CONTENTS

ACKNOWLEDGMENTS

William L. Andrews would like to
thank Robert G. Anthony, Jeffrey J. Crow, and
David S. Cecelski for sound advice and thoughtful
suggestions during the planning stages of this book,
the Center for the Study of the American South for grant
support, and Sian Hunter, David Perry, and Kate Torrey
for their interest in and support of this project at the
University of North Carolina Press. The editors
of this book are also grateful to the staff at
the North Carolina State Archives, and in
particular, Steve Massengill, for help
with photographic archives.

THE NORTH CAROLINA ROOTS OF
AFRICAN AMERICAN LITERATURE

INTRODUCTION

No other state in the American South has left a more indelible impression on African American literature before the twentieth century than has North Carolina. While white writers from the state produced little of lasting literary value before the twentieth century, nineteenth-century black North Carolina engendered poetry, autobiography, fiction, essays, and polemical writing that are still widely read and studied today. These classics by black North Carolina writers helped to form the bedrock of African American literature. Critics and historians now see many of these texts as foundational to the development of a truly national literature in the United States. This volume of writing by North Carolina's pioneering African American writers—George Moses Horton of Chatham County, David Walker of Wilmington, Moses Roper of Caswell County, Lunsford Lane of Raleigh, Harriet Jacobs of Edenton, Charles W. Chesnutt of Fayetteville, Anna Julia Cooper of Raleigh, and David Bryant Fulton of Wilmington—aims to provide for the first time a representative sampling of the breadth and richness of this literature.

The North Carolina Roots of African American Literature sheds light on many phases of black life in the state during the nineteenth century, from the slavery era to the turn of the century. Additional texts in this volume offer wider viewpoints on African American and inter-racial experience in the South, as well as in the North. Although the memories and imaginations of the eight men and women featured in this anthology were firmly rooted in North Carolina, all ultimately became literary expatriates from the state, a decision that was for most of them a prerequisite to their becoming writers. Traveling widely, in some cases internationally, after they left the state, they parlayed what might seem the relative disadvantages of their North Carolina beginnings into a seasoned and sophisticated perspective on the best and the worst of which humanity, black and white, South and North, was capable in America. The result, by the end of the nineteenth century, was a literary tradition whose distinctiveness, particularly insofar as its North Carolina common denominator is concerned, merits both attention and appreciation today.

❖   ❖   ❖

After exploring the remarkable quality and variety of black North Carolina writing from the nineteenth century, readers may ponder, as have the editors of this book, the tantalizing question of why: Why should North Carolina, among all the states of the old Confederacy, have given to African American and American literature such a disproportionate number of key black writers during the most turbulent century in the state's history? Is it merely a curious coincidence, this outpouring of African American literary talent from a state that embraced slavery in the first half of the nineteenth century and, by 1900, saw fit to humiliate its black citizenry by amending its constitution to ensure their effective disfranchisement?[1] At both the middle and the end of the nineteenth century, several states of the Old South, among them Virginia, South Carolina, Georgia, Alabama, and Mississippi, had larger African American populations than North Carolina's. None of these states, however, produced black writers in the numbers or of the caliber and reputation of North Carolina's classic African American literary pioneers.[2] If the American South or New England can lay claim to regionally specific literary traditions by virtue of the accomplishments of writers born in those regions, may individual states also make such claims on similar bases? Without advancing confident answers to these questions, this introduction to the writers and works featured in *The North Carolina Roots of African American Literature* will also comment on factors that seem germane to the rise in nineteenth-century North Carolina of the extraordinary contingent of African American writers represented in this book.

From the enslaved poet George Moses Horton, the first African American to publish a book in the South, to Charles W. Chesnutt, the first African American to win national critical acclaim for his fiction, black writers were responsible for putting North Carolina on the national literary map in the nineteenth century. Before 1829, when Horton's first book of verse, *The Hope of Liberty*, appeared in Raleigh, North Carolina's contribution to American literature had been all but negligible.[3] Dubbed "the state's first professional poet" by one historian of North Carolina literature,[4] Horton not only gave the state its first noteworthy poetic voice. He also became the first poet, and indeed the first belletristic writer, from North Carolina to attract more than a local reading audience. The fact that in 1828 Horton's verse could be found in the Lancaster, Massachusetts, *Gazette* and in *Freedom's Journal*, a New York African American newspaper, as well as in the Raleigh *Register*, testifies to the national attention that the slave poet from North Carolina earned even before his first book came out. Whether such notice, though a boon to Horton and to early African American literature, did North Carolina's social and political reputation much good is debatable. The poet's anguished chafing under the restraints of slavery was the most memorable theme of Horton's earliest published verse. Though blaming no one specifically for "the sad disgrace / In which enslaved I lie," "On Liberty and Slavery" (1828) left no doubt as to the poet's fervent desire for a better life in freedom. Whether that "blest asylum" might be found in North Carolina or elsewhere, Horton's poetry did not say.

The appearance of a slave poet in national newspapers and soon thereafter in his own volume of verse was astonishing enough in late-1820s America, but a black man using poetry actively to condemn his enslavement and to lobby for his freedom was quite unheard of, especially in the South. That this signal instance of African American poetic self-assertion came from a slave in the North Carolina Piedmont, rather than from the Virginia tidewater, the South Carolina low country, or the emerging cotton plantations of Georgia, Alabama, or Mississippi, was significant in itself. Horton's experience of bondage in central North Carolina was different from what the average enslaved black man of similar talents and aspirations would have known in many other parts of the South. These differences point up characteristics of slavery in North Carolina that both encouraged and frustrated Horton's endeavor to become a free man and a published author.

As a slave state, North Carolina was from its inception during the colonial era something of an anomaly, especially compared to neighboring South Carolina and Virginia. "The small farms of colonial North Carolina" never rivaled either in size or in slaveholding "the burgeoning tobacco plantations of Virginia" or "the swampy rice plantations of South Carolina."[5] In a few eastern North Carolina counties, where tobacco, rice, and the naval stores industries prospered, large plantations survived into the nineteenth century. But because slaveholding was an expensive proposition, which the predominantly yeoman farmers of North Carolina could ill afford, only one white household in four in the state ever claimed slaves.[6] By 1860, of the seven southern states in which the plantation system was well entrenched, North Carolina ranked next to last in slave population, just slightly ahead of Louisiana.[7] In a state in which slaveholding was plainly not the norm, notions of what a slave might do or aspire to were not as restrictive or dogmatic in the 1820s as they were in other southern states, or would be in North Carolina itself by the middle of the nineteenth century.

William Horton, George's master until he was eighteen years old, typified slaveholders in North Carolina in the early nineteenth century. When George was three years old, the 1800 census-taker in Chatham County recorded eight slaves in William Horton's possession.[8] All but one was a blood relative of George. The ratio of slaves to slaveholder in the Horton household was about average for the state at that time. Far from playing the lord of the manor, North Carolina farmers like William Horton usually worked alongside their slaves in the fields.[9] George recalled his master's penchant for inviting his slaves to share a dram with him after a day's work.[10] Under such circumstances, interpersonal relationships between masters and slaves were more likely to develop, for good and for ill, in North Carolina's regimen of slavery than in the routinized anonymity of labor required by the highly stratified plantation system in other southern states.

From his boyhood, George Moses Horton worked hard plowing his master's fields and tending to his stock. Seeking respite in his imagination, he began to teach himself to read. Although hard-bitten William Horton had little use for education for his children or his slaves, he did not punish George when he realized his slave was devoting his nonwork time to reading the Bible and his mother's Wesleyan hymnbook. By the time he was twenty years old, George had managed to secure another privilege from his master, the right to leave the Horton farm each Saturday and walk eight miles to Chapel Hill, home of the state university, to sell love poems, which the slave had composed while plowing during the week, to students eager for romantic rhymes that they could send to their sweethearts. Around the time *The Hope of Liberty* came out, the slave poet became a full-time resident of Chapel Hill, having negotiated with his master to hire his time—that is, to work independently, provide for his own needs, and return a portion of his earnings regularly to his master.[11] In the early nineteenth century, the practice of allowing skilled slaves to hire their time troubled many slaveholders, who believed, not without reason, that slaves granted so much control over their daily lives were primed to seize complete freedom as soon as they could.[12] Horton's early poetry testified to his deep yearning for freedom, but he was not desperate enough to attempt a risky escape to the North. Instead, he either sought or agreed to white sponsorship for a unique literary venture, the publication of a small book, *The Hope of Liberty*, the profits of which might prove substantial enough to allow the poet to purchase his freedom.

There was a catch, however, to the whole undertaking, which exemplifies the ironic mix of opportunity and denial that enslavement in North

Carolina entailed for George Moses Horton. On the one hand, the obscure farm worker from Chatham had managed to exploit the racial caste system very effectively, to the point at which he seemed on the verge of not only freedom but genuine fulfillment as an artist. On the other hand, in order to avail himself of the unprecedented chance to publish his way out of slavery and make a name for himself as an author, Horton had to promise, once his royalties had paid for his freedom, that he would depart from North Carolina and move permanently to Liberia. Was emigration to West Africa Horton's idea? Or was it a condition placed on the entire undertaking by his sponsor, Joseph Gales, editor of the Raleigh *Register*, which not only published several of Horton's poems but was also one of the leading antislavery newspapers in the state?[13] These questions are at present unanswerable. What we do know is that in the late 1820s Gales was secretary of the regional chapter of the American Colonization Society, which opposed slavery but also advocated enforced emigration to its colony, Liberia, for emancipated American slaves.

In one sense, Horton was fortunate to seek his freedom in a state whose antislavery credentials in the year of the publication of *The Hope of Liberty* were not inconsiderable. North Carolina had ten active branches of the American Colonization Society in the late 1820s and 100 chapters of a statewide Manumission Society (which also espoused Horton's cause).[14] On the other hand, Horton must have felt that exile was a painful price indeed for the kind of freedom his North Carolina antislavery supporters like Gales expected him to accept. This, in turn, may help to explain why Horton wrote his "Lines, On hearing of the intention of a gentleman to purchase the Poet's freedom" even before *The Hope of Liberty* came out. Perhaps this unknown "gentleman" represented to the poet a way of attaining his freedom that did not require him to uproot his life and pursue his destiny in a foreign land.

Nothing came of the campaign to secure Horton's freedom via the publication of *The Hope of Liberty*. A second volume, *The Poetical Works of George M. Horton, the Colored Bard of North-Carolina*, appeared from a Hillsborough, North Carolina, publisher in 1845, demonstrating Horton's continuing good standing with whites in and around Chapel Hill. In *The Poetical Works*, Horton's gift for homely comic verse, such as "Troubled with the Itch, and Rubbing with Sulphur," and his ability to assume multiple dramatic personae, such as the envious, exasperated creditor in "The Creditor to His Proud Debtor," show that he was much more than a poetic protester against slavery. Still, not until the Ninth Michigan Cavalry Volunteers occupied Chapel Hill in April 1865 did Horton achieve his freedom. In the summer of that year the 68-year-old poet published a final volume, *Naked Genius*, in Raleigh. The following year, he left North Carolina for Philadelphia. Despite the lingering fondness for North Carolina expressed in "The Southern Refugee" (1865), there is no evidence that Horton ever returned to the place he called "my ever devoted home."

Publicity in the North generated by Horton's poetic petitions for freedom caught the attention of Wilmington, North Carolina, native David Walker, in his adoptive home of Boston.[15] The principal subscription agent for *Freedom's Journal* in Boston, Walker was moved by the black newspaper's call for contributions to the poet's purchase price, reputedly $500, and in October 1828 made his own donation to his fellow North Carolinian's emancipation. What Walker thought of Horton's poetry is not known. But had he read Gales's introduction to *The Hope of Liberty*, in which the editor assured the reader that Horton had agreed to go to Liberia once emancipated, Walker, an avowed anti-emigrationist, would likely have felt serious reservations about donating to the slave poet's cause. In Boston's thriving black community, Walker had earned considerable respect as a defender of his race and an organizer of people of color for the purpose of social, political, and economic advancement. Fueling his vision of a united black America, militantly antislavery and dedicated unto the death to full civil and human rights for all black Americans, was Walker's conviction that every black man, especially those who could marshal the potent political weapon of literacy, had fundamental responsibilities to his people. Chief among them was to stay in the United States, develop a liberating self- and social awareness, and prepare himself, in Walker's own electrifying words, to "fight under our Lord and Master Jesus Christ, in the glorious and heavenly cause of freedom and of God."[16]

Walker issued this famous call to action, which thrilled black readers and alarmed whites, in a pamphlet, *Walker's Appeal, in Four Articles; Together with a Preamble, to the Colored Citizens of the World, but in Particular, and Very Expressly, to those of the United States of America*, which he published in Boston in 1829 only a few months after *The Hope of Liberty* was released. In this pamphlet of less than one hundred pages, Walker inveighed against slavery as nothing less than a crime against humanity, excoriated slaveholders, even those as respectable as Thomas Jefferson and Henry Clay, as tyrannous enemies of God, and denounced the American Colonization Society as hypocritical and deceitful. Whether Horton's first book had any effect on the tone or timing of *Walker's Ap-*

peal is not known. In several important ways the two men, like their two books, were strikingly different. Horton was born and raised a slave in rural North Carolina. Based on what little is known about Walker, he was born free around 1796 (about the same time as Horton) in Wilmington, North Carolina's biggest city and busiest seaport.

Wilmington's sizable and resourceful black community evidently had a strong impact on Walker.[17] The city's black population, which outnumbered whites by more than two to one, was notoriously difficult to monitor and control despite ordinances enacted by the city's commissioners and laws passed in the North Carolina General Assembly designed to regulate the conduct of urban blacks in the larger towns of eastern North Carolina, such as Wilmington, Washington, Edenton, and Fayetteville.[18] Before and since the triumph of the Haitian Revolution in 1802, rumors of uprisings against slavery pulsed through Wilmington, as well as other North Carolina seaports, galvanizing slaves to resist their oppression in countless ways.[19] In North Carolina's larger towns, enterprising and unruly slaves took their cue from free blacks and exploited the relative freedom of urban life to assert their social and economic interests. When Walker was still a small boy, white mechanics in Wilmington petitioned the North Carolina General Assembly to crack down on slaves who hired themselves out as free mechanics and took on building contracts from whites at a fraction of what a white mechanic would charge.[20] Wilmington's vibrant African American churches were also suspect in the eyes of many whites in the city. Walker's dynamic faith in a God who would deliver black people, as he had the Old Testament Israelites, from the injustice of slavery, was no doubt inculcated in him in a black church, probably of the Methodist persuasion, in Wilmington.

Despite all that black self-assertion had done to create a culture of resistance in early-nineteenth-century Wilmington, growing up in this racially tense coastal city must have constituted a contradictory and paradoxical heritage for a thoughtful black youth like David Walker. Unlike the enslaved George Moses Horton, who idealized freedom in his verse, Walker, though free from his birth, knew the real limitations that his color placed on his supposed freedom. He was never dependent on a particular white man for his basic necessities, or for those privileges—such as the right to read the Bible, or go to town on weekends, or hire his time—that Horton had to extract from his master, probably through careful cultivation. Nevertheless, Wilmington seems to have taught Walker that in some ways the free Negro's lot was more galling than that of the slave. A slave like Horton had to serve a particular white master.

Free Negroes like Walker were, in truth if not in title, slaves without masters.[21]

When David Walker was born in the late eighteenth century, free Negroes in North Carolina were a very small minority. Although Wilmington was a predominantly black city, only nineteen free Negroes lived there in 1800. Between 1790 and 1860 the free Negro population of North Carolina grew by 604 percent, faster than the white or the slave populations of the state. During Walker's residence in Wilmington, however, free Negroes remained virtually invisible. Though an endangered minority, free Negroes in North Carolina enjoyed a status before the law accorded few of their peers in other slave states. Until 1835, free blacks exercised the right to vote in North Carolina. By contrast, the free black populations of antebellum Virginia and South Carolina never had the franchise, while Connecticut, New Jersey, and Pennsylvania disfranchised their black citizenry well before North Carolina chose to do so. Free Negroes in North Carolina had the right to own firearms until 1840; their right to trial by jury was never denied during the antebellum era. "The lag of North Carolina behind the other states in the enactment of harsh free Negro legislation [during the antebellum era] and the laxity with which existing laws were enforced suggests a type of liberalism that existed in few other states in the South." But Walker probably knew, as the historian John Hope Franklin has concluded, that the state's apparent "liberalism" did not stem from "any humanitarianism peculiar to the State" but was attributable, more than likely, to socioeconomic factors, such as "the economic instability of the slave system" in North Carolina and "the presence of a large yeoman class" that did not benefit directly from slavery or have any direct investment in it.[22]

Growing up in the tiny free black minority in Wilmington, despite the advantages that free Negroes in North Carolina enjoyed relative to the situation of free people of color elsewhere in the South, must have made David Walker increasingly aware of the incapacitating isolation that threatened his future. Unlike the largely urbanized free Negroes of other southern states, North Carolina's free black population was dispersed and rural. In his home state, Walker could either be satisfied with a kind of desperate self-sufficiency or seek community elsewhere. Leaving the state in the mid-1820s, first for Charleston, South Carolina, one of the South's biggest cities (with one of its most spirited black communities), and ultimately for Boston, a sizable northern city with another thriving black community, let Walker search for a place where he could find a new kind of freedom based in a more fulfilling sense of community. *Walker's Appeal*

INTRODUCTION

exudes the sense of renewal its author found in Boston. It is also infused with a sense of mission: the redemption of free black Americans mentally, morally, and socially, so that they could lead an antislavery vanguard that would purge the United States, in blood if necessary, of the national crime of slavery.

It is not surprising, therefore, that a black man from North Carolina, who never experienced formal enslavement a day in his life but who never could call himself free either, conceived the most penetrating analysis and the most eloquent denunciation of slavery written during the first fifty years of U.S. history. Growing up in Wilmington and ending up in Boston, Walker understood that as long as slavery dictated the prospects of black people anywhere in America, every so-called free black person was condemned, whether aware of it or not, to a life-in-death sentence. Instead of seeing their quasi-freedom as something to be thankful for, or even to take pride in, Walker appealed to his fellow free blacks—"*My dearly beloved Brethren and Fellow Citizens,*" he called them in his Pre-amble—to adopt a more inclusive sense of identity, one that would not discriminate between them and the enslaved but would rather bind them, slave and quasi-free, in a mutually liberating African American national consciousness. "Your full glory and happiness," he assured his free black readership, "shall never be fully consummated, but with the *entire eman-cipation of your enslaved brethren all over the world.*"[23] This ideal of global solidarity among the peoples of the African diaspora is one of the main reasons why *Walker's Appeal* is considered the first major articulation of black nationalism in U.S. literature.

As if to model his ideal of African American solidarity, Walker an-nounced, "I am one of the oppressed, degraded and wretched sons of Af-rica, rendered so by the avaricious and unmerciful, among the whites.—If any wish to plunge me into the wretched incapacity of a slave, or murder me for the truth, know ye, that I am in the hand of God, and at your disposal. I count my life not dear unto me, but I am ready to be offered at any moment. For what is the use of living, when in fact I am dead."[24] Whether Walker was prophesying his own death or referring to what the historian Orlando Patterson has called the "social death" of the slaves in the eyes of American law,[25] less than a year after the appearance of the *Appeal*, its author was dead. North Carolina met the news of the covert circulation of the *Appeal* in its seaports with legislation that outlawed any book that might "excite insurrection, conspiracy or resistance in the slaves or free Negroes and persons of colour within the State." Fear of the *Appeal* also led to the enactment in 1830 of North Carolina's first statute criminalizing the teaching of slaves to read or write.[26] Outside the South, however, *Walker's Appeal* voiced the most compelling rallying cry ever heard in America for an immediate, uncompromising end to slavery.

Walker's unapologetic, "tell-it-like-it-is" brand of antislavery rhetoric, though not the violence that some felt he called for, energized and emboldened antislavery activism in the United States. As the American antislavery movement gravitated toward a more radical agenda, one that condemned slavery absolutely and demanded its immediate and total abolition, abolitionists became convinced that the eyewitness testimony of former slaves against slavery would touch the hearts and change the minds of many in the northern population of the United States who were either ignorant of or indifferent to the plight of African Americans in the South. Although autobiographies by ex-slaves had been introduced into the international debates over slavery in the late eighteenth century, by the late 1830s the antislavery movements in Britain and America were vying to see who could find actual fugitives from slavery willing to speak frankly about the evils of the system and their resistance to it. The goal was to heighten the pressure on the apologists for slavery by publishing hard-hitting narratives of fugitives from human bondage, whose testimony would highlight the violence and cruelty of the institution that slavery's defenders refused to acknowledge. In the late 1830s, the first shock wave of the fugitive slave narrative appeared, led by *A Narrative of the Adventures and Escape of Moses Roper, from American Slavery.*[27] The author of this unprecedented exposé was a twenty-two-year-old runaway whose career in slavery had begun in Caswell County, North Carolina.

Published in London in 1837, Roper's *Narrative* told a horrific story made all the more unsettling by the deadpan manner of its telling. Promising his readers "an impartial statement of facts" (p. 95), the author introduces himself in the opening scene as the son of a white man, identified only as Mr. Roper in the text,[28] whose wife, on the day of Moses's birth, attempts to murder him after being informed "that I was white, and resembled Mr. Roper very much" (p. 96). Instead of evincing the shame nineteenth-century white readers would have expected from the bastard son of an illicit interracial union, Roper simply recounts his story, leaving his reader to decide who should be held morally accountable for the circumstances of his birth. The farther the reader goes in Roper's *Narrative*, the more he or she realizes that, in marked contrast to David Walker, Roper was hesitant to denounce the monstrous behavior of slaveholders, despite an education in cruelty and brutality that would seem to justify fully Walker's characterization of whites as "acting more like devils than accountable men" (p. 87). As if to underline his commitment to Christian forgiveness, by the end of his *Narrative* Roper insists, "I bear no enmity even to the slave-holders, but regret their delusions" (p. 137). Roper's seemingly charitable disposition toward those who abused and exploited him may be genuine, or it may be a deliberate rhetorical stance constructed to allow the fugitive slave to posit a crucial difference between himself and those who once claimed him as their property. The difference has to do with control over the passionate, irrational, and destructive impulses that lie within humankind, waiting to be unleashed. By carefully maintaining a *dis*passionate, almost puzzlingly detached tone as he relates his life in slavery, Roper quietly but effectively draws a telling contrast between himself and the majority of the slaveholders profiled in his story. The former slave seems reliably self-controlled and evenhanded, while his antagonists, the slaveholders, goaded by absolute power and unbridled passions, succumb to the most appalling callousness and brutality. Thus Roper's *Narrative* seems designed to counter one of the principal assumptions about race on which slavery was based, namely, that because black people were supposedly subhuman and irrational, they needed the mastery and direction of their presumed intellectual superiors, the whites.

Roper says little about his day-to-day life as a slave in North and South Carolina. The early part of his *Narrative* portrays slavery as less a socio-economic institution than a nightmarish hell on earth presided over by malign, near-demonic slaveholders. In the face of such an all-out assault on his body and spirit, Roper has no choice but to run, even though he has little chance of gaining more than a temporary respite from his tormentors. The repetitive nature of his perilous "adventures and escape"—the more he runs away, the more savagely he is punished, which precipitates yet another escape attempt—suggests the slave's inevitable entrapment and defeat. Yet Roper survives, continues to resist, and ultimately finds his way to freedom. That this teenage slave, alone and largely unassisted, was able to beat the odds, traveling hundreds of miles across Georgia to Savannah before booking passage to New York, is eloquent testimony to Roper's faith, determination, and resilience. His successful passage from slavery to freedom also proves how resourceful Roper was in converting what initially seemed his greatest liability into what eventually became his greatest asset.

From the outset of his life, as well as of his *Narrative*, the fact "that I was white" portends nothing but trouble for Moses Roper. The harrowing account of the day of his birth demonstrates that Roper's incongruous whiteness could trigger anxious, even violent, reaction from slaveholders. The occasion of the white slave's first sale, when he was about seven, was because of "my resembling my father so very much, and being whiter than the other slaves" (p. 97). Purchased by a doctor to work in his shop mixing medicines, the slave boy finds himself unexpectedly dispatched to his master's cotton plantation, "that I might be burnt darker by the sun" (p. 97). The origins of the sadistic animus of Roper's chief tormentor, a South Carolina cotton planter named Mr. Gooch, seem hard to fathom until we remember the perturbing effect that the slave's skin color had on many of the whites he encountered. Thus, although Roper does not identify a motive, the most fiendish of Gooch's reprisals against Roper—pouring tar on the slave's head and face and then lighting it with a torch—can be interpreted as yet another attempt on the part of whites to burn and blacken Roper's skin, thereby denigrating him, quite literally, in order to differentiate him from themselves.

Characteristically, Roper declines to speculate on the anxieties his mere existence seems to have raised in many whites. He leaves it to his reader to discern how threatening his whiteness was to those in the American South for whom skin color provided the accepted basis for the prerogative they claimed to hold "blacks" as slaves. The autographed frontispiece of Roper's *Narrative*, depicting a well-dressed, dignified young gentleman whose evidently "white" facial features are crowned by a mass of well-groomed kinky hair, must have shocked thousands of readers who assumed they knew what a slave looked like. Even more confounding and distressing to slaveholding men and women in the South was the actual physical presence of a white Negro such as Roper, whose color, instead of registering a prescribed caste status in the slaveocracy (black or white), represented a blank, which could be filled in by anyone, including Roper himself.

As slaveholders try their best to fix the white slave's status by darkening him, Roper proves increasingly imaginative in exploiting his color, rather than being exploited by it. Emerging from the depressing cycle of futile escapes, capture, torture, and renewed flight, Roper the victim, to whom his color seems a kind of curse, evolves into Roper the victor, who adapts his appearance into protective coloration and disguise for a series of increasingly wily forays to freedom. On the back roads and byways of the rural and urban South, Roper becomes an accomplished trickster, reminiscent of the picaresque hero of European and American literature, skillfully turning white people's thoughtless prejudices about color and race to his benefit. Although his readers may find both justice and ironic delight in Roper's trickery, he professes from the outset of his story regret over certain aspects of his conduct on the road, "which I now deeply deplore" (p. 95). "The ignorance in which the poor slaves are kept by their masters, precludes almost the possibility of their being alive to any moral duties" (pp. 95–96), Roper assures his readers. We cannot be certain as to whether Roper truly repented of his duplicitous behavior while trying to elude his captors, or whether these sentiments were just another mask that he felt obliged to adopt as he penned his pioneering fugitive slave narrative. The literary journey that he charted for himself as a fugitive slave narrator, unsure of how much his white readers really wanted to know about his escape artistry or the slave community's survival ethic that justified it, was every bit as uncertain as the routes he took as a literal fugitive from the South to the North and ultimately to England.

A Narrative of the Adventures and Escape of Moses Roper, from American Slavery was the prototype for the classic American slave narratives of the 1840s as authored by internationally renowned fugitives such as Frederick Douglass, William Wells Brown, Henry Bibb, and James W. C. Pennington.[29] Less self-revealing and rhetorically contentious than its more famous successors, Roper's Narrative set a template, nevertheless, on which its literary descendants could build and capitalize in later years. Although his autobiography did not bestow on Roper the fame in the United States that the narratives of Douglass, Brown, Bibb, and Pennington gave these men a decade later, the publication of Roper's Narrative was by no means a small-gauge event. Quickly reprinted in Philadelphia, Roper's story became one of the hardiest sellers on the international antislavery booklist. The title page of the expanded 1848 edition (reprinted in this volume) announces that 36,000 copies of the Narrative were in circulation. Within twenty years of its initial appearance, the Narrative of the Adventures and Escape of Moses Roper had gone through ten British and American editions, including a translation into Celtic. Although Roper's narrative was one of the most influential books authored by an African American in the first half of the nineteenth century, he himself remains a shadowy figure about whom almost nothing is known after the publication of the expanded edition of his autobiography.

In the summer of 1842 a second fugitive from North Carolina slavery published his life story, this time in Boston, where the author had been banished for, the subtitle of his autobiography proclaimed, "the crime of wearing a colored skin." The Narrative of Lunsford Lane, formerly of Raleigh, N.C. could hardly be more different from the Narrative of the Adventures and Escape of Moses Roper, from American Slavery in terms of their portrayal of slavery and of slaveholders. Nevertheless, despite Lane's comparatively mild experience of bondage and his friendly relations with many influential whites in the state capitol of North Carolina, both Roper and Lane concluded their stories on a note of relief and gratitude after having eluded what Lane called "the stern, cruel, hated hand of slavery" (p. 168).[30] Lane was never menaced by the physical cruelties that Roper cataloged in excruciating detail in his story. Still, Lane engaged the sympathy of his northern readers with his account of the mental and emotional cruelty suffered daily by men like himself, slaves who were also husbands and fathers. Unlike Roper, who, being single and unattached, had only his own welfare to consult when he tried to flee his bondage, Lane, as husband and father, was so bound up in familial commitments that the idea of escaping slavery, if he pondered it at all, must have seemed either hopelessly impractical (how could one escape with a family in tow?) or emotionally self-defeating (what good was freedom apart from one's family?). The cruelly ironic outcome of Lane's successful purchase of his freedom in Raleigh, namely, his obligation to provide for his still-enslaved wife and children while remaining powerless to protect them from harm or sale, would not have been lost on Lane's readers either.

Published by its author rather than by an antislavery society, *The Narrative of Lunsford Lane* was well-received. It went through three additional reprintings within the first six years of its appearance. Twenty years after his autobiography came out, Lane remained important enough in the antislavery movement to warrant a full-length, white-authored biography, *Lunsford Lane; or, Another Helper from North Carolina*, which was published in Boston in 1863.[31] Nevertheless, by the late 1840s, with the advent of suspenseful narratives of struggle and flight authored by Douglass, Brown, Bibb, and Pennington, antislavery publishers evinced a decided preference for slave narratives by runaways cast in the Moses Roper mold. Such men struck more than one white reviewer as embodiments of nineteenth-century Romantic ideals of heroism, not to mention black American versions of rugged individualism.[32] By contrast, a man like Lunsford Lane, who had to pursue a more indirect and more compromised route to freedom, seemed a less gallant, though perhaps more representative, alternative to the ideal of unconquerable black masculinity retailed in more famous narratives such as Douglass's.

Although accounts of intrepid plantation rebels in quest of freedom were more thrilling than stories of men and women who worked day and night to buy their freedom, in fact the number of successful antebellum escapees to the North was extremely small. In North Carolina, for instance, between 1838 and 1860, researchers have identified only 114 black male runaways out of a slave population in 1840 of 245,817 and in 1850 of 288,548.[33] Yet between 1840 and 1850, the number of free Negroes living in North Carolina increased by more than 4,500.[34] While only a minority of this growing population of free Negroes in North Carolina were likely to have purchased their freedom (the majority were granted their freedom by their masters for "meritorious service"), it is unlikely that the number of slaves, like Roper, who successfully escaped to the North, was greater than the number of slaves, like Lane, who, through patience and diligence, managed to amass sufficient money to buy themselves. Thus, although the admiration accorded to escapees like Roper and Douglass remains both well-deserved and understandable, the perhaps less glorious example of Lunsford Lane reminds us that among the many routes to freedom, self-purchase, though it might seem today a compromise with slavery, was for some the only realistic option and the most effective means of resisting the threat of slavery to African American families.[35]

In addition to its remarkable focus on the plight of an enslaved family man, *The Narrative of Lunsford Lane* was also unprecedented for its examination of a form of slavery that abolitionist protest had hardly acknowledged before—urban slavery. While Roper's narrative shed light on the punishing daily routine and frightful atrocities endured by those worked dawn to dusk in the cotton fields of the Carolinas, Lane's account of his life in Raleigh showed that even the most favored of slaves—urban-dwellers with skills in the trades the South valued most—found enslavement all the more unbearable when viewed in the light of the degree of relative freedom they also enjoyed. Acknowledging that he was "comparatively happy" during his enslavement and expressing profound thanks to God "that I was not born a plantation slave, nor even a house servant under what is termed a hard and cruel master,"[36] Lane shows how persistent anxieties and suppressed resentments, belying an unscarred, apparently contented exterior, afflicted even the most fortunate among North Carolina's enslaved.

Born in Raleigh in 1803, the slave of Sherwood Haywood, a former clerk of the North Carolina Senate who owned three large plantations outside the city, Lane grew up largely exempt from field work on his master's plantations, although "any other business my master or any of his family had for me to do" kept Lunsford plenty busy (p. 146). Forestalling complacency about his lot in life was Lane's boyhood awareness of how much more his master's children could expect in and from the future than could he. Having grown up in an intact, though enslaved, family made Lane all the more troubled about the possibility that somehow he might yet be sold away from his kin. The more favored, Lane seems to suggest about slaves like himself, the more fearful they inevitably became about a future that could so quickly be snatched away from them.

Perhaps to allay these fears, Lane as a youth dedicated himself to making money. In the process of telling his story, Lane's *Narrative* becomes one of the rare firsthand antebellum accounts of a successful black entrepreneur who was also a slave. Ambitious, industrious, and well-connected through his master to other important whites, Lane and his father, Edward, took advantage of an 1826 North Carolina law that allowed slaves, with the permission of their masters, to trade in certain items, among them cotton, corn, and tobacco.[37] By 1829, having discovered a way to prepare a pleasing and increasingly popular blend of smoking tobacco, Lane had convinced his mistress, widowed and in debt, to let him hire his time for an annual payment of between $100 and $120. Having purchased, in effect, the independence he needed to become a full-time businessman, Lane along with his father set up their own private firm as retail tobacconists, which soon expanded via branches in Fayetteville, Salisbury, and Chapel Hill. A shrewd operator, Lane adapted the code of Benjamin Franklin, white America's archetypal man on the make, to his situation as an upwardly mobile city slave intent on gaining his freedom. "Ever after I entertained the first idea of being free," Lunsford wrote, "I had endeavored so to conduct myself as not to become obnoxious to the white inhabitants, knowing as I did their power, and their hostility to the colored people. The two points necessary in such a case I had kept constantly in mind. First, I had made no display of the little property or money I possessed, but in every way I wore as much as possible the aspect of poverty. Second, I had never appeared to be even so intelligent as I really was. This all colored people at the south, free and slaves, find it peculiarly necessary to their own comfort and safety to observe" (p. 159). Comments such as these indicate that, however accommodating Lane may have appeared on the streets of Raleigh, he had a private agenda too, which, if not in outright opposition to slavery, was subversive of its economic foundation, the concentration of wealth and power in the hands of whites alone.

The Narrative of Lunsford Lane is in many respects an extraordinary, but utterly American, success story. Unfortunately for Lane, the successes he earned for himself as a slave came at increasingly higher prices as he progressed steadily toward freedom. Indicative of the contradictions built into his status as first a slave and then a free Negro, Lane's strategy proved both a resounding success and a galling failure. Readers of his autobiography watch him evolve from upwardly mobile slave, who gets along by going along, into politic and ingratiating free man, who hopes that his connections among those whites whom he calls "the first men and the more wealthy" of Raleigh (p. 164) will help him circumvent North Carolina's repressive laws governing free blacks. (One of his white supporters, Weston R. Gales, son of the publisher of Horton's *Hope of Liberty*, co-signed a letter of recommendation for Lane.) Only at the climax of his *Narrative*, however, when he faces a crowd of white bullies in the shadow of the gallows in the Raleigh city commons, does Lane finally realize that all his hard work, political maneuvering, and careful cultivation of white patrons, instead of making his color and achievements less offensive, actually made him more vulnerable to white class, as well as caste, resentments. *The Narrative of Lunsford Lane* comes eventually to a satisfying ending. But the liberating disillusionment that highlights the climax of the story raises a question pondered by many subsequent narratives of middle-class striving in African American autobiography and fiction: do the acquisition of wealth and the social respectability that goes with it constitute a blow against white supremacy or a subtler co-optation by it?

The enslaved father of Harriet Jacobs, author of the first woman's slave narrative in the United States, experienced advantages and endured frustrations similar to those Lane recounted in his narrative. Elijah Jacobs, born and raised near the seacoast town of Edenton on the Albemarle Sound, was a skilled carpenter who, like George Moses Horton and Lunsford Lane, earned the privilege of hiring his time. He married into probably the most respected and well-connected African American family in Edenton, the Horniblow clan, headed by Elijah's mother-in-law, Molly Horniblow, who, although a slave, served as the unofficial manager of the town's most prominent tavern. Elijah and his wife, Delilah, were privileged enough to be allowed to set up housekeeping in their own home near the Horniblow tavern, which gave little Harriet the opportunity to grow up in the "hub of Edenton's slave society."[38] Sheltered by her parents, nurtured by her large extended family, and taught by her indulgent mistress to read and sew, Harriet was unaware until the age of six that she was a slave. By the time she was twelve, when she was willed by her dying mistress into the hands of Edenton's main physician, Dr. James Norcom, Harriet had imbibed her family's strong sense of self-esteem and their equally staunch belief in freedom as their ultimate right.

Installed in the Norcom household as a nursemaid, Harriet soon realized her master's concealed agenda—to make the light-skinned, attractive, and bright slave girl his concubine. Thus began what Jacobs called in her unique slave narrative, *Incidents in the Life of a Slave Girl*, "the war of my life."[39] The struggle, Jacobs makes clear in her narrative, was not simply over a teenage slave's virginity. Even more important to young Harriet—perhaps because she sensed it was also paramount to her abuser, Norcom—was the issue of power. Would Norcom browbeat his female slave into submission, or would Harriet resist with enough pride and tenacity to deny Norcom what he desired most, triumph over her will, as well as her body? Published in 1861 after she had lived in New England as a fugitive slave and later a free woman for almost twenty years, *Incidents* represents a singularly probing analysis of the sexual intimidation and exploitation that was endemic to slavery, though few even in the antislavery movement had dared to acknowledge, in Jacobs's words, "how deep, and dark, and foul is that pit of abominations" (pp. 178–79).

Harriet Jacobs broke this silence. Why this North Carolina woman took it upon herself to delve into slavery's special curse for women, exposing a topic that Moses Roper had declared was "too disgusting" to be broached in a public narrative (p. 104), a topic that was likely to scandalize and draw a blame-the-victim response from most readers of the time, is one of the most intriguing aspects of Jacobs's literary mission. We know that on making her escape from Edenton in 1842, Jacobs did not arrive in the North primed to write her autobiography, as had Roper, Lane, and other famous fugitives of the 1840s and 1850s. Jacobs took up the burden of writing her life's story only after her freedom had been secured in 1852 by a well-meaning employer who bought the fugitive slave's freedom to protect her from slave catchers. The preface to *Incidents* shows that its author was so uneasy about revealing her history that she refused to name names—even her own—preferring instead to give all the major characters in her story pseudonyms. Had her story exalted a virtuous slave girl's triumph over a lecherous master, Jacobs would have been much less disposed to write behind a mask. But *Incidents* could not be adapted to any established literary form or conventional moral standard. The truth, as well as her sense of responsibility to other slave women, demanded that Jacobs reveal the constricting ethical entanglements forged by slavery, which made "virtue," that is, sexual purity, traditionally considered woman's most sacred treasure, almost impossible for an enslaved woman to maintain.

The tenth chapter of *Incidents*, now one of the most famous passages in African American women's literature, tells how fifteen-year-old Harriet Jacobs decided that the only way to outwit and elude the repulsive Dr. Flint (Norcom) was to enter into a sexual liaison with a young unmarried Edenton attorney, who is called Mr. Sands in the autobiography. "I knew what I did," Jacobs admits unhesitatingly, "and I did it with deliberate calculation." "I will not try to screen myself behind the plea of compulsion from a master; for it was not so. Neither can I plead ignorance or thoughtlessness." This wording was risky, since it could have been construed as reinforcing contemporary stereotypes of black women as sexually aggressive, conniving, and promiscuous threats to white families. On the other hand, excusing herself as ignorant or thoughtless would have evoked an image of the author as merely a victim, the near-helpless object of a white man's desire. For Jacobs it was much more important to represent black American women, especially those once enslaved, as agents of their own destiny, no matter how compromised by their circumstances, than to acquiesce to the familiar image of slave women in antislavery propaganda as hopeless and humiliated victims. Even in the midst of her desperate dilemma—to become her master's concubine or another white man's mistress—Jacobs insisted she was still determined to *choose*, for there was "something akin to freedom" in making such a choice (p. 186). Ultimately, it was freedom young Harriet wanted more than either man. For her freedom she would use even her sexuality as leverage, having calculated that a jealously vengeful Dr. Flint would sell her, and, after Sands bought her, "I thought my freedom could be easily obtained from him" (p. 186).

Jacobs's adolescent calculations did not foresee the births of two children by the time she was twenty, let alone the eventual necessity of her escape to a crawlspace in the attic of Molly Horniblow's house, where the fugitive hid for seven years while secretly watching her children (cared for by their grandmother) and plotting her eventual flight to the North. The strength to persevere through what would become a near-incredible thirty-nine-year ordeal in slavery, followed by another decade on the run in the North, would have been virtually impossible had Jacobs not been able to count on her remarkable family, community, and heritage in Edenton. Her family had inculcated in her an abiding sense of self-respect and justice that nerved her to resist Norcom. Her grandmother Molly gave her an example of redoubtable black womanhood, uncowed by white intimidation, utterly dedicated to her black family. The founder of an independent home in the midst of violence and oppression, Molly also taught Harriet how to enlist sympathetic white women in her cause, ranging from a slaveholder's wife who gave Jacobs temporary shelter in Edenton to an employer who protected Jacobs from capture in New York City. Add to this strong and, when necessary, interracial network of support the assertive ethos of black Edenton itself, where as early as 1818 free blacks had established their own cemetery and their own church,[40] and where even enslaved families like the Jacobses and the Horniblows had become used to and indeed expected decent treatment. In the light of all these factors, we can begin to understand why Harriet Jacobs not only survived her ordeal in slavery but converted it into a classic American autobiography. Today almost certainly no book by a North Carolinian is read, studied, and discussed more than *Incidents in the Life of a Slave Girl*.

Published on the eve of the Civil War, *Incidents in the Life of a Slave Girl* was well received by the antislavery press at home and abroad. But the conflict that gripped the divided nation soon displaced whatever interest Jacobs's autobiography might have attracted in less momentous times. When the war ended, Jacobs and her daughter Louisa volunteered to teach the freedmen and -women in Savannah, Georgia. Disheartened by the unfair treatment the ex-slaves received at the hands of the Union army occupation, which remanded the labor and welfare of former plantation workers to their former masters for a pittance in compensation, Jacobs worried about mounting white violence against black community leaders like herself and decided Savannah was too dangerous. The spring of 1867 found her back in Edenton, where she penned a letter to a white friend while sitting under the roof of her deceased grandmother's house, only a few feet from the cramped crawlspace where she spent seven years in hiding as a fugitive slave. She wrote about the determined struggles of the ex-slaves on the farms around Edenton to avoid being "cheated out of their crop of cotton." Having visited one newly established school for blacks in her hometown, she noted admiringly, "some of the freedmen are very anxious to establish Plantation schools as soon as the more advanced Schools, can send out teachers." Although her sympathies were plainly with these efforts, Jacobs herself left Edenton soon after writing this letter and never again returned to North Carolina.[41]

Among the black North Carolina expatriates returning to their native state after the war in the hope of building a more just society in freedom were Andrew Jackson and Anne Maria Chesnutt, who resettled in their former hometown of Fayetteville about a year before Harriet Jacobs visited Edenton for the last time in 1867.[42] Having left Fayetteville along with other free Negroes in 1856 bound for Ohio, the Chesnutts believed ten years later that the Reconstruction policies of the ruling Republican Party in Washington, D.C., would ensure freedom and opportunity for them and their two sons, eight-year-old Charles and his younger brother, Lewis. Fayetteville had not suffered inordinately from the defeat of the Confederacy. Andrew Jackson Chesnutt's father was willing to help set him up in a grocery business; by 1868, Republican rule in Fayetteville enabled the enterprising young man to be elected a town commissioner and a justice of the peace in Cumberland County. Sharing the commitment to public school education for blacks that Harriet Jacobs and the majority of African Americans in the postwar South cherished, Jack Chesnutt used his political influence to found Fayetteville's Howard school, the town's first public school for African Americans, where his sons attended regularly, their rights to do so guaranteed by a new state constitution in 1868. In the spring of that year, Jack Chesnutt joined three other black Fayetteville leaders in purchasing the property on which was built the state's first normal school for the training of African American teachers. In 1880, at the age of twenty-two, Charles Waddell Chesnutt became the principal of the Fayetteville Colored Normal School. Before he had accepted this prized appointment, however, the ambitious young family man was already planning to abandon Fayetteville for better opportunities in a large northern city where, he confided to his journal, he hoped to "get employment in some literary avocation," "test the social problem," and "see if it's possible for talent, wealth, and genius to acquire social standing and distinction."[42]

Studious, bookish, and driven, Charles Chesnutt had wanted to be a writer since he was a teenager. "It is the dream of my life—to be an author!," he enthused in his journal on March 26, 1881 (p. 260). His motives, characteristically, sprang from a mix of personal ambition: "I want fame; I want money," he admitted to his journal; and social crusading: "I shall write for a purpose, a high holy purpose . . . for I consider the unjust spirit of caste which is so insidious as to pervade a whole nation, and so powerful as to subject a whole race and all connected with it to scorn and social ostracism—I consider this a barrier to the moral progress of the American people" (p. 260). "The unjust spirit of caste" was not simply an abstract idea to Chesnutt. He chafed daily under Fayetteville's unwritten but socially ingrained code of color hierarchy, which seemed designed to isolate people like himself. "I occupy here [in Fayetteville] a position similar to that of Mahomet's Coffin," he observed in his journal. "I am neither fish, flesh, nor fowl—neither 'nigger', poor white, nor 'buckrah.'

Too 'stuck-up' for the colored folks, and, of course, not recognized by the whites."[44] In other words, Chesnutt was what was termed locally a "bright mulatto." Light enough to pass for white but too proud to do so, Chesnutt in post-Reconstruction North Carolina experienced a similar brand of distaste, resentment, and denial that Moses Roper's unclassifiable whiteness had elicited from anxious whites in the slavery era. Fortunately for the respected Fayetteville principal, his reputation among local whites was such that he did not have to worry about physical intimidation. Unfortunately, the young principal also sensed that his betwixt-and-between status aroused little sympathy from whites or blacks in Fayetteville, who seemed even less interested in trying to understand what it was like to live in the uncharted twilight zone of the color line. Years later he would realize his dream of authorship partly by dramatizing in fiction the moral conflicts and psychological strains experienced by those who lived closest to the color line, namely, mixed-race persons like himself.

Concluding that people on neither side of the color line in North Carolina could appreciate him or his situation, Chesnutt left the South in 1883 at the age of twenty-five. In Cleveland, he built a profitable court stenography business, which allowed him and his family to live in increasing affluence. Much of his leisure time he devoted to writing. Concentrating on what he knew best, the folklore and history of his boyhood environs in eastern North Carolina,[45] in the late 1880s Chesnutt began to publish stories in Negro dialect that featured a wily old ex-slave storyteller well versed in the practice of conjure, or voodoo, among North Carolina's antebellum slaves. The popularity of Joel Chandler Harris's *Uncle Remus: His Songs and His Sayings* (1881) had proven that the folkways of southern black people could attract a sizable national literary audience. Chesnutt's realistic portrayal of the sand-hills region of eastern North Carolina also appealed to American readers' curiosity about the local color of the southern hinterlands. Revamping a voodoo tale told him by his father-in-law's gardener in Fayetteville, Chesnutt published his first "conjure story," titled "The Goophered Grapevine," in 1887 in the *Atlantic Monthly*, one of America's most prestigious literary magazines. The appearance less than a year later of another conjure story, "Po' Sandy," in the *Atlantic* confirmed that the new author's blend of realism and fantasy could be both honest in its assessment of the corrosive effects of slavery and inspirational in revealing the slaves' imaginative resources of resistance. One of the signature stories in *The Conjure Woman* (1899), Chesnutt's first book, "Po' Sandy" portrays slavery as a crucible that placed black people, especially enslaved women, under almost unbearable psychological pressures, demanding of them tenacity of purpose, firmness of character, and imaginative ingenuity in order to preserve themselves, their families, and their community. Appearing during an era when most whites questioned the African American's capacity for full and equal civil rights, Chesnutt's conjure stories suggested that, having confirmed their human dignity and heroic fortitude in the face of the worst that slavery could do, the free black man and woman were amply qualified for the rights and responsibilities of American citizenship.

The excellence of his conjure tales has led most historians of black American literature to applaud Chesnutt for almost single-handedly inaugurating a truly African American literary tradition in the short story. Yet in many ways, "The Sheriff's Children," the second story by Chesnutt reprinted in this volume, expresses more directly the author's most heartfelt social concerns and political aims. In its emphasis on the consequences of miscegenation, racial hatred, mob violence, and moral compromise in the post-Reconstruction South, this 1889 story became the germ of much of Chesnutt's later protest fiction, as well as his first significant study of the mulatto in American life. Similarly, his first major essay, "What Is a White Man?" (1889), articulates the challenge to racial (and racist) orthodoxy about whiteness that later impels Chesnutt's best-known and most controversial novels, *The House Behind the Cedars* (1900) and *The Marrow of Tradition* (1901). The latter novel, a trenchant analysis of the causes and effects of the Wilmington, North Carolina, racial massacre of 1898, registers Chesnutt's shock and dismay over the rise to power of unabashed white supremacists in a state that "I have been for a long time praising . . . for its superior fairness and liberality in the treatment of race questions."[46]

After a fact-finding mission to North Carolina in the winter of 1901 preparatory to the writing of *The Marrow of Tradition*, Chesnutt realized the grim social and political implications of the November 10, 1898, coup d'état in Wilmington. The city's black population had been terrorized by a violent takeover of the city government by an unelected cadre of white supremacist conspirators. Having kept abreast of racial developments in North Carolina since his departure in 1883, Chesnutt returned to Cleveland smoldering over the prospects for black people in the state and across the South. Before migrating to Cleveland, he had been among the African American voters who, according to historian Raymond Gavins, "helped to make North Carolina elections the most competitive and perhaps the most democratic among the southern states." After he left the state, black North Carolinians continued to exercise their voting rights vigorously—more than 75 percent of eligible black voters cast ballots in the state's gubernatorial contests between 1880 and 1896. As Joel Williamson has pointed out in his book *New People*, although the effects of Reconstruction in the upper South were relatively shallow and short-lived, "the one upper South state in which there was a second, very vigorous and briefly successful Reconstruction was North Carolina. There in the 1890s the Negro community joined Populists and white Republicans to win a significant share of power."[47]

"Fusion" politics spread across North Carolina in 1892 as agrarian revolt prompted disaffected white farmers to desert the "white man's party," the Democrats, for the new Populist Party. By 1894, a Populist-Republican coalition controlled the state legislature, making possible a revival of black political power not seen in the state since the late 1860s. Liberalizing election laws and removing obstacles to black voter registration, the ruling coalition set the stage for the election of a white Republican governor, Daniel Russell, for the first time in twenty years. In the same election, eleven African American representatives were elected to the North Carolina General Assembly, matching the total number of blacks in the General Assembly during the three previous sessions. A black congressman, George H. White, was elected in 1896 from North Carolina's Second District, known as the "Black Second" for its concentration of politically engaged black voters. Edgecombe County installed thirty-one black magistrates in office after the 1896 elections, Bertie County installed sixteen, and Halifax County, twenty-nine. "North Carolina was the only southern state at this time [1896] to tolerate so great a degree of black participation" in state and national politics.[48] While Mississippi and South Carolina had already disfranchised most of their black population, black North Carolinians went to the polls in 1896 to help elect three Republicans and five Populists to the U.S. House of Representatives.

This reassertion of black political power in North Carolina gave the state's Democrats an excuse to whip up hysteria among whites over the false specter of "Negro domination," opposition to which became the Democrats' rallying cry in 1898. The revolution in Wilmington, which Chesnutt called "the wholly superfluous slaughter of a harmless people" by whites possessed by the "raging devil of race hatred," served notice to the entire state, and indeed to the nation at large, that the color of politics in North Carolina was to be henceforth white only. With the state legislature securely in Democratic hands, the party of white supremacy proceeded to enact a constitutional amendment effectively stripping African Americans in the state of their voting rights. The disfranchisement law went into effect in 1900 after a political campaign of unprecedented race-baiting and fraud. Four years later, virtually no African American dared show his face on election day in North Carolina.[49]

In a 1903 essay titled "The Disfranchisement of the Negro," Chesnutt announced: "[T]he rights of the Negroes [in the South] are at a lower ebb than at any time during the thirty-five years of their freedom, and the race prejudice more intense and uncompromising." While southern black people appeared to Chesnutt largely defenseless against the onslaught of cradle-to-grave segregation, urban race riots, and lynchings that embroiled the region, he called on black writers in the North to seize the opportunity yet available to African Americans to prosecute a campaign for civil rights in the arena of national public opinion.[50] Few black writers active at this time needed to be recruited to enlist in this war of words. Although Chesnutt was one of only a handful of African Americans who could claim the ear of a national reading audience, a sense of mission and racial solidarity spurred blacks from across the spectrum of late-nineteenth-century African American society to address the intensifying "race problem." Writers from the small but vocal and well-educated middle class of black America, dubbed "the talented tenth" by W. E. B. Du Bois, made "uplifting the race," by which they meant primarily the less advantaged black masses, a near-evangelical responsibility.[51] The writing of two North Carolina expatriates—Anna Julia Cooper, a mixed-race member of the college-educated middle class, and David Bryant Fulton, a dark-skinned member of the self-educated working class—exemplifies diverse elements of the literature of racial uplift in the late nineteenth century. Their work is also prophetic of important directions in which twentieth-century African American literature would move.

Anna Julia Haywood Cooper was born in Raleigh in 1858 to Hannah Stanley, a slave, and George Washington Haywood, Hannah's master. Although G. W. Haywood is cited in the *Narrative of Lunsford Lane* as one of Lane's white supporters, Cooper is not known to have ever mentioned her father's name in print. Perhaps her refusal to acknowledge him publicly—even in private she dismissed him as someone to whom she owed nothing—was her way of returning in kind what appears to have been his refusal to acknowledge his slave-born, out-of-wedlock daughter. By contrast, Cooper revered her mother, whose "self-sacrificing toil to give me advantages she had never enjoyed is worthy the highest praise and undying gratitude."[52] Through her mother's efforts and a scholarship from a white benefactor, nine-year-old Anna Julia entered St. Augustine's Normal School in Raleigh, becoming a teacher when she was thirteen and the spouse of an Episcopal theology student at eighteen. Widowed two years later, she launched her pioneering career as a black woman in higher education when she moved to Ohio in 1881 to earn her Oberlin College A.B. (1884) and M.A. (1887) in classics. Unlike most of her female peers, she resolutely pursued the four-year "gentleman's course" of study at Oberlin, demonstrating her early commitment to equal educational opportunity for women, a theme she would practice as well as preach throughout her life. Eminently suited to intellectual leadership in black America, she excelled as a teacher in a variety of African American institutions, including St. Augustine's, Wilberforce University, the M Street High School in Washington, D.C. (where she also served as principal from 1902 to 1906), and Lincoln University. She welcomed the opportunity and the responsibility to speak on women's issues at important conferences, particularly during the 1890s, dubbed "the Woman's Era" by many historians because of the upsurge of agitation for women's rights during this decade led by Ida B. Wells-Barnett, Mary McLeod Bethune, Mary Church Terrell, and Cooper herself.[53]

Perhaps the most intellectually gifted U.S. woman writer of color in the late nineteenth century, Cooper led a busy life as a self-supporting professional woman (and the foster mother of two), which afforded her little time for expressly literary writing. Most of what we have from her pen are speeches and lectures composed for specific occasions and later published as essays. Although a collection of speeches and essays (like Du Bois's *The Souls of Black Folk* published eleven years later), Cooper's now-celebrated book, *A Voice from the South by a Black Woman of the South*, published by herself in 1892, is premised on a central metaphor: the idea of the "voice" of "the Black Woman," who sings the first section of her book in "Soprano Obligato" and the second in "Tutti ad Libitum."

The denotation of "Soprano Obligato" for the first section of Cooper's book, in which the speech "The Higher Education of Women" (reprinted in this anthology) appears, signifies the centrality of this section of *A Voice from the South*. All four of the "Soprano Obligato" essays key on the title of the first one, "Woman a Vital Element in the Regeneration and Progress of a Race." All four essays stress the unique role and responsibility of black women, when properly educated and fairly empowered to achieve all of which they are capable, to work in tandem with black men to uplift black America. The four "Soprano Obligato" essays address divergent audiences, from black Episcopal clergymen to white women's rights advocates. But regardless of whose platform she occupied, Cooper's emphasis remained consistent: black women, especially black women in the

South (where the majority of black American women lived in the 1890s), could not and would not remain voiceless onlookers while the fates of their people and their country were decided. Identifying herself from the title of her book as both prophet and exemplar of a new "black woman of the South," Cooper's voice models that of the educated, progressive, middle-class black woman she wished to inspire. This woman is at home in the study or in the parlor. She speaks confidently as informed social analyst, unflinching critic of injustice, and inspiring herald of an equal partnership with men.

At the same time that the essays in the "Soprano Obligato" section of *A Voice from the South* underscore the obligatory, or essential, role of full and equal educational opportunity for black American women, Cooper's choice of the obligato denotation for the key essays in her book also augments another important aim of *A Voice from the South*: to portray the assertive and aspiring African American woman as a complement, not a competitor, to the African American male. Just as a soprano obligato may provide an accompanying harmony above the melody line of a song, so Cooper is at pains in "The Higher Education of Women" to ensure that her prescriptions for the elevation of women will not be taken as detrimental to the interests of men. This led Cooper to endorse ideas about inherent emotional dispositions and sexually determined psychological traits that were widely presumed in the nineteenth century to differentiate women from men but are considered today highly suspect. Did Cooper truly believe, as she wrote in "The Higher Education of Women," that "as the man is more noble in reason, so the women is more quick in sympathy" (p. 277)? Or did she feel that her essay's seemingly radical thesis—that black women who had the ability to go to college ought to be encouraged and supported on a par with black men of equal ability—would have a better chance of winning converts if she endowed her new model of the educated black woman with plenty of familiar, nonthreatening attributes, such as "tenderness," "sensibility," "mercy," and "peace"? Scholars continue to debate the extent to which Cooper's feminist message was diluted or facilitated by her willingness to envision the postbaccalaureate black woman assuming traditional roles "as a teacher, as a home-maker, as wife, mother, or silent influence even" (p. 287). What all who read *A Voice from the South* agree on, however, is its author's absolute dedication to justice, opportunity, and equality, not just for black women or even black Americans, but for all those in U.S. society who had been marginalized and ignored by white America's turn-of-the-century fervor for racial separatism. Cooper would admit of no contradiction between her espousal of

African American rights and women's rights, though many in her own time felt obliged to choose between one or the other. She insisted that the only true and lasting crusade for any woman reformer was human rights. Thus her enduring legacy remains: "For woman's cause is the cause of the weak; and when all the weak shall have received their due consideration, then woman will have her 'rights,' and the Indian will have his rights, and the Negro will have his rights, and all the strong will have learned at last to deal justly, to love mercy, and to walk humbly; and our fair land will have been taught . . . the art, the science, and the religion of regarding one's neighbor as one's self."[54]

From Harriet Jacobs through Charles Chesnutt and Anna Julia Cooper, leading African American writers of the nineteenth century pled powerfully, and often highly personally, on behalf of those Cooper designated in the opening pages of *A Voice from the South* as "the *Colored Girls* of the South:—that large, bright, promising fatally beautiful class . . . so full of promise and possibilities, yet so sure of destruction." "Often without a father to whom they dare apply the loving term [here Cooper surely drew on her own experience], often without a stronger brother to espouse their cause and defend their honor with his life's blood," African American girls and women, the conduits of "the life-blood of the race," needed men of their race to stake their manhood on the defense of black womanhood.[55] As if in response to this call, David Bryant Fulton produced his 1912 essay, "A Plea for Social Justice for the Negro Woman,"[56] in which he indignantly asked why "the manhood and the racial pride of the Negro man" were not incensed over the contemptuous presumption on the part of white men that black women were still their sexual property. Portraying white violence against black women as an outrage to the masculinity of his black male reader put Fulton in danger of making black male honor, rather than the violation of black women's bodies, the overriding issue of "A Plea for Social Justice for the Negro Woman." Balancing his demand for black men "to begin the work of properly safeguarding the mother of our children," however, is Fulton's linkage of moral laxity in the area of black women's sexual "purity" to more insidious notions held by black men, as well as black women, that interbreeding with whites would somehow make America's blacks more socially acceptable. Fulton reserves special scorn for those who believe that "Amalgamation" of the white and black races would somehow bring an end to the "Race Problem."[57] Censuring a black professor at Wilberforce University for suggesting that "Race Blending" would "improve the stock" of black America, Fulton urged instead that black men recognize "all that is beautiful, all that is desirable, all that is lovable beneath and in the colored skin" (p. 310). Only by celebrating the beauty and nobility of blackness, which meant adopting proper self-respect and resisting, violently if necessary, white threats to "race integrity and strength," could black Americans, male and female, deliver themselves from insult and injustice.

Because so little is known about the life and work of David Bryant Fulton, we can only speculate as to the origins of his commitment to the defense of black womanhood in his writing. Devoted to his mother, Lavinia Robinson Fulton, who raised him in Wilmington from the time he was six years old, David chose a photograph of Lavinia as a frontispiece for his collection of sketches and newspaper articles, *Eagle Clippings*, which he published in Brooklyn, New York, in 1907. He also celebrated the African American woman as maternal ideal and standard-bearer "for equality in all things" in "Mother of Mine: An Ode to the Negro Woman," which Fulton delivered to the Empire State Federation of Colored Women's Clubs in Brooklyn in 1923. His dedication to black women was not limited to mothers of the race. A key character in his novel, *Hanover; or, The Persecution of the Lowly* (1900),[58] begins the story as the concubine of one of the main conspirators in the Wilmington massacre of 1898. Learning of the violence about to befall the black people of Wilmington, however, Molly Pierrepont spurns her white lover, warns her friends of the impending disaster, and, on the day of the coup d'état, brandishes a pistol to defend herself against marauding whites. Published a year before Chesnutt's much more famous *The Marrow of Tradition*, *Hanover* gives its beautiful mixed-race heroine a toughness, daring, and worldliness that do not exist in the equally beautiful, but considerably more conventional, mixed-race heroine of Chesnutt's novel. Although Fulton is not known to have extolled higher education for black women with Cooper's conviction and learning, he believed that an education that featured "knowledge of race history, race achievement, and the reading of race literature" would "enable us to see the need of as thoroughly trained women for wives and mothers as for teachers, lecturers, and business pursuits."[59] Thus, like Cooper, Fulton seems to have recognized that whether black women sought fulfillment in more traditional domestic roles or in careers outside the home, such women needed and deserved educational opportunities commensurate with their abilities, responsibilities, and goals.

Fulton's insistence on "race pride" as foundational to African American education and crucial to the united advancement of blacks in America recalls the appeal of his fellow Wilmingtonian, David Walker, for racial unity reinforced by racial pride. Other themes in Fulton's writing, such as his exhortations to an aroused black manhood, his commitment to a liberating knowledge of "race history," and his willingness to resist oppression by force, also ally him to the kind of black nationalism pioneered by Walker. Like Walker, Fulton left Wilmington as a largely self-educated young man in search of better prospects outside the South. Both men settled in the urban North, their relatively inconspicuous occupations—Walker as a dealer in used clothes, Fulton as a porter for the Pullman Palace Car Company—veiling their fervent commitment to black community-building and their strong desire to make a name for themselves as writers. The fact that neither man claimed professional status through either advanced education or white-collar job status (Fulton also worked for the Brooklyn YMCA, a music publishing house in New York, and for Sears, Roebuck, though in what capacities is unknown)[60] gave both Fulton and Walker an affinity with and appreciation of working-class African Americans that is considerably less pronounced in the writing of Lunsford Lane, Harriet Jacobs, Charles Chesnutt, or Ann Julia Cooper. While most of his predecessors in African American literature treated the rank-and-file black worker of the South with sympathy, Fulton's portrayal of working-class black people reflects more respect and less condescension than is typical of nineteenth-century black American writing on intraracial class matters. More than likely Fulton's distinctiveness in this regard is due to his willingness to write from his own work experience, particularly after arriving in New York City. His autobiographical *Eagle Clippings* sketch, "A Dock Laborer: Experiences of One Man Who Came to the Metropolis in the Late Eighties, Looking for Honest Employment," offers insight into the daily working lives of black stevedores, many of whom, like Fulton, had been obliged to seek work in the shipping industry as strikebreakers. Fulton's *Recollections of a Sleeping Car Porter* (1892) provides pungent characterizations of white travelers from the North and South as only a shrewd black porter, schooled to penetrate pretense by many miles on the road, could present them.

The eight writers featured in this book do not comprise the full measure of black North Carolina's contribution to the founding of African American literature in the nineteenth century. Both before and after the Civil War, a number of North Carolinians who had once been enslaved published autobiographies that were widely read during their own time and, in several cases, are still available in print today.[61] The narratives of Roper, Lane, and Jacobs constitute singular achievements in the slave narrative tradition, but they by no means represent the full richness of North Carolina's contribution to African American autobiography in the nineteenth and early twentieth centuries. Several black natives of North Carolina published volumes of verse in the late nineteenth century, although none achieved the reputation of George Moses Horton.[62] In 1880, New Bern–born John Patterson Green published *Recollections of the Inhabitants, Localities, Superstitions, and KuKlux Outrages of the Carolinas. By a "Carpet-Bagger" Who Was Born and Lived There*, a rare blend of travel narrative, local-color sketchbook, amateur ethnography, and socio-political commentary on African American life in the South during the Reconstruction era. Yet like his cousin, Charles Chesnutt, Green left North Carolina, which he considered backward and unsophisticated, despite the "extensive, well-regulated society of colored people" he found in towns such as Fayetteville, to seek a better life in Cleveland, Ohio.[63] Among those black North Carolinians who made a literary name for themselves in the North, Greensboro's James Ephraim McGirt also merits notice, if not for his efforts in poetry and short fiction, then in recognition of his editorial work, chiefly the publication of *McGirt's Magazine* (1903–10), an illustrated monthly that followed the activities of black Americans in art, literature, science, and public affairs.[64]

As for the role that their native state played in the intellectual and artistic development of the writers selected for this volume, it is hard to say, finally, what sort of credit North Carolina may justifiably claim for the accomplishments of Horton, Walker, Roper, Lane, Jacobs, Chesnutt, Cooper, and Fulton. Without question, *black* North Carolina—represented most notably by the families, communities, churches, and educational institutions that nurtured the talents and helped to fuel the ambitions of each of these writers—provided a fertile cultural topsoil in which the genius of all eight took root. By contrast, nineteenth-century white North Carolina, in a corporate sense at least, made life sufficiently unpleasant, if not downright dangerous, for all eight aspiring men and women that, independent of each other, they came to the same conclusion—to leave the state pretty much as soon as they could. It is true that some of these writers were able to look back to a departed home, kinfolk, and fond North Carolina memories with palpable nostalgia, as two poems in this volume, Horton's "The Southern Refugee" and Fulton's "De Coonah Man," plainly attest. Just as incontestable is the fact that the majority of the eight acknowledged advantages that accrued to them by virtue of comparatively fortunate birth circumstances, family connections, and/or white benevolence. Such advantages put leverage into the hands of town slaves and family servants like Lunsford Lane and Harriet Jacobs who, once they had tasted freedom however slightly, were determined to have more. Yet if North Carolina could reward the enterprise of a slave like Lane, it could just as easily deny it in the case of Horton. If Chesnutt, while tracing his free black family history in North Carolina, could compliment the state for not restricting by law "the right of marriage between whites and free persons of color" until 1830,[65] Roper, Jacobs, and Cooper could just as readily show cause, from their family histories, for lifelong resentment of the indifference of their native state to the lawless violation of enslaved women by white men, some of them among the so-called best people of the state. If Walker and Fulton left North Carolina to become exponents of African American pride, solidarity, and uncompromising struggle, was their dedication to these ideals as much attributable to the frustrations and humiliations they felt at the hands of white North Carolina as to the support and inspiration they experienced from black North Carolina?

More than likely, the debt all eight of these classic African American writers owe collectively to North Carolina is both twofold and contradictory. We can identify in the lives of most of these writers conditions in their North Carolina youth that gave each of them resources of various kinds on which to build a sense of expectation and hope for individual fulfillment. We can also identify in the lives of almost all of these writers instances in which white North Carolina tried to restrict or rescind the emotional, spiritual, intellectual, or economic resources on which each writer's hope for a fulfilling future depended. From this fundamental contradiction, which made North Carolina a symbol of all that was best and worst in the South, came at least one strong impetus for most of the writing included in this book. Evoking memories of sacrifice and struggle, suffering and resistance, rejection and redemption, North Carolina gave these eight talented men and women their formative lessons in the intricacies of color, caste, and class—and then dismissed them. Finding their literary voices elsewhere, they recreated what they learned in North Carolina into unforgettable metaphors of the intersection of black America's hopes and white America's fears along the nation's enduring color line. Because of the energy and commitment of these writers, North Carolina, for better, as well as for worse, has a role and a place in African American literary history unmatched by any other state in the Old South.

Notes

1 In "North Carolina Slave Narratives and the Politics of Place," *North Carolina Literary Review* 1 (Summer 1992), pp. 115–31, Gay Wilentz argues that

because the North Carolina system of slavery was "unique," many of the auto-biographical narratives that emerged from the experience of slavery in North Carolina do not conform to the generalizations about the slave narrative that various literary critics have applied to the genre as a whole. In his introduction to *North Carolina Slave Narratives: The Lives of Moses Roper, Lunsford Lane, Moses Grandy, and Thomas H. Jones* (Chapel Hill: University of North Carolina Press, 2003), William L. Andrews ponders the relationship of slavery as practiced in North Carolina to the four narratives of enslavement by North Carolinians included in his book. These are the only two scholars thus far to have considered the effect of state origin on writing by black people from nineteenth-century North Carolina.

2 The only slave state that rivaled North Carolina in the production of important African American writers in the nineteenth century was Maryland, which saw its slave population decline dramatically in the half century before the outbreak of the Civil War, while the ranks of its black literary leaders grew: Benjamin Banneker (1731–1806), almanac maker; Daniel Coker (1780–1846), pamphleteer; Josiah Henson (1789–1883), slave narrator; James W. C. Pennington (1807–70), essayist and slave narrator; Henry Highland Garnet (1815–82), orator; Frederick Douglass (1818–95), editor and author of the most famous slave narrative of his era; Frances Ellen Watkins Harper (1825–1911), poet, novelist, and essayist; and Amanda Berry Smith (1837–1915), spiritual autobiographer.

3 For a review of early North Carolina writing, see Richard Walser and E. T. Malone Jr., *Literary North Carolina* (Raleigh: Division of Archives and History, North Carolina Department of Cultural Resources, 1986), pp. 6–10.

4 Ibid., p. 10.

5 Jeffrey J. Crow, *The Black Experience in Revolutionary North Carolina* (Raleigh: Division of Archives and History, North Carolina Department of Cultural Resources, 1977), p. 1.

6 This ratio held up throughout the antebellum period, although the evidence suggests that as the nineteenth century progressed, most North Carolina slaveholders claimed fewer human beings as their property. In 1790, only 31 percent of North Carolina families held slaves. As Jeffrey Crow notes, "The concentration of slaveholders and slaves appeared in counties where tobacco, rice, and naval stores prospered." But in even large slaveholding counties, such as Warren and New Hanover, the average number of slaves per white slaveholding family was 10.3. In Randolph County in the Piedmont, the average was 3.5. See Crow, *Black Experience*, p. 6. By 1830, of the approximately 15,000 slaveholding families in North Carolina, 85 percent owned fewer than ten human beings (Freddy L. Parker, *Running for Freedom* [New York: Garland, 1993], 9–11, 21–22). In 1860, "the typical slaveholder in North Carolina owned only one slave. Fifty-three percent of the state's slave owners held five or fewer slaves, and in the total population of slaves a modest 2.6 percent lived on plantations with fifty or more slaves" (Jeffrey J. Crow, Paul D. Escott, and Flora J. Hatley, *African Americans in North Carolina* [Raleigh: Division

of Archives and History, North Carolina Department of Cultural Resources, 1992], p. 56).

7 Guion Griffs Johnson, *Ante-Bellum North Carolina: A Social History* (Chapel Hill: University of North Carolina Press, 1937), p. 468.

8 Biographical information on George Moses Horton is drawn from George Moses Horton, "Life of George M. Horton. The Colored Bard of North Carolina," in Horton, *The Poetical Works of George M. Horton, the Colored Bard of North Carolina* (Hillsborough, N.C.: Heartt, 1845), pp. iii–xx; Joan R. Sherman, ed. *The Black Bard of North Carolina: George Moses Horton and His Poetry* (Chapel Hill: University of North Carolina Press, 1997); and Richard Walser, *The Black Poet* (New York: Philosophical Library, 1966).

9 Johnson, *Ante-Bellum North Carolina*, p. 492; Parker, *Running for Freedom*, p. 22.

10 Horton, "Life of George M. Horton," p. xii.

11 The practice of hiring slaves out for stipulated periods of time to do certain kinds of work began during the colonial era. Usually the most skilled and trustworthy of slaves would be allowed "to contact a potential employer, make arrangements for wages and working conditions, and secure their own food and lodging." The practice had benefits for both slave and master. Required to return to their masters a monthly or yearly percentage of their wages, slaves could keep the remainder for themselves. In exchange, however, the hired slaves had to provide their own food, lodging, clothes, and tools (Loren Schweninger, *Black Property Owners in the South, 1790–1915* [Urbana: University of Illinois Press, 1990], pp. 38–44). The most famous self-hired slave was Frederick Douglass, who explained the advantages and disadvantages of the practice from the standpoint of the slave in his autobiography, *My Bondage and My Freedom* (1855).

12 Crow, *Black Experience*, p. 43. Because slaves who were allowed to hire their time "moved into a twilight zone between bondage and freedom," they "often demonstrated an independence, self-esteem, and at times arrogance, which grated on whites who believed slaves should be docile, self-deprecating, and humble" (Schweninger, *Black Property Owners*, p. 43).

13 Johnson, *Ante-Bellum North Carolina*, pp. 562–63.

14 John Hope Franklin, *The Free Negro in North Carolina, 1790–1860* (Chapel Hill: University of North Carolina Press, 1995), pp. 25–26, 199.

15 Biographical information on David Walker is drawn from Peter P. Hinks, *To Awaken My Afflicted Brethren: David Walker and the Problem of Antebellum Slave Resistance* (University Park: Pennsylvania State University Press, 1997).

16 David Walker, *Walker's Appeal, in Four Articles; Together With a Preamble, to the Colored Citizens of the World, But in Particular, and Very Expressly, to Those of the United States of America* (Boston: the Author, 1829). The quotation appears on p. 83 in this volume. The standard edition of *Walker's Appeal* is Peter P. Hinks, ed., *David Walker's Appeal to the Coloured Citizens of the*

World (University Park: Pennsylvania State University Press, 2000), which reprints the final edition of the *Appeal* published in 1830.

17 For information on African American life in Wilmington and other seaports on the North Carolina coast, see Lawrence Lee, *The Lower Cape Fear in Colonial Days* (Chapel Hill: University of North Carolina Press, 1965), and David S. Cecelski, *The Waterman's Song: Slavery and Freedom in Maritime North Carolina* (Chapel Hill: University of North Carolina Press, 2001).

18 Crow, *Black Experience*, p. 29.

19 Jeffrey J. Crow, "Slave Rebelliousness and Social Conflict in North Carolina, 1775–1802," *William and Mary Quarterly*, 3rd ser., 37 (January 1980): 79–102; Hinks, ed., *David Walker's Appeal*, pp. 40–47.

20 Schweninger, *Black Property Owners*, p. 48.

21 The standard study of free Negroes in the South is Ira Berlin's *Slaves Without Masters: The Free Negro in the Antebellum South* (New York: Pantheon, 1974).

22 Franklin, *Free Negro in North Carolina*, pp. 15, 84, 193, 222–23, 225.

23 Hinks, ed., *Walker's Appeal*, p. 32.

24 Ibid., pp. 74–75.

25 Orlando Patterson, *Slavery and Social Death* (Cambridge, Mass.: Harvard University Press, 1982).

26 Franklin, *Free Negro in North Carolina*, p. 68.

27 The first edition of Roper's narrative was *A Narrative of Moses Roper's Adventures and Escape from American Slavery* (London: Darton, Harvey and Darton, 1837). For this volume, the revised and expanded 1848 edition has been selected. See the Note on the Text to the *Narrative of the Adventures and Escape of Moses Roper, from American Slavery*. For a discussion of Roper's *Narrative* in the context of other contemporary North Carolina slave narratives, see Ian Frederick Finseth's introduction to Roper's *Narrative* in Andrews, ed., *North Carolina Slave Narratives*, pp. 23–34. Further quotations from Roper's *Narrative* are taken from the edition reprinted in this volume.

28 Henry H. Roper, a slave-owning farmer in a predominantly agricultural county in central North Carolina just south of the Virginia state line, was about thirty years old when his son was born. See Andrews, ed., *North Carolina Slave Narratives*, pp. 74–75. According to L. David Roper's genealogy of his forebears, "Most of the Ropers in the South were not wealthy enough to own slaves. Moses's father Henry is the only one I know about" (e-mail from L. David Roper to William L. Andrews, December 1, 1993).

29 *Narrative of the Life of Frederick Douglass, An American Slave* (1845), the most famous slave narrative of the nineteenth century, exists in a number of modern reprint editions. See William L. Andrews and William S. McFeely, eds., *Narrative of the Life of Frederick Douglass, An American Slave, Written by Himself* (New York: W. W. Norton, 1997). William Wells Brown's *Narrative of William W. Brown*, which rivaled Douglass's narrative in popularity, is available in William L. Andrews, ed., *From Fugitive Slave to Free Man:*

The Autobiographies of William Wells Brown (Columbia, Mo.: University of Missouri Press, 2003). Two other widely read narratives of the 1840s are also available in convenient editions: Charles Heglar, ed., *The Life and Adventures of Henry Bibb, An American Slave* (Madison, Wisc.: University of Wisconsin Press, 2001), and James W. C. Pennington's *The Fugitive Blacksmith*, in Arna Bontemps, ed., *Great Slave Narratives* (Boston: Beacon, 1969).

30 Lunsford Lane, *The Narrative of Lunsford Lane, Formerly of Raleigh, N.C.* (Boston: J. G. Torrey, 1842). Further quotations from Lane's narrative are taken from the edition reprinted in this volume unless otherwise noted. For a discussion of Lane's *Narrative* in the context of other contemporary North Carolina slave narratives, see Tampathia Evans's introduction to Lane's *Narrative* in Andrews, ed., *North Carolina Slave Narratives*, pp. 79–92.

31 William G. Hawkins, *Lunsford Lane; or, Another Helper from North Carolina* (Boston: Crosby & Nichols, 1863).

32 For summaries of reviews of fugitive slave narratives that linked them to the *Odyssey*, to "the romance of the time," and to America's reverence for "the force and working of the native love of freedom in the individual mind," see William L. Andrews, *To Tell a Free Story: The First Century of Afro-American Autobiography, 1760–1865* (Urbana: University of Illinois Press, 1986), pp. 98–99.

33 John Hope Franklin and Loren Schweninger, *Runaway Slaves* (New York: Oxford University Press, 1999), pp. 210–13, 332.

34 Franklin, *Free Negro in North Carolina*, p. 18.

35 For more accounts of enslaved family men and women who chose self-purchase as the safest means of securing their freedom, see *Narrative of the Life of Moses Grandy* (1843) and *The Experience of Rev. Thomas H. Jones, Who Was a Slave for Forty-Three Years* (1885) in Andrews, ed., *North Carolina Slave Narratives*, pp. 131–279, and Elizabeth Keckley, *Behind the Scenes; or, Thirty Years a Slave, and Four Years in the White House*, ed. William L. Andrews (1868; reprint, New York: Penguin, 2005).

36 *Narrative of Lunsford Lane*, in Andrews, ed., *North Carolina Slave Narratives*, p. 99.

37 Evans, intro. to *Narrative of Lunsford Lane*, in Andrews, ed., *North Carolina Slave Narratives*, p. 129.

38 Jean Fagan Yellin, *Harriet Jacobs: A Life* (New York: Basic Civitas, 2004), p. 10.

39 Harriet Jacobs, *Incidents in the Life of a Slave Girl*, ed. Jean Fagan Yellin (Cambridge, Mass.: Harvard University Press, 2000), p. 19. Further quotations from *Incidents* are taken from the text of Jacobs's autobiography in this volume.

40 Yellin, *Harriet Jacobs*, pp. 18–19.

41 This summary of Jacobs's life in the 1860s is drawn from Yellin, *Harriet Jacobs*, pp. 140–209. Jacobs's April 25, 1867, letter from Edenton to Ednah Dow Cheney appears in Jacobs, *Incidents*, pp. 271–73.

42 Frances Richardson Keller, *An American Crusade: The Life of Charles Wad-*

dell Chesnutt (Provo, Utah: Brigham Young University Press, 1978), p. 30. Further details of Chesnutt's life are taken from this biography.

43 Richard H. Brodhead, ed., *The Journals of Charles W. Chesnutt* (Durham, N.C.: Duke University Press, 1993), p. 106. Further quotations from Chesnutt's journals, unless otherwise noted, are taken from the excerpts from the journals reprinted in this volume.

44 Brodhead, ed., *Journals*, pp. 157–58.

45 In her early article "Tar Heelia in Chesnutt," *College Language Association Journal* 9 (1965): 39–50, Sylvia Lyons Render identifies various aspects of North Carolina folk life and culture in Chesnutt's fiction. See also John W. Parker's reminiscence of Chesnutt's ties to Fayetteville in "Chesnutt as a Southern Town Remembers Him," *Crisis* 56 (1949): 205–6, 221.

46 Chesnutt to Walter Hines Page, November 11, 1898, in Joseph R. McElrath Jr. and Robert C. Leitz, eds., *"To Be an Author": Letters of Charles W. Chesnutt, 1889–1905* (Princeton, N.J.: Princeton University Press, 1997), p. 116.

47 For discussions of the Wilmington massacre from various scholarly standpoints, see David S. Cecelski and Timothy B. Tyson, eds., *Democracy Betrayed: The Wilmington Race Riot of 1898 and Its Legacy* (Chapel Hill: University of North Carolina Press, 1998); Raymond Gavins, "The Meaning of Freedom: Black North Carolina in the Nadir, 1880–1900," in *Race, Class, and Politics in Southern History: Essays in Honor of Robert F. Durden*, ed. Jeffrey J. Crow, Paul D. Escott, and Charles L. Flynn Jr. (Baton Rouge: Louisiana State University Press, 1989), p. 207; and Joel R. Williamson, *New People: Miscegenation and Mulattoes in the United States* (New York: Free Press, 1980), p. 79.

48 Eric Anderson, *Race and Politics in North Carolina, 1872–1901* (Baton Rouge: Louisiana State University Press, 1981), 227.

49 Ibid., pp. 145, 245–48; Charles W. Chesnutt, *The Marrow of Tradition* (Boston: Houghton Mifflin, 1901), pp. 290, 297; Gavins, "Meaning of Freedom," p. 208.

50 Charles W. Chesnutt, "The Disfranchisement of the Negro," in Booker T. Washington et al., *The Negro Problem* (New York: James Pott & Co., 1903), pp. 104, 114.

51 Du Bois describes the character and responsibilities of the black leadership vanguard he envisioned in "The Talented Tenth," in Washington et al., *Negro Problem*, pp. 33–75. A thorough examination of the ideology of racial uplift in post–Civil War African American cultural history appears in Kevin K. Gaines, *Uplifting the Race: Black Leadership, Politics, and Culture in the Twentieth Century* (Chapel Hill: University of North Carolina Press, 1996).

52 George Washington Haywood (1802–90) was the Raleigh attorney who cosigned a November 3, 1840, letter on behalf of Lunsford Lane (whose *Narrative* appears in this book), requesting an exemption in his case from a law requiring free Negroes to leave the state (see p. 155). Anna Julia Cooper's statements about her parents appear in Louise Daniel Hutchinson, *Anna J. Cooper, A Voice from the South* (Washington, D.C.: Smithsonian Institution

Press, 1981), p. 4. Additional details of Cooper's biography are taken from Hutchinson's book.

53 For a compact review of the Woman's Era, see the article devoted to it authored by Claudia Tate in William L. Andrews, Frances Smith Foster, and Trudier Harris, eds., *The Oxford Companion to African American Literature* (New York: Oxford University Press, 1997), pp. 785–87. For more discussion of Cooper's role in the development of African American movements for women's rights, see Paula Giddings, *When and Where I Enter: The Impact of Black Women on Race and Sex in America* (New York: William Morrow, 1984), and Karen Ann Johnson, *Uplifting the Women and the Race: The Lives, Educational Philosophies, and Social Activism of Anna Julia Cooper and Nannie Helen Burroughs* (New York: Garland, 2000).

54 This often-quoted statement by Cooper comes from her essay "Woman Versus the Indian," in *A Voice from the South* (Xenia, Ohio: the Author, 1892), p. 117.

55 "Womanhood a Vital Element in the Regeneration and Progress of a Race," in *A Voice from the South*, pp. 24–25.

56 Jack Thorne, "A Plea for Social Justice for the Negro Woman," Occasional Paper No. 2 (Yonkers, N.Y.: Negro Society for Historical Research, 1912). Further quotations from this essay are taken from the text reprinted in this volume. Jack Thorne was David Bryant Fulton's pen name, which he chose evidently to suggest his determination to be a literary thorn in the side of those who published attacks against black people.

57 Chesnutt was one African American writer who argued that amalgamation of the two races through intermarriage was desirable, as it would eventually bring an end to America's race problem. See his "The Future American: A Complete Race-Amalgamation Likely to Occur," Boston *Evening Transcript*, September 1, 1900, p. 24.

58 Jack Thorne, *Eagle Clippings* (Brooklyn, N.Y.: the Author, 1907); David B. Fulton, *Mother of Mine: Ode to the Negro Woman* (New York: the Author, 1923); Jack Thorne, *Hanover; or, The Persecution of the Lowly. A Story of the Wilmington Massacre* (Philadelphia: the Author, 1900).

59 Jack Thorne, "Race Unification; How It May Be Accomplished," *African Times and Orient Review* 2 (Nov–Dec. 1913): 234.

60 Biographical information on Fulton is drawn from the sketch by William L. Andrews in Rayford Logan and Michael R. Winston, eds., *Dictionary of American Negro Biography* (New York: W. W. Norton, 1982), pp. 589–90.

61 In addition to the narratives of Moses Grandy of Pasquotank County and Thomas H. Jones of Wilmington, whose life stories are reprinted in Andrews, ed., *North Carolina Slave Narratives*, North Carolina plays an important part in the life of teenage Elizabeth Keckley, whose *Behind the Scenes* was one of the most controversial African American autobiographies of the Reconstruction era. A few months after the appearance of *Incidents in the Life of a Slave Girl*, Harriet Jacobs's brother, John S., published *A True Tale of Slavery*, a narrative of his experience as a slave in North Carolina, in a British magazine.

A True Tale of Slavery is reprinted in Yellin's edition of *Incidents*. Among the post–Civil War narratives of slavery and freedom produced by North Carolinians are London Ferebee, *A Brief History of the Slave Life of Rev. L. R. Ferebee, and the Battles of Life, and Four Years of His Ministerial Life* (Raleigh, N.C.: Edwards, Broughton, Printers, 1882); Friday Jones, *Days of Bondage* (1883; reprint, Greenville, N.C.: Joyner Library, East Carolina University, 1999); Allen Parker, *Recollections of Slavery Times* (Worcester, Mass.: Chas. W. Burbank & Co., 1895); William Mallory, *Old Plantation Days*, [Hamilton, Ontario]: s.n., [1902?]; Morgan L. Latta, *The History of My Life and Work. Autobiography by Rev. M. L. Latta, A.M., D.D.* (Raleigh, N.C.: the Author, 1903); William H. Robinson, *From Log Cabin to the Pulpit; or, Fifteen Years in Slavery* (Eau Claire, Wisc.: James H. Tifft, 1913); and William Henry Singleton, *Recollections of My Slavery Days*, ed. Katherine Mellen Charron and David S. Cecelski (1922; reprint, Raleigh: North Carolina Department of Cultural Resources, 1999). A diary written by William Gould, a fugitive slave from Wilmington, North Carolina, who became a sailor in the U.S. Navy during the Civil War, has been edited by his great-grandson, William B. Gould IV, and published as *Diary of a Contraband* (Stanford, Calif.: Stanford University Press, 2002). Two collections of transcribed narratives containing oral histories by former slaves from North Carolina are worthy of note: Benjamin Drew, ed., *The Refugee: A North-Side View of Slavery* (Boston: John P. Jewett, 1856), and Belinda Hurmence, ed., *My Folks Don't Want Me to Talk about Slavery* (Winston-Salem, N.C.: John F. Blair, 1984).

62 For samples of the poetry of Alfred Island Walden of Randolph County, Josephine Henderson Heard of Salisbury, and Greensboro's James Ephraim McGirt, see Joan R. Sherman, ed., *African-American Poetry of the Nineteenth Century* (Urbana: University of Illinois Press, 1992), pp. 221–33, 360–64, and 456–63.

63 John Patterson Green, *Recollections of the Inhabitants, Localities, Superstitions, and KuKlux Outrages of the Carolinas. By a "Carpet-Bagger" Who Was Born and Lived There* (Cleveland, Ohio: the Author, 1880), p. 204.

64 For more information on McGirt, see the sketch by William L. Andrews in Logan and Winston, eds., *Dictionary of American Negro Biography*, p. 416.

65 Charles W. Chesnutt, "The Free Colored People of North Carolina" (1902), in Joseph R. McElrath Jr., Robert C. Leitz III, and Jesse S. Crisler, eds., *Charles W. Chesnutt: Essays and Speeches* (Stanford, Calif.: Stanford University Press, 1999), p. 175.

STATEMENT OF EDITORIAL PRACTICE

The "Note on the Text" that precedes the selections from the works of the eight authors represented in *The North Carolina Roots of African American Literature* identifies the sources for each of the texts in this book. The aim of this anthology is to reprint each text as a faithful reproduction of its original. Texts that have been abridged, namely, those by Roper, Lane, and Jacobs, have been abbreviated because their length does not permit their full inclusion in this volume. In every other respect these abbreviated texts accurately follow their originals.

The editors of *The North Carolina Roots of African American Literature* have not attempted to modernize or regularize inconsistencies in spelling, capitalization, italicization, or paragraphing among the texts in this book. Obvious inconsistencies in spelling within a given text, indicative of a printer's error, have been silently corrected. Terms such as "Negro," "Christian," or "the Bible" sometimes appear in lower case in some of the texts in this book, reflecting varying capitalization practices among writers and publishers in the nineteenth century. Although punctuation in some of the texts in this book diverges from contemporary practice, to preserve the intention and flavor of the originals, we have left them unaltered. Renditions of so-called Negro dialect in various texts in this book, most noticeably in Chesnutt's "Po' Sandy" and Fulton's "De Coonah Man," are reproduced exactly as they were originally published. In the hands of nineteenth-century black writers such dialect was often a deliberately crafted medium and mask that allowed a marginalized writer to exploit popular tastes of the time.

All footnotes to the texts in *The North Carolina Roots of African American Literature*, unless otherwise indicated, are provided by individual contributing editors to this volume. Writing that appears within brackets—[ ]—is provided by the editors.

WILLIAM L. ANDREWS
GENERAL EDITOR

AMANDA M. PAGE

union to the end

ter soul in soul

break the soft control

is the thought to me

a nymph as thee

language into song

delightful soft alon

a soft reply

I must with joy rely

hand and then th

ght not to part

BORN A SLAVE IN Northampton County around 1797, George Moses Horton, the "colored bard of North Carolina," became the first African American to publish in the South and the first American slave to protest his enslavement in poetry. While the names of Horton's parents are unknown, he was the sixth of ten children. Horton lived on the tobacco farm of his master, William Horton, until 1800, when his master moved to Chatham County. Horton disliked farm work, but during his free time, he taught himself to read using spelling books, the Bible, and his mother's Wesley hymnal. In 1814, William Horton gave George to his son James. When William Horton died five years later, his estate was eventually broken up among relatives, with George Moses Horton's family scattered among them. Horton's wrenching poem "Division of an Estate," written decades after the event, was based on this experience.

Around 1817, Horton began to walk to the nearby university at Chapel Hill, where he sold love poems to students for twenty-five to seventy-five cents apiece. "Acrostics" is a fine example of Horton's early made-to-order verse. He was so successful in selling his poems that, by the 1830s, his master allowed him to hire his time so as to devote himself to poetry.

At Chapel Hill, Horton met novelist Caroline Lee Hentz, wife of university language professor Nicholas Hentz, who taught him to write. She sent his poem "Liberty and Slavery" to her hometown newspaper, the Lancaster, Massachusetts, *Gazette*, where it was published on April 8, 1828. Soon thereafter, Horton's poetry was published in newspapers as varied as the proslavery Raleigh *Register* and the black-owned New York *Freedom's Journal*. Both newspapers subsequently tried to raise money for Horton's purchase, but James Horton refused to sell.

The interest of the *Register*'s publishers, Joseph and Weston Gales, in Horton's poetry led directly to the 1829 publication of his first book, *The Hope of Liberty*. While the preface of the collection has led scholars to believe that the sale of this book was intended to free Horton, research by critic Leon Jackson suggests that *The Hope of Liberty* was likely published as a fund-raiser for the American Colonization Society, of which Joseph Gales was regional secretary. The American Colonization Society was a nationwide organization that advocated the emigration of free blacks to African colonies such as Liberia in an effort to maintain white dominance in the United States. The degree of control that Horton exercised over the publication of his first book is unknown. It is remarkable, nevertheless, that the first book by a slave published in the South, in which poems such as "On Liberty and Slavery" and "A Slave's Complaint" directly protest against slavery, was probably published under the auspices of a colonizationist, rather than abolitionist, agenda.

Though the publication of his first book appears to have had little effect on his life, Horton continued to hire his time from his master and write poetry. Sometime in the 1830s, Horton married a slave belonging to Franklin Snipes of Chatham County. The couple had two children, a son named Free and a daughter named Rhody. Little else is known about Horton's family. His second book, *The Poetical Works of George Moses Horton*, was published in 1845. Because the social climate of North Carolina had grown more restrictive in the years before the Civil War, the book contained no explicitly antislavery verse. Poems such as "Division of an Estate" and "The Creditor to His Proud Debtor," however, have subtle messages of protest lurking below the surface.

Horton's life changed dramatically when the Ninth Michigan Cavalry Volunteers swept through Chapel Hill in 1865 in the waning weeks of the Civil War. Finally emancipated, Horton traveled with Captain William Banks, who published Horton's last collection of poems, *Naked Genius*, in Raleigh that year. Though Horton had the liberty he longed for, poems in *Naked Genius* reveal he found his new freedom bittersweet. "George Moses Horton, Myself" and "Death of an Old Carriage Horse" encapsulate the frustration Horton felt at gaining his freedom so late in life. "The Southern Refugee" also reveals that Horton was reluctant to leave North Carolina for the first time in his sixty-eight years.

Horton did leave his native North Carolina, living for a time in Philadelphia. "Forbidden to Ride on the Street Cars," published in the *Christian Recorder* in 1866, shows that Horton continued to protest unjust treatment of African Americans in his poetry after emancipation. Though most accounts of Horton's life speculate that he died in obscurity in Philadelphia in 1883, research by scholar Reginald H. Pitts suggests that Horton emigrated to Liberia in 1866. His fate thereafter is unknown.

The literary legacy of George Moses Horton is both impressive and permanent. From his forceful protest poetry to his lively folk verse, such as "Troubled with the Itch and Rubbing with Sulphur," Horton's varied spectrum of poetry demonstrates his range and talent. Horton's poetic achievements, notable in themselves, are only made more extraordinary because of his decades of enslavement.

Suggested Readings

Horton's three books have been long out of print. Copies of *The Hope of Liberty* are rare but, along with Horton's second book, *The Poetical Works of George M. Horton, the Colored Bard of North Carolina, to which is Prefixed The Life of the Author, Written by Himself*, are now available in electronic form through Documenting the American South, an electronic database sponsored by The Academic Affairs Library at the University of North Carolina at Chapel Hill at <http://docsouth.unc.edu>. *Naked Genius* was reprinted in small numbers in 1982 by the Chapel Hill Historical Society. The best available collection of Horton's poems is listed below under Joan R. Sherman.

Jackson, Blyden. *A History of Afro-American Literature: The Long Beginning, 1746–1895*. Baton Rouge: Louisiana State University Press, 1989. [Jackson devotes a chapter to Horton, providing critical interpretations of Horton's life and selected poems.]

Pitts, Reginald H. "'Let Us Desert This Friendless Place': George Moses Horton in Philadelphia—1866." *Journal of Negro History* 80, no. 4 (Autumn 1995): 145–56. [Pitts's article offers a compelling alternative ending to Horton's life story.]

Richmond, Merle A. *Bid the Vassal Soar: Interpretative Essays on the Life and Poetry of Phillis Wheatley (ca. 1753–1784) and George Moses Horton (ca. 1797–1883)*. Washington, D.C.: Howard University Press, 1974. [The most complete critical evaluation to date.]

Sherman, Joan R. ed. *The Black Bard of North Carolina: George Moses Horton and His Poetry*. Chapel Hill: University of North Carolina Press, 1997. [This collection includes a thorough biographical and critical introduction.]

Walser, Richard. *The Black Poet: Being the Remarkable Story (Partly Told My [sic] Himself) of George Moses Horton a North Carolina Slave*. New York: Philosophical Library, 1966. [While the only book-length biography, Walser's account of Horton's life and work is marred by the author's patronizing and often prejudiced perspective.]

Note on the Text

The poems of George Moses Horton that appear in *The North Carolina Roots of African American Literature* are reprinted in chronological order of publication, with the exception of "Acrostics," which has been transcribed from the original handwritten copy, dated c. 1844, in the Simpson and Biddle Family Papers at the North Carolina Division of Archives and History, Raleigh. "On Liberty and Slavery," "The Slave's Complaint," and "On hearing of the intention of a gentleman to purchase the Poet's freedom" are reprinted from the first edition of *The Hope of Liberty*, published in 1829. Reprinted from the first edition of *The Poetical Works of George Moses Horton* (1845) are "Troubled with the Itch, and

Rubbing with Sulphur," "The Creditor to His Proud Debtor," and "Division of an Estate." "George Moses Horton, Myself," "The Southern Refugee," "Death of an Old Carriage Horse," and "Snaps for Dinner, Snaps for Breakfast and Snaps for Supper" are reprinted from *Naked Genius*, first published in 1865. "Forbidden to Ride on the Street Cars" is reprinted from the *Christian Recorder* of Philadelphia, Pennsylvania, where the poem first appeared on November 10, 1866.

ACROSTICS

Mistress of green in flowers arrayed
Alluring all my heart away
Replete with glory not to fade
Yet flourish in eternal May—
Eternalized by distant fame—
Void of a shade in bloom divine—
Pleasures await thy sacred name
Or bid thee still proceed (s) to shine
Who has surpassed thy heavenly mein
Expression will forbear to tell
Like thee not one I yet have seen
Let all adore thee lovely belle

So let our names togather blend
In floods of union to the end
Or flow togather soul in soul
Nor distance break the soft control—
How pleasing is the thought to me
A thought of such a nymph as thee
Reverts my language into song
That flows delightful soft along—
Return to me a soft reply
On which I must with joy rely
Give me thy hand and then thy heart
Entirely mingled not to part
Relume[1] the tapor[2] near expired
Seeking a friend so long desired—

ca. 1844

1 Rekindle.
2 A wax candle, commonly spelled "taper."

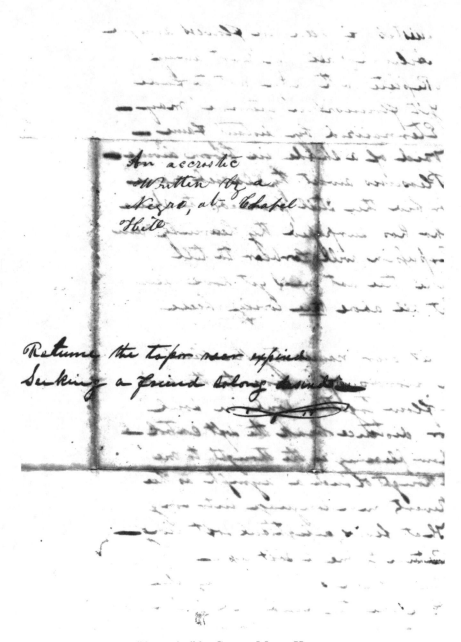

"Acrostics" by George Moses Horton

(North Carolina Department of Cultural Resources,
Office of Archives and History, Raleigh)

Acrostics

Mistress of green in flowers arrayed
Alluring all my heart away
Replete with glory not to fade
Yet flourish in eternal may —
Eternalized by distant fame —
Void of a shade in bloom divine —
Pleasures await thy sacred name
Or bid thee still proceed(s) to shine
Who has surpassed thy heavenly mien
Expression will forbear to tell
Like thee not one I yet have seen
Let all adore thee lovely belle

So let our names together blend
In floods of union to the end
Or flow together soul in soul
Nor distance break the soft control —
How pleasing is the thought to me
A thought of such a nymph as thee
Reverts my language into song
That flows delightful soft along —
Return to me a soft reply
On which I must with joy rely
Give me thy hand and then thy heart
Entirely mingled not to part

ON LIBERTY AND SLAVERY

Alas! and am I born for this,
  To wear this slavish chain?
Deprived of all created bliss,
  Through hardship, toil and pain!

How long have I in bondage lain,
  And languished to be free!
Alas! and must I still complain—
  Deprived of liberty.

Oh, Heaven! and is there no relief
  This side the silent grave—
To soothe the pain—to quell the grief
  And anguish of a slave?

Come Liberty, thou cheerful sound,
  Roll through my ravished ears!
Come, let my brief in joys be drowned,
  And drive away my fears.

Say unto foul oppression, Cease:
  Ye tyrants rage no more,
And let the joyful trump of peace,
  Now bid the vassal soar.

Soar on the pinions of that dove
  Which long has cooed for thee,
And breathed her notes from Afric's grove,
  The sound of Liberty.

Oh, Liberty! thou golden prize,
  So often sought by blood—
We crave thy sacred sun to rise,
  The gift of nature's God!

Bid Slavery hide her haggard face,
  And barbarism fly:
I scorn to see the sad disgrace
  In which enslaved I lie.

Dear Liberty! upon thy breast,
  I languish to respire;
And like the Swan unto her nest,
  I'd to thy smiles retire.

Oh, blest asylum—heavenly balm!
  Unto thy boughs I flee—
And in thy shades the storm shall calm,
  With songs of Liberty!

Lancaster *Gazette*, April 8, 1828
The Hope of Liberty (1829)
Emancipator, October 12, 1857

THE SLAVE'S COMPLAINT

Am I sadly cast aside,
On misfortune's rugged tide?
Will the world my pains deride
　　Forever?

Must I dwell in Slavery's night,
And all pleasure takes its flight,
Far beyond my feeble sight,
　　Forever?

Worst of all, must Hope grow dim,
And withhold her cheering beam?
Rather let me sleep and dream
　　Forever!

Something still my heart surveys,
Groping through this dreary maze;
Is it Hope?—then burn and blaze
　　Forever!

Leave me not a wretch confined,
Altogether lame and blind—
Unto gross despair consigned,
　　Forever!

Heaven! in whom can I confide?
Canst thou not for all provide?
Condescend to be my guide
　　Forever:

And when this transient life shall end,
Oh, may some kind eternal friend
Bid me from servitude ascend,
　　Forever!

The Hope of Liberty (1829)

Caroline Lee Hentz,
George Moses Horton's first literary sponsor
*(North Carolina Collection, University of North Carolina
Library at Chapel Hill)*

❖

ON HEARING OF THE INTENTION
OF A GENTLEMAN TO PURCHASE
THE POET'S FREEDOM

When on life's ocean first I spread my sail,
I then implored a mild auspicious gale;
And from the slippery strand I took my flight,
And sought the peaceful haven of delight.

Tyrannic storms arose upon my soul,
And dreadful did their mad'ning thunders roll;
The pensive muse[3] was shaken from her sphere,
And hope, it vanish'd in the clouds of fear.

At length a golden sun broke thro' the gloom,
And from his smiles arose a sweet perfume—
A calm ensued, and birds began to sing,
And lo! the sacred muse resumed her wing.

With frantic joy she chaunted as she flew,
And kiss'd the clement[4] hand that bore her thro';
Her envious foes did from her sight retreat,
Or prostrate fall beneath her burning feet.

'Twas like a proselyte,[5] allied to Heaven—
Or rising spirits' boast of sins forgiven,
Whose shout dissolves the adamant away
Whose melting voice the stubborn rocks obey.

'Twas like the salutation of the dove,
Borne on the zephyr[6] thro' some lonesome grove,
When Spring returns, and Winter's chill is past,
And vegetation smiles above the blast.

---

3 Greek goddess of the arts, responsible for inspiring poets.
4 Kind, merciful.

5 A convert to a religion.
6 A gentle breeze or wind.

'Twas like the evening of a nuptial pair,
When love pervades the hour of sad despair—
'Twas like fair Helen's sweet return to Troy,[7]
When every Grecian bosom swell'd with joy.

The silent harp which on the osiers[8] hung,
Was then attuned, and manumission[9] sung:
Away by hope the clouds of fear were driven,
And music breathed my gratitude to heaven.

Hard was the race to reach the distant goal,
The needle oft was shaken from the pole;
In such distress who could forbear to weep?
Toss'd by the headlong billows of the deep!

The tantalizing beams which shone so plain,
Which turn'd my former pleasures into pain—
Which falsely promised all the joys of fame,
Gave way, and to a more substantial flame.

Some philanthropic souls as from afar,
With pity strove to break the slavish bar;
To whom my floods of gratitude shall roll,
And yield with pleasure to their soft control.

And sure of Providence this work begun—
He shod my feet this rugged race to run;
And in despite of all the swelling tide,
Along the dismal path will prove my guide.

Thus on the dusky verge of deep despair,
Eternal Providence was with me there;
When pleasure seemed to fade on life's gay dawn,
And the last beam of hope was almost gone.

Raleigh *Register*, October 7, 1828
The Hope of Liberty (1829)

7 The Greeks waged war on Troy
  to return the beautiful Helen in
  Homer's *Iliad*.

8 Branches of a willow tree.
9 Emancipation.

University of North Carolina campus
during George Moses Horton's lifetime
*(North Carolina Collection, University of North Carolina
Library at Chapel Hill)*

❖

TROUBLED WITH THE ITCH,
AND RUBBING WITH SULPHUR

'Tis bitter, yet 'tis sweet,
   Scratching effects but transient ease;
Pleasure and pain together meet,
   And vanish as they please.

My nails, the only balm,
   To ev'ry bump are oft applied,
And thus the rage will sweetly calm
   Which aggravates my hide.

It soon returns again;
   A frown succeeds to ev'ry smile;
Grinning I scratch and curse the pain,
   But grieve to be so vile.

In fine, I know not which
   Can play the most deceitful game,
The devil, sulphur,[10] or the itch;
   The three are but the same.

The devil sows the itch,
   And sulphur has a loathsome smell,
And with my clothes as black as pitch,
   I stink where'er I dwell.

Excoriated[11] deep,
   By friction play'd on ev'ry part,
It oft deprives me of my sleep,
   And plagues me to my heart.

The Poetical Works of
George Moses Horton (1845)

10 A nonmetallic substance sometimes
used in skin ointments; also known
as brimstone.

11 Stripped or peeled of skin.

❖

THE CREDITOR TO HIS PROUD DEBTOR

Ha, tott'ring Johny, strut and boast,
But think of what your feathers cost;
Your crowing days are short at most,
   You bloom but soon to fade;
Surely you could not stand so wide,
If strictly to the bottom tried,
The wind would blow your plume aside
   If half your debts were paid.
     Then boast and bear the crack,
     With the sheriff at your back;
     Huzza for dandy Jack,
     My jolly fop,[12] my Joe.

The blue smoke from your segar[13] flies,
Offensive to my nose and eyes;
The most of people would be wise
   Your presence to evade;
Your pocket jingles loud with cash,
And thus you cut a foppish dash,
But, alas! dear boy, you would be trash,
   If your accounts were paid.
     Then boast and bear the crack, &c.

My duck bill boots[14] would look as bright,
Had you in justice served me right;
Like you I then could step as light,
   Before a flaunting maid;
As nicely could I clear my throat,
And to my tights my eyes devote;
But I'd leave you bare without that coat,
   For which you have not paid.
     Then boast and bear the crack, &c.

---

12 A vain, foolish man; a dandy.   14 Broad-toed boots.
13 Cigar.

I'd toss myself with a scornful air,
And to a poor man may pay no care;
I could rock cross-leg'd on my chair
   Within the cloister[15] shade;
I'd gird my neck with a light cravat,
And creaning[16] wear my bell-crown hat;
But away my down would fly at that,
  If once my debts were paid.
    Then boast and bear the crack,
    With a sheriff at your back;
    Huzza for dandy Jack,
    My jolly fop, my Joe.

The Poetical Works of
George Moses Horton (1845)

---

15 A place of seclusion.   16 Possibly a variant of crooning.

DIVISION OF AN ESTATE

It well bespeaks a man beheaded, quite
Divested of the laurel[17] robe of life,
When every member struggles for its base,
The head; the power of order now recedes,
Unheeded efforts rise on every side,
With dull emotion rolling through the brain
Of apprehending slaves. The flocks and herds,
In sad confusion, now run to and fro,
And seem to ask, distressed, the reason why
That they are thus prostrated. Howl, ye dogs!
Ye cattle, low! ye sheep, astonish'd, bleat!
Ye bristling swine, trudge squealing through the glades,
Void of an owner to impart your food!
Sad horses, lift your head and neigh aloud,
And caper frantic from the dismal scene;
Mow the last food upon your grass-clad lea,[18]
And leave a solitary home behind,
In hopeless widowhood no longer gay!
The trav'ling sun of gain his journey ends
In unavailing pain; he sets with tears;
A king sequester'd sinking from his throne,
Succeeded by a train of busy friends,
Like stars which rise with smiles, to mark the flight
Of awful Phoebus[19] to another world;
Stars after stars in fleet succession rise
Into the wide empire of fortune clear,
Regardless of the donor of their lamps,
Like heirs forgetful of parental care,
Without a grateful smile or filial tear,
Redound in rev'rence to expiring age.
But soon parental benediction flies

17 A symbol of honor.
18 Meadow or pasture.
19 A name for the Greek sun god
Apollo, who was also the god of
music and poetry.

Like vivid meteors; in a moment gone,
As though they ne'er had been. But O! the state,
The dark suspense in which poor vassals[20] stand,
Each mind upon the spire of chance hangs fluctuant;
The day of separation is at hand;
Imagination lifts her gloomy curtains,
Like ev'ning's mantle at the flight of day,
Thro' which the trembling pinnacle we spy,
On which we soon must stand with hopeful smiles,
Or apprehending frowns; to tumble on
The right or left forever.

The Poetical Works of
George Moses Horton (1845)

20 Servants or subordinates; in this case, slaves.

GEORGE MOSES HORTON, MYSELF

I feel myself in need
  Of the inspiring strains of ancient lore,
My heart to lift, my empty mind to feed,
  And all the world explore.

I know that I am old
  And never can recover what is past,
But for the future may some light unfold
  And soar from ages blast.

I feel resolved to try,
  My wish to prove, my calling to pursue,
Or mount up from the earth into the sky,
  To show what Heaven can do.

My genius from a boy,
  Has fluttered like a bird within my heart;
But could not thus confined her powers to employ,
  Impatient to depart.

She like a restless bird,
  Would spread her wing, her power to be unfurl'd,
And let her songs be loudly heard,
  And dart from world to world.

Naked Genius (1865)

THE SOUTHERN REFUGEE

What sudden ill the world await,
   From my dear residence I roam;
I must deplore the bitter fate,
   To straggle from my native home.

The verdant[21] willow droops her head,
   And seems to bid a fare thee well;
The flowers with tears their fragrance shed,
   Alas! their parting tale to tell.

'Tis like the loss of Paradise,
   Or Eden's garden left in gloom,[22]
Where grief affords us no device,
   Such is thy lot, my native home.

I never, never shall forget,
   My sad departure far away,
Until the sun of life is set,
   And leaves behind no beam of day.

How can I from my seat remove
   And leave my ever devoted home,
And the dear garden which I love,
   The beauty of my native home.

Alas! sequestered, set aside,
   It is a mournful tale to tell;
'Tis like a lone deserted bride
   That bade her bridegroom fare thee well.

I trust I soon shall dry the tear
   And leave forever hence to roam,
Far from a residence so dear,
   The place of beauty—my native home.

Naked Genius (1865)

21 Green with vegetation.
22 As told in Genesis 3:22–24, Adam and Eve lived in the Garden of Eden, or Paradise, until expelled for eating from the Tree of Knowledge of Good and Evil.

DEATH OF AN OLD CARRIAGE HORSE

I was a harness horse,
   Constrained to travel weak or strong,
With orders from oppressing force,
   Push along, push along.

I had no space of rest,
   And took at forks the roughest prong,
Still by the cruel driver pressed,
   Push along, push along.

Vain strove the idle bird,
   To charm me with her artless song,
But pleasure lingered from the word,
   Push along, push along.

The order of the day
   Was push, the peal of every tongue,
The only word was all the way,
   Push along, push along.

Thus to my journey's end,
   Had I to travel right or wrong,
'Till death my sweet and favored friend,
   Bade me from life to push along.

Naked Genius (1865)

❖

SNAPS FOR DINNER, SNAPS FOR BREAKFAST
AND SNAPS FOR SUPPER

Come in to dinner squalls the dame,
   You need it now perhaps,
But hear the husband's loud exclaim,
   I do not like your snaps,
'Tis the snaps when at your breakfast meal,
   And snaps when at your spinning wheel,
Too many by a devilish deal,
   For all your words are snaps.

Why do you tarry, tell me why?
   The chamber door she taps,
Eat by yourself, my dear, for I
   Am surfeited with snaps,
For if I cough it is the cry,
   You always snap at supper time,
I'd rather lave in vats of lime,[23]
   Than face you with your snaps.

How gladly would I be a book,
   To your long pocket flaps,
That you my face may read and look,
   And learn the worth of snaps,
I'm sorry that I learning lack,
   To turn you to an almanac,
Next year I'll hang you on the rack,
   And end the date of snaps.

Naked Genius (1865)

23 To wash in tubs of a highly caustic lime solution.

FORBIDDEN TO RIDE ON THE STREET CARS[24]

Why wilt thou from the right revolt?
   I wish to ride not far;
Why wilt thou fear the mild result,
Nor bid the humble horses halt,
   But spurn me from the car?

And though I wish to travel fleet,
   Regardless of a jar,
A short mile's journey to complete,
I dare not ride along the street,
   Within a rattling car.

What retribution wilt thou meet,
   When summon'd to the bar!
Wilt thou not from the call retreat?
Leave not the traveller on his feet,
   Alone to watch the car.

Like thee, we bravely fought our way,
   Before the shafts of war;
Lest thou shouldst fall the rebels' prey;
Why canst thou not a moment stay,
   And take one on the car?

E'er long, we trust, the time will come,
   We'll ride, however far;
And all ride on together home,
When freedom will be in full bloom,
   Regardless of the car!

Philadelphia, *Christian Recorder*,
November 10, 1866

24. This poem originally appeared with a note from the editor of the *Christian Recorder* that read: "The writer, widely known as 'The Slave Poet,' recently saw a colored person enter a Philadelphia passenger railway car, which had stopped for a passenger, but the conductor immediately compelled her to leave. The following lines were suggested."

JENNIFER LARSON

WALKER'S

APPEAL,

IN FOUR ARTICLES;

TOGETHER WITH

A PREAMBLE,

TO THE

COLOURED CITIZENS OF THE WORLD,

BUT IN PARTICULAR, AND VERY EXPRESSLY, TO THOSE OF

THE UNITED STATES OF AMERICA,

WRITTEN IN BOSTON, STATE OF MASSACHUSETTS,
SEPTEMBER 28, 1829.

―――――

THIRD AND LAST EDITION,
WITH ADDITIONAL NOTES, CORRECTIONS, &C.

―――――

Boston:

REVISED AND PUBLISHED BY DAVID WALKER.

· · · · · · · · · · · · · · · ·

1830.

Title page of David Walker's *Appeal*

(Documenting the American South, <http://docsouth.unc.edu>,
The University of North Carolina at Chapel Hill Libraries, North Carolina Collection)

DAVID WALKER'S strident, unprecedented call for African American racial pride and human rights has influenced generations of activists, writers, and historians. Whether hailed as the father of black nationalism or dismissed as a racial extremist, Walker endures, holding a key role in the African American literary tradition. Borrowing its structure from the U.S. Constitution, Walker's *Appeal in Four Articles; Together with a Preamble, to the Colored Citizens of the World, but in Particular and Very Expressly, to Those of the United States of America* challenges black and white readers to recognize how much the America of 1829 failed to live up to the ideal America envisioned in its founding documents.

Despite the *Appeal*'s notoriety, the life of its author remains largely a mystery. Walker was born in Wilmington, North Carolina, around 1796 to a free black mother and enslaved father whose identities are as yet unverified. Census records and comments in the *Appeal* suggest that Walker left the city in his late twenties and eventually settled in Charleston, South Carolina, a city that at the time had more free black citizens than any other in the South. After the failure of the Denmark Vesey conspiracy (in which Walker may have been involved) to take control of Charleston, Walker, like many free blacks, headed north. The *Appeal* indicates that Walker traveled the country widely, often witnessing racial atrocities, but we know little about these journeys. Around 1825, Walker settled in Boston and opened a used-clothing store. In 1826, he married Eliza Butler, a Boston native and daughter of one of the city's prominent black families; they had three children. Walker soon became highly involved in Boston's black community. He joined the Prince Hall, or African, Masonry Lodge No. 459, the May Street Methodist Church, and the Massachusetts General Colored Association, a social organization later absorbed into the New England Anti-Slavery Society. Earning a reputation as a dedicated, fiery activist, Walker served, beginning in 1827, as the principal agent in Boston for *Freedom's Journal*, the first black newspaper in the United States. The source of Walker's education is also unknown, but he was likely self-educated.

With his own funds, Walker published the first edition of his *Appeal* as a pamphlet in 1829 and revised it twice, releasing the final edition in 1830. The pamphlets were likely produced with the aid of white printers and distributed by mail or sewn into the linings of clothes sold at Walker's store. The first notice of the *Appeal*'s appearance in the South came when the Savannah, Georgia, police announced the seizure of sixty copies. Soon after, Georgia's governor urged the state legislature to enact laws forbidding further distribution of the *Appeal* and related literature. The *Appeal* was also banned by lawmakers in North Carolina, South Carolina, Louisiana, and Virginia. White abolitionists as radical as William Lloyd Garrison welcomed the *Appeal*'s message but rejected its angry tone.

The *Appeal* circulated widely in the South and North. Because of high illiteracy rates among blacks, Walker may have designed the text to be read aloud, like a sermon, to large groups of enslaved people. Christianity's influence on Walker is evident throughout the text, particularly in his insistence that "the colored citizens of the world" were God's chosen people, morally superior to whites and destined to be delivered out of slavery by divine justice. Fearing black ministers would deploy the argument of the *Appeal* in their preaching, white authorities in some southern localities outlawed unsupervised black religious services. These fears were not unwarranted, in light of the fact that many contemporary slaveholders, as well as later historians, believe that Walker's *Appeal* played an inspirational role in Nat Turner's 1831 slave rebellion in Southampton County, Virginia. Indeed, anxieties about the influence of the *Appeal* were so rampant that southern planters are rumored to have plotted Walker's assassination. Many scholars still believe that these plots were successful, although Walker's death certificate suggests he died of consumption in 1830, only days after his daughter succumbed to the same disease.

Walker's *Appeal* has been celebrated for its catalogs of slavery's brutalities, its denunciations of white religious and political hypocrisy, and, most important, its vehement exhortation to black Americans to claim their rights and dignity as citizens, by force if necessary. Though the militant aspects of the *Appeal* dominate critical attention to the text, it is important to realize that Walker ends his text with hope for healing. In the *Appeal*'s final article, "Article IV: Our Wretchedness in Consequence of the Colonization Plan," he asserts that racial reconciliation is possible as long as America grants its black citizens the freedom and human rights they deserve.

Suggested Readings

Aptheker, Herbert. *One Continual Cry; David Walker's Appeal to the Colored Citizens of the World, 1829–1830, its Setting and its Meaning, Together with the Full Text of the Third, and Last, Edition of the Appeal.* New York: Humanities Press, 1965.

Berson, Robin Kadison. *Marching to a Different Drummer: Unrecognized Heroes of American History*. Westport, Conn.: Greenwood Press, 1994.

Brawley, Benjamin Griffith. *Early Black American Writers: Selections with Biographical and Critical Introductions*. Mineola, N.Y.: Dover, 1992. Originally published as *Early Negro American Writers*. New York: Dover, 1970.

Hinks, Peter P. *To Awaken My Afflicted Brethren: David Walker and the Problem of Antebellum Slave Resistance*. University Park: Pennsylvania State University Press, 1997. [The most complete cultural and biographical source.]

——, ed. *David Walker's Appeal to the Coloured Citizens of the World*. University Park: Pennsylvania State University Press, 2002. [The most complete and thoroughly annotated edition of the *Appeal*.]

Jacobs, Donald M., ed. *Courage and Conscience: Black and White Abolitionists in Boston*. Bloomington: Indiana University Press, 1993.

Vogel, Todd, ed. *The Black Press: New Literary and Historical Essays*. New Brunswick: Rutgers University Press, 2001. See pp. 17–36.

Walker, David. *Walker's Appeal, In Four Articles; Together with a Preamble, to the Coloured Citizens of the World, but in Particular and Very Expressly, to Those of The United States of America*. 3rd ed. Boston: the Author, 1830.

Note on the Text

The following selections from Walker's *Appeal* are reprinted from the third edition. Published in the spring of 1830 only a few months before Walker's death, the third edition reflects the author's final revisions and polish. These revisions intensified Walker's condemnation of slavery while reinforcing the spiritual basis of both his charges against whites and his call to black Americans.

❖

From DAVID WALKER'S APPEAL, IN FOUR ARTICLES; TOGETHER WITH A PREAMBLE, TO THE COLOURED CITIZENS OF THE WORLD, BUT IN PARTICULAR, AND VERY EXPRESSLY, TO THOSE OF THE UNITED STATES OF AMERICA

Preamble.

My dearly beloved Brethren and Fellow Citizens.

Having travelled over a considerable portion of these United States, and having, in the course of my travels, taken the most accurate observations of things as they exist—the result of my observations has warranted the full and unshaken conviction, that we, (coloured people of these United States,) are the most degraded, wretched, and abject set of beings that ever lived since the world began; and I pray God that none like us ever may live again until time shall be no more. They tell us of the Israelites in Egypt,[1] the Helots in Sparta,[2] and of the Roman Slaves,[3] which last were made up from almost every nation under heaven, whose sufferings under those ancient and heathen nations, were, in comparison with ours, under this enlightened and Christian nation, no more than a cypher—or, in other words, those heathen nations of antiquity, had but little more among them than the name and form of slavery; while wretchedness and endless miseries were reserved, apparently in a phial, to be poured out upon our fathers, ourselves and our children, by *Christian* Americans!

These positions I shall endeavour, by the help of the Lord, to demonstrate in the course of this *Appeal*, to the satisfaction of the most incredulous mind—and may God Almighty, who is the Father of our Lord Jesus Christ, open your hearts to understand and believe the truth.

The *causes*, my brethren, which produce our wretchedness and miser-

1 The most complete account of the Israelites in Egypt that Walker would have known is the book of Exodus in the Old Testament.
2 State-owned agricultural serfs in Sparta, an ancient Greek city-state.
3 The Roman slave population con- sisted primarily of war prisoners, kidnapped foreigners, and the progeny of other slaves (children followed the condition of the mother). In Rome, however, slaves were allowed to buy their own freedom and become citizens.

ies, are so very numerous and aggravating, that I believe the pen only of a Josephus or a Plutarch,[4] can well enumerate and explain them. Upon subjects, then, of such incomprehensible magnitude, so impenetrable, and so notorious, I shall be obliged to omit a large class of, and content myself with giving you an exposition of a few of those, which do indeed rage to such an alarming pitch, that they cannot but be a perpetual source of terror and dismay to every reflecting mind.

I am fully aware, in making this appeal to my much afflicted and suffering brethren, that I shall not only be assailed by those whose greatest earthly desires are, to keep us in abject ignorance and wretchedness, and who are of the firm conviction that Heaven has designed us and our children to be slaves and *beasts of burden* to them and their children. I say, I do not only expect to be held up to the public as an ignorant, impudent and restless disturber of the public peace, by such avaricious creatures, as well as a mover of insubordination—and perhaps put in prison or to death, for giving a superficial exposition of our miseries, and exposing tyrants. But I am persuaded, that many of my brethren, particularly those who are ignorantly in league with slave-holders or tyrants, who acquire their daily bread by the blood and sweat of their more ignorant brethren—and not a few of those too, who are too ignorant to see an inch beyond their noses, will rise up and call me cursed—Yea, the jealous ones among us will perhaps use more abject subtlety, by affirming that this work is not worth perusing, that we are well situated, and there is no use in trying to better our condition, for we cannot. I will ask one question here.—Can our condition be any worse?—Can it be more mean and abject? If there are any changes, will they not be for the better, though they may appear for the worst at first? Can they get us any lower? Where can they get us? They are afraid to treat us worse, for they know well, the day they do it they are gone. But against all accusations which may or can be preferred against me, I appeal to Heaven for my motive in writing—who knows that my object is, if possible, to awaken in the breasts of my afflicted, degraded and slumbering brethren, a spirit of inquiry and investigation respecting our miseries and wretchedness in this *Republican Land of Liberty!!!!!!*

The sources from which our miseries are derived, and on which I shall comment, I shall not combine in one, but shall put them under distinct heads and expose them in their turn; in doing which, keeping truth on

4. Greek biographer and moral philosopher (46–120? C.E.); Josephus: Jewish statesman and historian (37–100? C.E.).

my side, and not departing from the strictest rules of morality, I shall endeavour to penetrate, search out, and lay them open for your inspection. If you cannot or will not profit by them, I shall have done *my* duty to you, my country and my God.

And as the inhuman system of *slavery*, is the *source* from which most of our miseries proceed, I shall begin with that *curse to nations*, which has spread terror and devastation through so many nations of antiquity, and which is raging to such a pitch at the present day in Spain and in Portugal. It had one tug in England, in France, and in the United States of America yet the inhabitants thereof, do not learn wisdom, and erase it entirely from their dwellings and from all with whom they have to do. The fact is, the labour of slaves comes so cheap to the avaricious usurpers, and is (as they think) of such great utility to the country where it exists, that those who are actuated by sordid avarice only, overlook the evils, which will as sure as the Lord lives, follow after the good. In fact, they are so happy to keep in ignorance and degradation, and to receive the homage and the labour of the slaves, they forget that God rules in the armies of heaven and among the inhabitants of the earth, having his ears continually open to the cries, tears and groans of his oppressed people; and being a just and holy Being will at one day appear fully in behalf of the oppressed, and arrest the progress of the avaricious oppressors; for although the destruction of the oppressors God may not effect by the oppressed, yet the Lord our God will bring other destructions upon them—for not unfrequently will he cause them to rise up one against another, to be split and divided, and to oppress each other, and sometimes to open hostilities with sword in hand. Some may ask, what is the matter with this united and happy people?—Some say it is the cause of political usurpers, tyrants, oppressors, &c. But has not the Lord an oppressed and suffering people among them? Does the Lord condescend to hear their cries and see their tears in consequence of oppression? Will he let the oppressors rest comfortably and happy always? Will he not cause the very children of the oppressors to rise up against them, and oftimes put them to death? "God works in many ways his wonders to perform."[5]

I will not here speak of the destructions which the Lord brought upon Egypt, in consequence of the oppression and consequent groans of the oppressed—of the hundreds and thousands of Egyptians whom God

---

5 Adapted from William Cowper's hymn "Light Shining Out of Darkness" (1772). The actual lines read, "God moves in a mysterious way, / His wonders to perform."

hurled into the Red Sea for afflicting his people in their land—of the Lord's suffering people in Sparta or Lacedaemon,[6] the land of the truly famous Lycurgus[7]—nor have I time to comment upon the cause which produced the fierceness with which Sylla usurped the title, and absolutely acted as dictator of the Roman people—the conspiracy of Cataline—the conspiracy against, and murder of Cæsar in the Senate house—the spirit with which Marc Antony made himself master of the commonwealth— his associating Octavius and Lipidus with himself in power—their divid- ing the provinces of Rome among themselves—their attack and defeat, on the plains of Phillippi, of the last defenders of their liberty, (Brutus and Cassius)—the tyranny of Tiberius,[8] and from him to the final overthrow of Constantinople by the Turkish Sultan, Mahomed II.[9] A.D. 1453. I say, I shall not take up time to speak of the *causes* which produced so much wretchedness and massacre among those heathen nations, for I am aware that you know too well, that God is just, as well as merciful!—I shall call your attention a few moments to that *Christian* nation, the Spaniards— while I shall leave almost unnoticed, that avaricious and cruel people, the Portuguese, among whom all true hearted Christians and lovers of Jesus Christ, must evidently see the judgments of God displayed. To show the judgments of God upon the Spaniards, I shall occupy but a little time, leaving a plenty of room for the candid and unprejudiced to reflect.

All persons who are acquainted with history, and particularly the Bible, who are not blinded by the God of this world, and are not actu- ated solely by avarice—who are able to lay aside prejudice long enough to view candidly and impartially, things as they were, are, and probably will be—who are willing to admit that God made man to serve Him *alone*, and that man should have no other Lord or Lords but Himself—that God Almighty is the *sole proprietor* or *master* of the WHOLE human family, and will not on any consideration admit of a colleague, being unwilling to divide his glory with another—and who can dispense with prejudice long enough to admit that we are *men*, notwithstanding our *improminent noses* and *woolly heads*, and believe that we feel for our fathers, mothers,

6 A region of ancient Greece; Sparta: capital of Lacedaemon.
7 A reformer and legislator of Sparta, descended from Hercules (c. 800 B.C.E.).
8 Walker is tracing the major events and leaders of the civil wars that, during the last century B.C.E., trans- formed Rome from a republic into a dictatorship under the emperor Augustus (31 B.C.E.–14 C.E.) and his successor Tiberius (d. 37 C.E.).
9 Muhammad II (1429–81 C.E.) con- quered the Byzantine Empire in 1453.

wives and children, as well as the whites do for theirs.—I say, all who are permitted to see and believe these things, can easily recognize the judgments of God among the Spaniards. Though others may lay the cause of the fierceness with which they cut each other's throats, to some other circumstance, yet they who believe that God is a God of justice, will believe that SLAVERY *is the principal cause.*

While the Spaniards are running about upon the field of battle cutting each other's throats, has not the Lord an afflicted and suffering people in the midst of them, whose cries and groans in consequence of oppression are continually pouring into the ears of the God of justice? Would they not cease to cut each other's throats, if they could? But how can they? The very support which they draw from government to aid them in perpetrating such enormities, does it not arise in a great degree from the wretched victims of oppression among them? And yet they are calling for *Peace!—Peace!!* Will any peace be given unto them? Their destruction may indeed be procrastinated awhile, but can it continue long, while they are oppressing the Lord's people? Has He not the hearts of all men in His hand? Will he suffer one part of his creatures to go on oppressing another like brutes always, with impunity? And yet, those avaricious wretches are calling for *Peace!!!!* I declare, it does appear to me, as though some nations think God is asleep, or that he made the Africans for nothing else but to dig their mines and work their farms, or they cannot believe history, sacred or profane. I ask every man who has a heart, and is blessed with the privilege of believing—Is not God a God of justice to *all* his creatures? Do you say he is? Then if he gives peace and tranquillity to tyrants, and permits them to keep our fathers, our mothers, ourselves and our children in eternal ignorance and wretchedness, to support them and their families, would he be to us a God of *justice?* I ask, O ye *Christians!!!* who hold us and our children in the most abject ignorance and degradation, that ever a people were afflicted with since the world began—I say, if God gives you peace and tranquillity, and suffers you thus to go on afflicting us, and our children, who have never given you the least provocation—would he be to us *a God of justice?* If you will allow that we are MEN, who feel for each other, does not the blood of our fathers and of us their children, cry aloud to the Lord of Sabaoth against you, for the cruelties and murders with which you have, and do continue to afflict us. But it is time for me to close my remarks on the suburbs, just to enter more fully into the interior of this system of cruelty and oppression.

Our Wretchedness in Consequence of Slavery

My beloved brethren:—The Indians of North and of South America—the Greeks—the Irish, subjected under the king of Great Britain—the Jews, that ancient people of the Lord—the inhabitants of the islands of the sea—in fine, all the inhabitants of the earth, (except however, the sons of Africa) are called *men*, and of course are, and ought to be free. But we, (coloured people) and our children are *brutes!!* and of course are, and *ought to be* SLAVES to the American people and their children forever!! to dig their mines and work their farms; and thus go on enriching them, from one generation to another with our *blood* and our *tears!!!!*

I promised in a preceding page to demonstrate to the satisfaction of the most incredulous, that we, (coloured people of these United States of America) are the *most wretched, degraded* and *abject* set of beings that *ever lived* since the world began, and that the white Americans having reduced us to the wretched state of *slavery*, treat us in that condition *more cruel* (they being an enlighted and Christian people,) than any heathen nation did any people whom it had reduced to our condition. These affirmations are so well confirmed in the minds of all unprejudiced men, who have taken the trouble to read histories, that they need no elucidation from me. But to put them beyond all doubt, I refer you in the first place to the children of Jacob, or of Israel in Egypt, under Pharaoh and his people. Some of my brethren do not know who Pharaoh and the Egyptians were—I know it to be a fact, that some of them take the Egyptians to have been a gang of *devils*, not knowing any better, and that they (Egyptians) having got possession of the Lord's people, treated them *nearly* as cruel as *Christian Americans* do us, at the present day. For the information of such, I would only mention that the Egyptians, were Africans or coloured people, such as we are—some of them yellow and others dark—a mixture of Ethiopians and the natives of Egypt—about the same as you see the coloured people of the United States at the present day.—I say, I call your attention then, to the children of Jacob, while I point out particularly to you his son Joseph, among the rest, in Egypt.

"And Pharaoh, said unto Joseph, thou shalt be over my house, and according unto thy word shall all my people be ruled: only in the throne will I be greater than thou."[10]

10 See Genesis, chap. xli. [Walker's note]. See verses 39–40.

"And Pharaoh said unto Joseph, see, I have set thee over all the land of Egypt."[11]

"And Pharaoh said unto Joseph, I am Pharaoh, and without thee shall no man lift up his hand or foot in all the land of Egypt."[12]

Now I appeal to heaven and to earth, and particularly to the American people themselves, who cease not to declare that our condition is not *hard*, and that we are comparatively satisfied to rest in wretchedness and misery, under them and their children. Not, indeed, to show me a coloured President, a Governor, a Legislator, a Senator, a Mayor, or an Attorney at the Bar. — But to show me a man of colour, who holds the low office of a Constable, or one who sits in a Juror Box, even on a case of one of his wretched brethren, throughout this great Republic!! — But let us pass Joseph the son of Israel a little farther in review, as he existed with that heathen nation.

"And Pharaoh called Joseph's name Zaphnath paaneah; and he gave him to wife Asenath the daughter of Potipherah priest of On. And Joseph went out over all the land of Egypt."[13]

Compare the above, with the American institutions. Do they not institute laws to prohibit us from marrying among the whites? I would wish, candidly, however, before the Lord, to be understood, that I would not give a *pinch of snuff* to be married to any white person I ever saw in all the days of my life. And I do say it, that the black man, or man of colour, who will leave his own colour (provided he can get one, who is good for any thing) and marry a white woman, to be a double slave to her, just because she is *white*, ought to be treated by her as he surely will be, viz: as a NIGGER!!!! It is not, indeed, what I care about inter-marriages with the whites, which induced me to pass this subject in review; for the Lord knows, that there is a day coming when they will be glad enough to get into the company of the blacks, notwithstanding, we are, in this generation, levelled by them, almost on a level with the brute creation: and some of us they treat even worse than they do the brutes that perish. I only made this extract to show how much lower we are held, and how much more cruel we are treated by the Americans, than were the children of Jacob, by the Egyptians. — We will notice the sufferings of Israel some further, under *heathen Pharaoh*, compared with ours under the *enlightened Christians of America*.

"And Pharaoh spoke unto Joseph, saying, thy father and thy brethren are come unto thee:

11 xli. 41. [Walker's note]   13 xli. 45. [Walker's note]
12 xli. 44. [Walker's note]

"The land of Egypt is before thee: in the best of the land make thy father and brethren to dwell; in the land of Goshen let them dwell: and if thou knowest any men of activity among them, then make them rulers over my cattle."[14]

I ask those people who treat us so *well*, Oh! I ask them, where is the most barren spot of land which they have given unto us? Israel had the most fertile land in all Egypt. Need I mention the very notorious fact, that I have known a poor man of colour, who laboured night and day, to ac-quire a little money, and having acquired it, he vested it in a small piece of land, and got him a house erected thereon, and having paid for the whole, he moved his family into it, where he was suffered to remain but nine months, when he was cheated out of his property by a white man, and driven out of door! And is not this the case generally? Can a man of co-lour buy a piece of land and keep it peaceably? Will not some white man try to get it from him, even if it is in a *mud hole?* I need not comment any farther on a subject, which all, both black and white, will readily admit. But I must, really, observe that in this very city, when a man of colour dies, if he owned any real estate it most generally falls into the hands of some white person. The wife and children of the deceased may weep and lament if they please, but the estate will be kept snug enough by its white possessor.

But to prove farther that the condition of the Israelites was better under the Egyptians than ours is under the whites. I call upon the pro-fessing Christians, I call upon the philanthropist, I call upon the very tyrant himself, to show me a page of history, either sacred or profane, on which a verse can be found, which maintains, that the Egyptians heaped the *insupportable insult* upon the children of Israel, by telling them that they were not of the *human family*. Can the whites deny this charge? Have they not, after having reduced us to the deplorable condition of slaves under their feet, held us up as descending originally from the tribes of *Monkeys* or *Orang-Outangs?* O! my God! I appeal to every man of feel-ing—is not this insupportable? Is it not heaping the most gross insult upon our miseries, because they have got us under their feet and we can-not help ourselves? Oh! pity us we pray thee, Lord Jesus, Master.—Has Mr. Jefferson declared to the world, that we are inferior to the whites, both in the endowments of our bodies and of minds?[15] It is indeed sur-

14 Genesis, chap. xlvii. 5, 6. [Walker's note]

15 In Query xiv of his *Notes on the State of Virginia* (1787), Jefferson

(1743–1826) records his observations regarding the mental and physical characteristics of African-descended people.

prising, that a man of such great learning, combined with such excellent natural parts, should speak so of a set of men in chains. I do not know what to compare it to, unless, like putting one wild deer in an iron cage, where it will be secured, and hold another by the side of the same, then let it go, and expect the one in the cage to run as fast as the one at liberty. So far, my brethren, were the Egyptians from heaping these insults upon their slaves, that Pharoah's daughter took Moses, a son of Israel for her own, as will appear by the following.

"And Pharoah's daughter said unto her, [Moses' mother] take this child away, and nurse it for me, and I will pay thee thy wages. And the woman took the child [Moses] and nursed it.

"And the child grew, and she brought him unto Pharoah's daughter and he became her son. And she called his name Moses: and she said because I drew him out of the water."[16]

In all probability, Moses would have become Prince Regent to the throne, and no doubt, in process of time but he would have been seated on the throne of Egypt. But he had rather suffer shame, with the people of God, than to enjoy pleasures with that wicked people for a season. O! that the coloured people were long since of Moses' excellent disposition, instead of courting favour with, and telling news and lies to our *natural enemies*, against each other—aiding them to keep their hellish chains of slavery upon us. Would we not long before this time, have been respectable men, instead of such wretched victims of oppression as we are? Would they be able to drag our mothers, our fathers, our wives, our children and ourselves, around the world in chains and hand-cuffs as they do, to dig up gold and silver for them and theirs? This question, my brethren, I leave for you to digest; and may God Almighty force it home to your hearts. Remember that unless you are united, keeping your tongues within your teeth, you will be afraid to trust your secrets to each other, and thus perpetuate our miseries under the *Christians!!!!*

☞ADDITION.—Remember, also to lay humble at the feet of our Lord and Master Jesus Christ, with prayers and fastings. Let our enemies go on with their butcheries, and at once fill up their cup. Never make an attempt to gain our freedom of *natural right*, from under our cruel oppressors and murderers, until you see your way clear[17]—when that hour

16 See Exodus, chap. ii. 9, 10. [Walker's note]

17 It is not to be understood here, that I mean for us to wait until God shall take us by the hair of our heads and drag us out of abject wretchedness and slavery, nor do I mean to convey the idea for us to wait until our enemies shall make preparations, and call us to seize those preparations,

arrives and you move, be not afraid or dismayed; for be you assured that Jesus Christ the King of heaven and of earth who is the God of justice and of armies, will surely go before you. And those enemies who have for hundreds of years stolen our *rights*, and kept us ignorant of Him and His divine worship, he will remove. Millions of whom, are this day, so ignorant and avaricious, that they cannot conceive how God can have an attribute of justice, and show mercy to us because it pleased Him to make us black—which colour, Mr. Jefferson calls unfortunate!!!!!! As though we are not as thankful to our God, for having made us as it pleased himself, as they, (the whites,) are for having made them white. They think because they hold us in their infernal chains of slavery, that we wish to be white, or of their color—but they are dreadfully deceived—we wish to be just as it pleased our Creator to have made us, and no avaricious and unmerciful wretches, have any business to make slaves of, or hold us in slavery. How would they like for us to make slaves of, and hold them in cruel slavery, and murder them as they do us?—But is Mr. Jefferson's assertions true? viz. "that it is unfortunate for us that our Creator has been pleased to make us *black*." We will not take his say so, for the fact. The world will have an opportunity to see whether it is unfortunate for us, that our Creator *has made us* darker than the *whites*.

Fear not the number and education of our *enemies*, against whom we shall have to contend for our lawful right; guaranteed to us by our Maker; for why should we be afraid, when God is, and will continue, (if we continue humble) to be on our side?

The man who would not fight under our Lord and Master Jesus Christ, in the glorious and heavenly cause of freedom and of God—to be delivered from the most wretched, abject and servile slavery, that ever a people was afflicted with since the foundation of the world, to the present day—ought to be kept with all of his children or family, in slavery, or in chains, to be butchered by his *cruel enemies*. ❧

I saw a paragraph, a few years since, in a South Carolina paper, which, speaking of the barbarity of the Turks, it said: "The Turks are the most

---

take it away from them, and put every thing before us to death, in order to gain our freedom which God has given us. For you must remember that we are men as well as they. God has been pleased to give us two eyes, two hands, two feet, and some sense in our heads as well as they. They have no more right to hold us in slavery than we have to hold them, we have just as much right, in the sight of God, to hold them and their children in slavery and wretchedness, as they have to hold us, and no more. [Walker's note] barbarous people in the world—they treat the Greeks more like *brutes* than human beings." And in the same paper was an advertisement, which said: "Eight well built Virginia and Maryland *Negro fellows* and four *wenches* will positively be *sold* this day, *to the highest bidder!*" And what astonished me still more was, to see in this same *humane* paper!! the cuts of three men, with clubs[18] and budgets on their backs, and an advertisement offering a considerable sum of money for their apprehension and delivery. I declare, it is really so amusing to hear the Southerners and Westerners of this country talk about *barbarity*, that it is positively, enough to make a man *smile*.

The sufferings of the Helots among the Spartans, were somewhat severe, it is true, but to say that theirs, were as severe as ours among the Americans, I do most strenuously deny—for instance, can any man show me an article on a page of ancient history which specifies, that, the Spartans chained, and hand-cuffed the Helots, and dragged them from their wives and children, children from their parents, mothers from their suckling babes, wives from their husbands, driving them from one end of the country to the other? Notice the Spartans were heathens, who lived long before our Divine Master made his appearance in the flesh. Can Christian Americans deny these barbarous cruelties? Have you not, Americans, having subjected us under you, added to these miseries, by insulting us in telling us to our face, because we are helpless, that we are not of the human family? I ask you, O! Americans, I ask you, in the name of the Lord, can you deny these charges? Some perhaps may deny, by saying, that they never thought or said that we were not men. But do not actions speak louder than words?—have they not made provisions for the Greeks, and Irish? Nations who have never done the least thing for them, while *we*, who have enriched their country with our blood and tears—have dug up gold and silver for them and their children, from generation to generation, and are in more miseries than any other people under heaven, are not seen, but by comparatively, a handful of the American people? There are indeed, more ways to kill a dog, besides choking it to death with butter. Further—The Spartans or Lacedaemonians, had some frivolous pretext, for enslaving the Helots, for they (Helots) while being free inhabitants of Sparta, stirred up an intestine commotion, and were, by the Spartans subdued, and made prisoners of war. Consequently they and their children were condemned to perpetual slavery.[19]

18 "Clubs": leather bags. "Cuts": images from woodcuts.

19 See Dr. Goldsmith's History of Greece—page 9. See also, Plutarch's

DAVID WALKER

I have been for years troubling the pages of historians, to find out what our fathers have done to the *white Christians of America*, to merit such condign punishment as they have inflicted on them, and do continue to inflict on us their children. But I must aver, that my researches have hitherto been to no effect. I have therefore, come to the immoveable conclusion, that they (Americans) have, and do continue to punish us for nothing else, but for enriching them and their country. For I cannot conceive of any thing else. Nor will I ever believe otherwise, until the Lord shall convince me.

The world knows, that slavery as it existed among the Romans, (which was the primary cause of their destruction) was, comparatively speaking, no more than a *cypher*,[20] when compared with ours under the Americans. Indeed I should not have noticed the Roman slaves, had not the very learned and penetrating Mr. Jefferson said, "when a master was murdered, all his slaves in the same house, or within hearing, were condemned to death."[21]—Here let me ask Mr. Jefferson, (but he is gone to answer at the bar of God, for the deeds done in his body while living,) I therefore ask the whole American people, had I not rather die, or be put to death, than to be a slave to any tyrant, who takes not only my own, but my wife and children's lives by the inches? Yea, would I meet death with avidity far! far!! in preference to such *servile submission* to the murderous hands of tyrants. Mr. Jefferson's very severe remarks on us have been so extensively argued upon by men whose attainments in literature, I shall never be able to reach, that I would not have meddled with it, were it not to solicit each of my brethren, who has the spirit of a man, to buy a copy of Mr. Jefferson's "Notes on Virginia," and put it in the hand of his son. For let no one of us suppose that the refutations which have been written by our white friends are enough—they are *whites*—we are *blacks*. We, and the world wish to see the charges of Mr. Jefferson refuted by the blacks *themselves*, according to their chance; for we must remember that what the whites have written respecting this subject, is other men's labours, and did not emanate from the blacks. I know well, that there are some talents and learning among the coloured people of this country, which we have not a chance to develope, in consequence of oppression; but our oppression ought not to hinder us from acquiring all we can. For we will

Lives. The Helots subdued by Agis, king of *Sparta*. [Walker's note]. Walker is referring to Oliver Goldsmith's *History of Greece* (1774).

20 Something of no consequence.

21 See his Notes on Virginia, page 210. [Walker's note]

have a chance to develope them by and by. God will not suffer us, always to be oppressed. Our sufferings will come to an *end*, in spite of all the Americans this side of *eternity*. Then we will want all the learning and talents among ourselves, and perhaps more, to govern ourselves.—"Every dog must have its day," the American's is coming to an end.

But let us review Mr. Jefferson's remarks respecting us some further. Comparing our miserable fathers, with the learned philosophers of Greece, he says: "Yet notwithstanding these and other discouraging circumstances among the Romans, their slaves were often their rarest artists. They excelled too, in science, insomuch as to be usually employed as tutors to their master's children; Epictetus, Terence and Phædrus,[22] were slaves,—but they were of the race of whites. It is not their *condition* then, but *nature*, which has produced the distinction."[23]

See this, my brethren!! Do you believe that this assertion is swallowed by millions of the whites? Do you know that Mr. Jefferson was one of as great characters as ever lived among the whites? See his writings for the world, and public labours for the United States of America. Do you believe that the assertions of such a man, will pass away into oblivion unobserved by this people and the world? If you do you are much mistaken—See how the American people treat us—have we souls in our bodies? Are we men who have any spirits at all? I know that there are many *swell-bellied* fellows among us, whose greatest object is to fill their stomachs. Such I do not mean—I am after those who know and feel, that we are MEN, as well as other people; to them, I say, that unless we try to refute Mr. Jefferson's arguments respecting us, we will only establish them.

But the slaves among the Romans. Every body who has read history, knows, that as soon as a slave among the Romans obtained his freedom, he could rise to the greatest eminence in the State, and there was no law instituted to hinder a slave from buying his freedom. Have not the Americans instituted laws to hinder us from obtaining our freedom? Do any deny this charge? Read the laws of Virginia, North Carolina, &c. Further: have not the Americans instituted laws to prohibit a man of colour from obtaining and holding any office whatever, under the government of the United States of America? Now, Mr. Jefferson tells us, that our condition is not so hard, as the slaves were under the Romans!!!!!!

22 An author of fables, Roman; Epictetus: a classical Roman philosopher and teacher (55–135 C.E.); Terence: early Roman dramatist (d. 159 B.C.E.). Each was born into slavery.

23 See his Notes on Virginia, page 211. [Walker's note]

It is time for me to bring this article to a close. But before I close it, I must observe to my brethren that at the close of the first Revolution in this country, with Great Britain, there were but thirteen States in the Union, now there are twenty-four, most of which are slave-holding States, and the whites are dragging us around in chains and in handcuffs, to their new States and Territories to work their mines and farms, to enrich them and their children—and millions of them believing firmly that we being a little darker than they, were made by our Creator to be an inheritance to them and their children for ever—the same as a parcel of *brutes*.

Are we MEN!!—I ask you, O my brethren! are we MEN? Did our Creator make us to be slaves to dust and ashes like ourselves? Are they not dying worms as well as we? Have they not to make their appearance before the tribunal of Heaven, to answer for the deeds done in the body, as well as we? Have we any other Master but Jesus Christ alone? Is he not their Master as well as ours?—What right then, have we to obey and call any other Master, but Himself? How we could be so *submissive* to a gang of men, whom we cannot tell whether they are *as good* as ourselves or not, I never could conceive. However, this is shut up with the Lord, and we cannot precisely tell—but I declare, we judge men by their works.

The whites have always been an unjust, jealous, unmerciful, avaricious and blood-thirsty set of beings, always seeking after power and authority.—We view them all over the confederacy of Greece, where they were first known to be any thing, (in consequence of education) we see them there, cutting each other's throats—trying to subject each other to wretchedness and misery—to effect which, they used all kinds of deceitful, unfair, and unmerciful means. We view them next in Rome, where the spirit of tyranny and deceit raged still higher. We view them in Gaul,[24] Spain, and in Britain.—In fine, we view them all over Europe, together with what were scattered about in Asia and Africa, as heathens, and we see them acting more like devils than accountable men. But some may ask, did not the blacks of Africa, and the mulattoes of Asia, go on in the same way as did the whites of Europe. I answer, no—they never were half so avaricious, deceitful and unmerciful as the whites, according to their knowledge.

But we will leave the whites or Europeans as heathens, and take a view of them as Christians, in which capacity we see them as cruel, if not more so than ever. In fact, take them as a body, they are ten times more cruel,

24. France.

avaricious and unmerciful than ever they were; for while they were hea-thens, they were bad enough it is true, but it is positively a fact that they were not quite so audacious as to go and take vessel loads of men, women and children, and in cold blood, and through devilishness, throw them into the sea, and murder them in all kind of ways. While they were hea-thens, they were too ignorant for such barbarity. But being Christians, enlightened and sensible, they are completely prepared for such hellish cruelties. Now suppose God were to give them more sense, what would they do? If it were possible, would they not *dethrone* Jehovah and seat themselves upon his throne? I therefore, in the name and fear of the Lord God of Heaven and of earth, divested of prejudice either on the side of my colour or that of the whites, advance my suspicion of them, whether they are *as good by nature* as we are or not. Their actions, since they were known as a people, have been the reverse, I do indeed suspect them, but this, as I before oberved, is shut up with the Lord, we cannot exactly tell, it will be proved in succeeding generations.—The whites have had the es-sence of the gospel as it was preached by my master and his apostles—the Ethiopians have not, who are to have it in its meridian splendor—the Lord will give it to them to their satisfaction. I hope and pray my God, that they will make good use of it, that it may be well with them.[25]

25 It is my solemn belief, that if ever the world becomes Christianized, (which must certainly take place before long) it will be through the means, under God of the *Blacks*, who are now held in wretchedness, and degradation, by the white *Christians* of the world, who before they learn to do justice to us before our Maker—and be reconciled to us, and reconcile us to them, and by that means have clear consciences before God and man.—Send out Missionar-ies to convert the Heathens, many of whom after they cease to worship gods, which neither see nor hear, be-come ten times more the children of Hell, then ever they were, why what is the reason? Why the reason is obvious, they must learn to do justice at home, before they go into distant lands, to display their charity, Chris-tianity, and benevolence; when they learn to do justice, God will accept their offering, (no man may think that I am against Missionaries for I am not, my object is to see justice done at home, before we go to con-vert the Heathens.) [Walker's note]

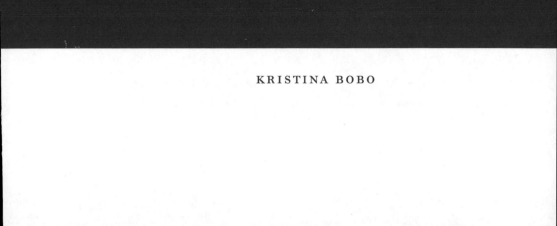

KRISTINA BOBO

Moses Roper (from the 1848 edition of his *Narrative*)

"I HAVE NEVER READ nor heard of any thing connected with slavery so cruel as what I have myself witnessed," the author of *The Narrative of the Adventures and Escape of Moses Roper from American Slavery* states early in his disturbingly graphic portrayal of man's inhumanity to man. One reason why Roper's *Narrative* was so widely read in England and America after its initial appearance in 1837 is its unprecedented candor about the evils of slavery. The few autobiographical accounts of slavery before Roper's call slavery unjust but rarely document its violation of the slave's body and mind, as well as his rights as a human being. Roper's *Narrative*, by contrast, demanded the attention of readers on both sides of the Atlantic because of its author's exceptionally detailed and yet curiously deadpan accounts of the violence inflicted on him by his masters. Two distinguishing characteristics of Roper emerge, both of which seem to have aroused slaveholders to special viciousness toward him: his light skin and his incorrigible determination to escape. Roper's *Narrative* contains perhaps the earliest accounts of racial passing in African American literature. Roper's thrilling stories of his repeated escape attempts anticipate what made the fugitive slave narrative, later popularized by Frederick Douglass and William Wells Brown, one of the most widely read forms of autobiography in mid-nineteenth-century America.

Moses Roper was born in 1815 in Caswell County, North Carolina, on a plantation belonging to a man sometimes identified as John Farley. His mother, Nancy, was a slave on the plantation; his father, Henry Roper, was Farley's son-in-law. At the age of six, Moses was sold away from his mother. Over the next fourteen years he passed through the hands of at least fifteen different owners and traders in North Carolina, South Carolina, Georgia, and Florida. The child of a mother who was, according to Roper, "part Indian and part African" and a father who was fully white, Roper was often mistaken for white, which presented a great handicap for him in slavery. However, during his escapes he used his appearance to his advantage by passing for a white traveler when the opportunity arose. The brutality he endured as a slave motivated Roper to make numerous escape attempts, which began when he was thirteen and ended only when he successfully fled the South in 1834. After fifteen months of insecure freedom in the North, Roper left the United States for England in November 1835.

In England, Roper was warmly received by the white abolitionist community, whose members helped him attend school and find work. Here he began to deliver lectures about his experience on behalf of antislavery efforts. Encouraged by his antislavery sponsors, Roper produced his *Narrative*, apparently his only publication, when he was twenty-one years old. Published in London and Philadelphia, the *Narrative* went through ten editions between 1837 and 1856, and was translated into Celtic.

In the original publication of the *Narrative*, Rev. Thomas Price, one of Roper's British sponsors, explicitly dismisses any fears that the *Narrative* might have been written or heavily edited by Roper's white supporters. Price states that Roper had "drawn up the following narrative" and it was "his own production." In later editions, including the 1848 version reprinted here, Roper testifies to his authorial independence by dispensing with prefatory authentication by prominent whites in favor of composing his own preface. Roper did not abandon the text of his original *Narrative* in the later editions, another sign that he was, as he and his sponsors claimed, the author of the *Narrative* from its beginning. The 1848 edition of Roper's *Narrative* is, nevertheless, importantly different from the original edition, especially because of the explanatory notes Roper adds to his original text and because of the appendix that brings his life story up to the mid-1840s.

Little is known of Roper's life after the 1848 edition of his autobiography appeared. We know he married an Englishwoman in 1839. After a failed attempt to become a missionary in Africa, he and his wife and small child moved to Canada. Beyond a trip to England to lecture in 1854, nothing further is known about Roper's life or death.

Suggested Readings

Andrews, William L. *To Tell a Free Story: The First Century of Afro-American Autobiography, 1760–1865*. Urbana: University of Illinois Press, 1986.

Bruce, Dickson D., Jr. *The Origins of African American Literature 1680–1865*. Charlottesville: University Press of Virginia, 2001.

Finseth, Ian Frederick. Introduction to "The Narrative of the Adventures and Escape of Moses Roper from American Slavery." In *North Carolina Slave Narratives: The Lives of Moses Roper, Lunsford Lane, Moses Grandy, and Thomas H. Jones*, edited by William L. Andrews, 23–34. Chapel Hill: University of North Carolina Press, 2003. [Finseth's introduction is the most extended critical treatment of the narrative.]

Foster, Frances Smith. *Witnessing Slavery: The Development of Antebellum Slave Narratives*. Madison: University of Wisconsin Press, 1994.

Nichols, Charles H. *Many Thousand Gone: The Ex-Slaves' Account of Their Bondage and Their Freedom*. Bloomington: Indiana University Press, 1963.

Roper, Moses. "Letter to the Committee of the British and Foreign Anti-Slavery Society." May 9, 1844. Available in electronic form through Documenting the American South, an electronic database sponsored by The Academic Affairs Library at the University of North Carolina at Chapel Hill, <http://docsouth.unc.edu/roper/support3.html>.

———. "Speeches Delivered at Baptist Chapel, Devonshire Square, 26 May 1836 and at Finsbury Chapel, London, England, 30 May 1836." Available in electronic form through Documenting the American South, an electronic database sponsored by The Academic Affairs Library at the University of North Carolina at Chapel Hill, <http://docsouth.unc.edu/roper/support4.html>.

Starling, Marian Wilson. *The Slave Narrative: Its Place in American History*. Washington, D.C.: Howard University Press, 1988.

Note on the Text

The version of Moses Roper's *Narrative* included here was published by Roper himself in England in 1848. This is the first time since its original publication that this edition has been reprinted. Although the most familiar versions of Roper's *Narrative* are the first British and American editions, published in 1837 and 1838, respectively, the 1848 edition features more information about Roper's life after his escape to England, and about the fates of several other enslaved persons mentioned in the *Narrative*. The 1848 edition also includes an appendix that briefly updates Roper's life, a series of letters from readers debating the propriety of Roper's escape, several poems penned by eager admirers, and a list of several hundred British churches Roper lectured in.

While this appended matter illustrates just how much Roper's narrative and lectures captivated the British public in the early 1840s, in the interest of conciseness only the appendix updating Roper's life has been reprinted in this volume. Interested readers can find the full text of the 1838 edition of Roper's *Narrative* in William L. Andrews, ed., *North Carolina Slave Narratives* (Chapel Hill: University of North Carolina Press, 2003). The entire 1848 edition, with all appended matter, is available online on Documenting the American South, http://docsouth.unc.edu/neh/roper/menu.html.

References to page numbers in Roper's notes to the 1848 edition of his *Narrative* have been changed to correspond to the pagination of this volume.

NARRATIVE

OF THE

ADVENTURES AND ESCAPE

OF

MOSES ROPER,

FROM

AMERICAN SLAVERY.

WITH AN APPENDIX,

CONTAINING A LIST OF PLACES VISITED BY THE AUTHOR IN
GREAT BRITAIN AND IRELAND AND THE BRITISH ISLES;
AND OTHER MATTER.

THIRTY-SIXTH THOUSAND.

(ENTERED AT STATIONERS' HALL.)

BERWICK-UPON-TWEED:
PUBLISHED FOR THE AUTHOR, AND PRINTED
AT THE WARDER OFFICE.
MDCCCXLVIII.

Published in England at 2s. Sterling.
The Price of this Edition is 1s. 10½d. Currency (Three York Shillings.)

Title page of the 1848 edition of Moses Roper's *Narrative*
(Documenting the American South, <http://docsouth.unc.edu>, The University of
North Carolina at Chapel Hill Libraries, North Carolina Collection)

NARRATIVE OF THE ADVENTURES AND ESCAPE OF
MOSES ROPER, FROM AMERICAN SLAVERY. WITH AN
APPENDIX, CONTAINING A LIST OF PLACES VISITED
BY THE AUTHOR IN GREAT BRITAIN AND IRELAND
AND THE BRITISH ISLES; AND OTHER MATTER.

Preface to the First Edition

The determination of laying this little narrative before the public, did not arise from any desire to make myself conspicuous, but with the view of exposing the cruel system of slavery, as will here be laid before my readers; from the urgent calls of nearly all the friends to whom I had related any part of my story, and also from the recommendation of anti-slavery meetings, which I have attended, through the suggestion of many warm friends of the cause of the oppressed.

The general narrative, I am aware, may seem to many of my readers, and especially to those who have not been before put in possession of the actual features of this accursed system, somewhat at variance with the dictates of humanity. But the facts related here do not come before the reader unsubstantiated by collateral evidence, nor highly coloured to the disadvantage of our cruel taskmasters.

My readers may be put in possession of facts respecting this system which equal in cruelty my own narrative, on an authority which may be investigated with the greatest satisfaction. Besides which, this little book will not be confined to a small circle of my own friends in London, or even in England. The slave-holder, the colonizationist, and even Mr. Gooch himself, will be able to obtain this document, and be at liberty to draw from it whatever they are honestly able, in order to set me down as the tool of a party. Yea, even Friend Brechenridge, a gentleman known at Glasgow, will be able to possess this, and to draw from it all the forcible arguments on his own side, which in his wisdom, honesty, and candour, he may be able to adduce.

The earnest wish to lay this narrative before my friends as an impartial statement of facts, has led me to develope some part of my conduct, which I now deeply deplore. The ignorance in which the poor slaves are kept by their masters, precludes almost the possibility of their being alive to any moral duties.

With these remarks, I leave the statement before the public. May this little volume be the instrument of opening the eyes of the ignorant of the system—of convincing the wicked, cruel, and hardened slaveholder—and of befriending generally the cause of oppressed humanity.

MOSES ROPER

LONDON, 1839.

NARRATIVE, &C.
CHAPTER I
*Birth-place of the Author.—The first time he was sold from
his Mother, and passed through several other hands.*

I was born in North Carolina, in Caswell County,[1] I am not able to tell in what month or year. What I shall now relate, is what was told me by my mother and grandmother. A few months before I was born, my father[2] married my mother's young mistress. As soon as my father's wife heard of my birth, she sent one of my mother's sisters to see whether I was white or black, and when my aunt had seen me, she returned back as soon as she could, and told her mistress that I was white, and resembled Mr. Roper very much. Mr. Roper's wife not being pleased with this report, she got a large club-stick and knife, and hastened to the place in which my mother was confined. She went into my mother's room with a full intention to murder me with her knife and club, but as she was going to stick the knife into me, my grandmother happening to come in, caught the knife and saved my life. But as well as I can recollect from what my mother told me, my father sold her and myself, soon after her confinement. I cannot recollect anything that is worth notice till I was six or seven years of age. My mother being half white, and my father a white man, I was at that time very white. Soon after I was six or seven years of age, my mother's old master died, that is, my father's wife's father.[3] All his slaves had to be divided among the children.[4] I have mentioned before

1 Located in north central North Carolina, on the Virginia state line.
2 Henry H. Roper (1784?–1845?), Moses Roper's biological father.
3 Possibly John Farley. Henry Roper was married to Rachel Farley (1792?–1831?).

4 Slaves are usually a part of the marriage portion, but lent rather than given, to be returned to the estate at the decease of the father, in order that they may be divided equally among his children. [Roper's note]

of my father disposing of me; I am not sure whether he exchanged me and my mother for another slave or not, but think it very likely he did exchange me with one of his wife's brothers or sisters, because I remember when my mother's old master died, I was living with my father's wife's brother-in-law, whose name was Mr. Durham. My mother was drawn with the other slaves.

The way they divide their slaves is this: they write the names of different slaves on a small piece of paper, and put it into a box, and let them all draw. I think that Mr. Durham drew my mother, and Mr. Fowler drew me, so we were separated a considerable distance, I cannot say how far. My resembling my father so much, and being whiter than the other slaves, caused me to be soon sold to what they call a negro trader, who took me to the Southern States of America, several hundred miles from my mother. As well as I can recollect I was then about six years old. The trader, Mr. Mitchell, after travelling several hundred miles, and selling a good many of his slaves, found he could not sell me very well, (as I was so much whiter than other slaves were) for he had been trying several months—left me with a Mr. Sneed, who kept a large boarding-house, who took me to wait at table, and sell me if he could. I think I stayed with Mr. Sneed about a year, but he could not sell me. When Mr. Mitchell had sold his slaves, he went to the north, and brought up another drove, and returned to the south with them, and sent his son-in-law into Washington, in Georgia, after me; so he came and took me from Mr. Sneed, and met his father-in-law with me, in a town called Lancaster, with his drove of slaves. We stayed in Lancaster a week, because it was court week, and there were a great many people there, and it was a good opportunity for selling the slaves; and there he was enabled to sell me to a gentleman, Dr. Jones, who was both a Doctor and a Cotton Planter. He took me into his shop to beat up and mix medicines, which was not a very hard employment, but I did not keep it long, as the Doctor soon sent me to his cotton plantation, that I might be burnt darker by the sun. He sent me to be with a tailor to learn the trade, but the journeymen being white men, Mr. Bryant, the tailor, did not let me work in the shop; I cannot say whether it was the prejudice of his men in not wanting me to sit in the shop with them, or whether Mr. Bryant wanted to keep me about the house to do the domestic work, instead of teaching me the trade. After several months, my master came to know how I got on with the trade: I am not able to tell Mr. Bryant's answer, but it was either that I could not learn, or that his journeymen were unwilling that I should sit in the shop with them. I was only once in the shop all the time I was there, and then only for an hour or two before his wife called me out to do some other work. So my master took me home, and as he was going to send a load of cotton to Camden, about forty miles distance, he sent me with the bales of cotton to be sold with it, where I was sold to a gentleman, named Allen; but Mr. Allen soon exchanged me for a female slave to please his wife. The traders who bought me, were named Cooper and Lindsey, who took me for sale, but could not sell me, people objecting to my being rather white. They then took me to the city of Fayetteville, North Carolina, where he swopt me for a boy, that was blacker than me, to Mr. Smith, who lived several miles off.

I was with Mr. Smith nearly a year. I arrived at the first knowledge of my age when I lived with him. I was then between twelve and thirteen years old; it was when President Jackson was elected the first time,[5] and he has been President eight years, so I must be nearly twenty-one years of age. At this time I was quite a small boy, and was sold to Mr. Hodge, a negro trader. Here I began to enter into hardships.

CHAPTER II

The Author's being sold to Mr. J. Gooch.—The cruel treatment he both received and witnessed while on his estate.—Repeated attempts at running away.—Escapes to his mother after being absent from her about ten years.—Meets with his sister, whom he had never seen before, on the road, who conducted him to his mother.

After travelling several hundred miles, Mr. Hodge sold me to Mr. Gooch,[6] the Cotton Planter, Cashaw County,[7] South Carolina; he purchased me at a town called Liberty Hill, about three miles from his home. As soon as he got home, he immediately put me on his cotton plantation to work, and put me under overseers, gave me an allowance of meat and bread with the other slaves, which was not half enough for me to live upon, and very laborious work; here my heart was almost broke with grief at leaving my fellow-slaves. Mr. Gooch did not mind my grief, for he flogged me nearly every day, and very severely. Mr. Gooch bought me for his son-in-law, Mr. Hammans,[8] about five miles distance from his residence. This man had but two slaves besides myself; he treated me very kindly for a week

5 Andrew Jackson was elected president of the United States in 1828.
6 John Gooch (1793?–1840), South Carolina planter.

7 Kershaw County in north central South Carolina.
8 Leroy Hammond (1801?–81), reportedly married to John Gooch's daughter, Nancy Robinson Gooch.

or two, but in summer, when cotton was ready to hoe, he gave me task work, connected with this department, which I could not get done, not having worked on cotton farms before. When I failed in my task he commenced flogging me, and set me to work without any shirt, in the cotton field, in a very hot sun, in the month of July. In August, Mr. Condell, his overseer, gave me a task at pulling fodder; having finished my task before night, I left the field, the rain came on which soaked the fodder; on discovering this, he threatened to flog me for not getting in the fodder before the rain came. I attempted to run away, knowing that I should get a flogging. I was then between thirteen and fourteen years of age; I ran away to the woods half naked; I was caught by a slave-holder who put me in Lancaster Gaol. When they put slaves in gaol, they advertise for their masters to own them; but if the master does not claim his slave in six months from the time of imprisonment, the slave is sold for gaol fees. When the slave runs away, the master always adopts a more rigorous system of flogging; this was the case in the present instance. After this, having determined from my youth to gain my freedom, I made several attempts, was caught, and got a severe flogging of one hundred lashes, each time. Mr. Hammans was a very severe and cruel master, and his wife still worse; she used to tie me up and flog me while naked.

After Mr. Hammans saw that I was determined to die in the woods, and not live with him, he tried to obtain a piece of land from his father-in-law, Mr. Gooch: not having the means of purchasing it, he exchanged me for the land.

As soon as Mr. Gooch had possession of me again, knowing that I was averse to going back to him, he chained me by the neck to his chaise.[9] In this manner he took me to his home at Mac Daniels Ferry, in the County of Chester, a distance of fifteen miles. After which, he put me into a swamp to cut trees, the heaviest work, which men of twenty-five or thirty years of age have to do, I being but sixteen. Here I was on very short allowance of food, and having heavy work, was too weak to fulfil my tasks. For this, I got many severe floggings: and, after I had got my irons off, I made another attempt at running away. He took my irons off, in the full anticipation that I could never get across the Catarba River,[10] even when at liberty. On this, I procured a small Indian canoe, which was tied to a tree, and ultimately got across the river in it. I then wandered through the wilderness for several days without any food, and but a drop

9 A horse-drawn carriage.
10 The Catawba River flows from North Carolina through York, Lan-

caster, and Chester counties in north central South Carolina.

of water to allay my thirst, till I become so starved, that I was obliged to go to a house to beg for something to eat, when I was captured, and again imprisoned.

Mr. Gooch having heard of me through an advertisement, sent his son after me; he tied me up, and took me back to his father. Mr. Gooch then obtained the assistance of another slaveholder, and tied me up in his blacksmith's shop, and gave me fifty lashes with a cow-hide.[11] He then put a log chain, weighing twenty-five pounds, round my neck, and sent me into a field, into which he followed me with a cow-hide, intending to set his slaves to flog me again. Knowing this, and dreading to suffer again in this way, I gave him the slip, and got out of his sight, he having stopped to speak with the other slaveholder.

I got to a canal on the Catarba River, on the banks of which, and near to a loch, I procured a stone and a piece of iron, with which I forced the ring off my chain, and got it off, and then crossed the river, and walked about twenty miles, when I fell in with a slave-holder, named Ballad, who had married the sister of Mr. Hammans. I knew that he was not so cruel as Mr. Gooch, and therefore begged of him to buy me. Mr. Ballad, who was one of the best planters in the neighbourhood, said that he was not able to buy me, and stated that he was obliged to take me back to my master, on account of the heavy fine attaching to a man harbouring a slave. Mr. Ballad proceeded to take me back; as we came in sight of Mr. Gooch's all the treatment that I had met with there, came forcibly upon my mind, the powerful influence of which is beyond description. On my knees, with tears in my eyes, with terror in my countenance, and fervency in all my features, I implored Mr. Ballad to buy me, but he again refused, and I was taken back to my dreaded and cruel master. Having reached Mr. Gooch's he proceeded to punish me. This he did, by first tying my wrists together and placing them over the knees, he then put a stick through, under my knees and over my arms, and having thus secured my arms, he proceeded to flog me, and gave me five hundred lashes on my bare back. This may appear incredible, but the marks which they left at present remain on my body, a standing testimony to the truth of this statement of his severity. He then chained me down in a log-pen[12] with a forty pounds chain, and made me lie on the damp earth all night. In the morning, after his breakfast, he came to me, and without giving me any

---

11 A whip made from rawhide or braided leather.
12 A building or unit of a building built of horizontal logs interlocking at the corners (*Dictionary of American Regional English*).

breakfast, tied me to a large heavy barrow,[13] which is usually drawn by a horse, and made me drag it to the cotton field for the horse to use in the field. Thus, the reader will see, that it was of no possible use to my master to make me drag it to the cotton field and not through it; his cruelty went so far, as actually to make me the slave of his horse, and thus to degrade me. He then flogged me again, and set me to work in the cotton field the whole of that day, and at night chained me down in the log-pen as before. The next morning he took me to the cotton field, and gave me a third flogging, and sent me to hoe cotton. At this time I was dreadfully sore and weak with the repeated floggings and cruel treatment I had endured. He put me under a black man, with orders, that if I did not keep up my row in hoeing with this man, he was to flog me. The reader must recollect here, that not being used to this kind of work, having been a domestic slave, it was impossible for me to keep up with him, and therefore I was repeatedly flogged during the day.

Mr. Gooch had a female servant about eighteen years old, who had also been a domestic slave, and, through not being able to fulfill her task, had run away: which slave he was at this time punishing for that offence. On the third day, he chained me to this female slave, with a large chain of forty pounds[14] weight round my neck. It was most harrowing to my feelings thus to be chained to a young female slave, for whom I would rather have suffered one hundred lashes than she should have been thus treated; he kept me chained to her during the week, and repeatedly flogged us both, while thus chained together, and forced us to keep up with the other slaves, although retarded by the heavy weight of the log-chain.

Here again, words cannot describe the misery which possessed both body and mind whilst under this treatment, and which was most dreadfully increased by the sympathy which I felt for my poor, degraded fellow-sufferer. On the Friday morning, I entreated my master to set me free from my chains, and promised him to do the task which was given me, and more if possible, if he would desist from flogging me. This he refused to do until Saturday night, when he did set me free.—This must rather be ascribed to his own interest in preserving me from death, as it was very evident I could no longer have survived under such treatment.

After this, though still determined in my own mind to escape, I stayed with him some months, during which he frequently flogged me, but not so severely as before related.—During this time, I had opportunity for

13 A cart.

14. This was a chain that they used to draw logs with from the woods, when they clear their land. [Roper's note]

recovering my health, and using means to heal my wounds. My master's cruelty was not confined to me, it was his general conduct to all his slaves. I might relate many instances to substantiate this, but will confine myself to one or two. Mr. Gooch, it is proper to observe, was a member of a Baptist Church, called Black Jack Meeting House, in Cashaw County, which church I attended for several years, but was never inside. This is accounted for by the fact, that the coloured population are not permitted to mix with the white population. In the Roman Catholic Church no distinction is made. Mr. Gooch had a slave named Phil, who was a member of a Methodist Church; this man was between seventy and eighty years of age; he was so feeble that he could not accomplish his tasks, for which his master used to chain him round the neck, and run him down a steep hill; this treatment he never relinquished to the time of his death. Another case was that of a slave, named Peter, who, for not doing his task, he flogged nearly to death, and afterwards pulled out his pistol to shoot him, but his (Mr. Gooch's) daughter snatched the pistol from his hand. Another mode of punishment which this man adopted, was that of using iron horns, with bells, attached to the back of the slave's neck. The following is the instrument of torture:—

This instrument he used to prevent the negroes running away, being a very ponderous machine, several feet in height, and the cross pieces being two feet four, and six feet in length. This custom is generally adopted among the slave-holders in South Carolina, and other slave States. One morning, about an hour before day break, I was going on an errand for my master; having proceeded about a quarter of a mile, I came up to a man named King, (Mr. Sumlin's overseer,) who had caught a young girl that had run away with the above machine on her. She had proceeded four miles from her station, with the intention of getting into the hands of a more humane master. She came up with this overseer nearly dead, and could get no farther; he immediately secured her, and took her back to her master, a Mr. Johnson.

Having been in the habit of going over many slave States with my master, I had good opportunities of witnessing the harsh treatment which was adopted by masters towards their slaves. As I have never heard or read anything connected with slavery, so cruel as what I have myself witnessed, it will be as well to mention a case or two.

A large farmer, Colonel McQuiller in Cashaw county, South Carolina, was in the habit of driving nails into a hogshead[15] so as to leave the point

15 A large barrel.

Woman with iron horns

(Documenting the American South, <http://docsouth.unc.edu>,
The University of North Carolina at Chapel Hill Libraries,
North Carolina Collection)

of the nail just protruding in the inside of the cask; into this, he used to put his slaves for punishment, and roll them down a very long and steep hill. I have heard from several slaves, (though I had no means of ascertaining the truth of this statement,) that in this way he had killed six or seven of his slaves. This plan was first adopted by a Mr. Perry, who lived on the Catarba River, and has since been adopted by several planters. Another was that of a young lad, who had been hired by Mr. Bell, a member of a holding church, to hoe three-quarters of an acre of cotton per day. Having been brought up as a domestic slave, he was not able to accomplish the task assigned to him. On the Saturday night, he left three or four rows to do on the Sunday; on the same night it rained very hard, by which the master could tell that he had done some of the rows on the Sunday; on Monday, his master took and tied him up to a tree in the field, and kept him there the whole of that day and flogged him at intervals. At night, when he was taken down, he was so weak that he could not get home, having a mile to go. Two white men who were employed by Mr. Bell, put him on a horse, took him home, and threw him, down on the kitchen floor, while they proceeded to their supper. In a little while, they heard some deep groans proceeding from the kitchen; they went to see him die; he had groaned his last. Thus, Mr. Bell flogged the poor boy, even to death, for what? for breaking the Sabbath, when he (his master) had set him a task, on Saturday, which it was not possible for him to do, and which, if he did not do, no mercy would be extended towards him! The general custom in this respect is, that if a man kills his own slave, no notice is taken of it by the civil functionaries; but if a man kills a slave belonging to another master, he is compelled to pay the worth of the slave. In this case, a jury met, returned a verdict of "Wilful Murder" against this man, and ordered him to pay the value. Mr. Bell was unable to do this, but a Mr. Cunningham paid the debt, and took this Mr. Bell, with this recommendation for cruelty, to be his overseer.

It will be observed that most of the cases here cited, are those in respect to males. Many instances, however, in respect to females,[16] might be mentioned, but are too disgusting to appear in this narrative. The cases here brought forward are not rare, but the continued feature of slavery. But I must now follow up the narrative as regards myself in peculiar. I stayed with this master for several months, during which time we went on very well in general. In August, 1831, (this was my first acquaintance with any

16 In her 1861 autobiography, *Incidents in the Life of a Slave Girl* (excerpted in this anthology), Harriet Jacobs documents a variety of abuses of female slaves.

date), I happened to hear a man mention this date, and, as it excited my curiosity, I asked what it meant; they told me it was the number of the year from the birth of Christ. On this date, August 1831, some cows broke into a crib where the corn is kept, and ate a great deal. For this, his slaves were tied up, and received several floggings: but myself and another man, hearing the groans of those who were being flogged, stayed back in the field, and would not come up. Upon this, I thought to escape punishment. On the Monday morning, however, I heard my master flogging the other man who was in the field; he could not see me, it being a field of Indian corn, which grows to a great height. Being afraid that he would catch me, and dreading a flogging more than many other, I determined to run for it; and, after travelling forty miles, I arrived at the estate of Mr. Crawford, in North Carolina, Mecklinburgh county.[17] Having formerly heard people talk about the Free States, I determined upon going thither, and, if possible, in my way to find out my poor mother, who was in slavery, several hundred miles from Chester; but the hope of doing the latter was very faint, and, even if I did, it was not likely that she would know me, having been separated from her when between five and six years old.

The first night I slept in a barn, upon Mr. Crawford's estate, and, having overslept myself, was awoke by Mr. Crawford's overseer, upon which I was dreadfully frightened; he asked me what I was doing there? I made no reply to him then; and he making sure that he had secured a runaway slave, did not press me for an answer. On my way to his house, however, I made up the following story, which I told him in the presence of his wife:—I said that I had been bound to a very cruel master when I was a little boy, and that having been treated very badly I wanted to get home to see my mother. This statement may appear to some to be untrue, but as I understood the word *bound*,[18] I considered it to apply to my case, having been sold to him, and thereby bound to serve him; though still, I did rather hope that he would understand it, that I was bound when a boy till twenty-one years of age. Though I was white at that time, he would not believe my story, on account of my hair being curly and wooly, which led him to conclude I was possessed of enslaved blood. The overseer's

17 A county in south central North Carolina in which the city of Charlotte is located.

18 Roper refers to the practice of indentured servitude, by which a person contracted to work for another exclusively, often under restricted conditions, for a period of years. Many whites were "bound" in this way via a practice that began in the Americas in the seventeenth century as a way to finance the emigration of poor English workers.

wife, however, who seemed much interested in me, said she did not think I was of the African origin, and that she had seen white men still darker than me; her persuasion prevailed; and after the overseer had given me as much butter-milk as I could drink, and something to eat, which was very acceptable, having had nothing for two days, I set off for Charlotte, in North Carolina, the largest town in the county. I went on very quickly the whole of that day, fearful of being pursued. The trees were thick on each side of the road, and only a few houses, at the distance of two or three miles apart; as I proceeded, I turned round in all directions to see if I was pursued, and if I caught a glimpse of any one coming along the road, I immediately rushed into the thickest part of the wood, to elude the grasp of what, I was afraid, might be my master. I went on in this way the whole day; at night, I came up with two waggons, they had been to market; the regular road waggons do not generally put up at inns, but en-camp in the roads and fields. When I came to them, I told them the same story I had told Mr. Crawford's overseer, with the assurance that the statement would meet the same success. After they had heard me, they gave me something to eat, and also a lodging in the camp with them.

I then went on with them about five miles, and they agreed to take me with them as far as they went, if I would assist them. This I promised to do. In the morning, however, I was much frightened by one of the men putting several questions to me—we were then about three miles from Charlotte. When within a mile of the town, we stopped at a brook to water the horses; while stopping there I saw the men whispering, and fancying I overheard them say they would put me in Charlotte gaol when they got there, I made my escape into the woods, pretending to be looking after something till I got out of their sight. I then ran on as fast I could, but did not go through the town of Charlotte, as had been my in-tention; being a large town I was fearful it might prove fatal to my escape. Here I was at a loss how to get on, as houses were not very distant from each other for nearly two hundred miles.

While thinking what I should do, I observed some waggons before me, which I determined to keep behind, and never go nearer to them than a quarter of a mile—in this way I travelled till I got to Salisbury. If I hap-pened to meet any person on the road, I was afraid they would take me up, I asked them how far the waggons had gone on before me? to make them suppose I belonged to the waggons. At night, I slept on the ground in the woods, some little distance from the waggons, but not near enough to be seen by the men belonging to them. All this time, I had but little food, principally fruit, which I found on the road. On Thursday night, I got into Salisbury, having left Chester on the Monday preceding. After this, being afraid my master was in pursuit of me, I left the usual line of road, and took another direction, through Huntsville and Salem, principally through fields and woods; on my way to Caswell Court-House, a distance of nearly two hundred miles from Salisbury,[19] I was stopped by a white man, to whom I told my old story, and again succeeded in my escape. I also came up with a small cart, driven by a poor man, who had been moving into some of the western territories, and was going back to Virginia, to move some more of his luggage. On this I told him I was going the same way to Hilton, thirteen miles from Caswell Court-House; he took me up in his cart, and went to the Red House, two miles from Milton, the place where Mr. Mitchell took me from, when six years old, to go to the Southern States. This was a very providential circumstance, for it happened, that at the time I had to pass through Caswell Court-house, a fair or election was going on, which caused the place to be much crowded with people, and rendered it more dangerous for me to pass through.

At the Red House I left the cart, and wandered about a long time, not knowing which way to go and find my mother. After some time, I took the road leading over Ikeo Creek. I shortly came up with a little girl, about six years old, and asked her where she was going; she said, to her mother's, pointing to a house on a hill, half a mile off. She had been at the overseer's house, and was returning to her mother. I then felt some emotions arising in my breast, which I cannot describe, but will be explained in the sequel. I told her I was very thirsty, and would go with her to get something to drink. On our way I asked her several questions, such as her name, that of her mother; she said hers was Maria, and that of her mother's Nancy. I inquired, if her mother had any more children? she said five besides herself, and that they had been sold, that one had been sold when a little boy. I then asked the name of this child? she said it was Moses. These answers, as we approached the house, led me nearer and nearer to the finding out the object of my pursuit, and of recognising in the little girl the person of my own sister.

19 The distance from Salisbury to Caswell Court-house is not so far, but I had to go a round-about way. [Roper's note]

CHAPTER III

An account of the Author's meeting with his Mother,
who did not know him, but was with her a very short time
before he was taken by armed men, and imprisoned for
thirty-one days, and then taken back to his master.

At last I got to my mother's house! my mother was at home. I asked her if she knew me? she said, no. Her master was having a house built close by, and as the men were digging a well, she supposed that I was one of the diggers. I told her, I knew her very well, and thought that if she looked at me a little, she would know me, but this had no effect. I then asked her if she had any sons? she said, yes; but none so large as me. I then waited a few minutes, and narrated some circumstances to her, attending my being sold into slavery, and how she grieved at my loss. Here the mother's feelings on that dire occasion, and which a mother can only know, rushed to her mind; she saw her own son before her, for whom she had so often wept; and, in an instant, we were clasped in each other's arms, amidst the ardent interchange of caresses and tears of joy. Ten years had elapsed since I had seen my dear mother. My own feelings, and the circumstances attending my coming home, have been often brought to mind since, on a perusal of the 42d, 43d, 44th, and 45th chapters of Genesis.[20] What could picture my feelings so well, as I once more beheld the mother who had brought me into the world, and had nourished me, not with the anticipation of my being torn from her maternal care, when only six years old, to become the prey of a mercenary and blood-stained slave-holder: I say, what picture so vivid in description of this part of my tale, as the 7th and 8th verses of the 42d chapter of Genesis, "And Joseph saw his brethren, and he knew them, but made himself strange unto them. And Joseph knew his brethren, but they knew not him." After the first emotion of the mother, on recognising her first-born, had somewhat subsided, could the reader not fancy the little one, my sister, as she told her simple tale of meeting with me to her mother, how she would say, while the parent listened with intense interest: "The man asked me straitly of our state and our kindred, saying, is your father yet alive, and have ye another brother." Or, when at last, I could no longer refrain from making myself known, I say I was ready to burst into a frenzy of joy. How applicable the 1st, 2d, and 3d verses of the 45th chapter, "Then Joseph could not refrain himself before all that stood by him, and he wept aloud, and said unto his breth-

---

20 These chapters of Genesis recount the reunion of the Hebrew patriarch Joseph with his brothers in Egypt after years of separation.

ren, I am Joseph, doth my father still live." Then when the mother knew her son, when the brothers and sisters owned their brother; "he kissed all his brethren and wept over them, and after that his brethren talked with him," 15th verse. At night my mother's husband, a blacksmith, belonging to Mr. Jefferson at the Red House, came home; he was surprised to see me with the family, not knowing who I was. He had been married to my mother, when I was a babe, and had always been very fond of me. After the same tale had been told him, and the same emotions filled his soul, he again kissed the object of his early affection. The next morning I wanted to go on my journey, in order to make sure of my escape to the Free States. But as might be expected, my mother, father, brothers, and sisters, could ill part with their long lost one; and persuaded me to go into the woods in the day time, and at night come home and sleep there. This I did for about a week; on the next Sunday night, I laid me down to sleep between my two brothers, on a pallet, which my mother had prepared for me; about twelve o'clock I was suddenly awoke, and found my bed surrounded by twelve slave-holders with pistols in hand, who took me away (not allowing me to bid farewell to those I loved so dearly) to the Red House, where they confined me in a room the rest of the night, and in the morning lodged me in the gaol of Caswell Court-House.

What was the scene at home, what sorrow possessed their hearts, I am unable to describe, as I never after saw any of them more. I heard, however, that my mother was, soon after I left, confined,[21] and was very long before she recovered the effects of this disaster.[22] I was told afterwards, that some of those men who took me were professing Christians, but, to me, they did not seem to live up to what they professed; they did not seem, by their practice, at least, to recognise that God as their God, who hath said, "thou shalt not deliver unto his master, the servant which is escaped from his master unto thee, he shall dwell with thee, even among you, in that place which he shall choose, in one of thy gates, where it liketh him best; thou shalt not oppress him."—Deut. xxiii, 15, 16.

I was confined here in a dungeon under ground, the grating of which looked to the door of the gaoler's house. His wife had a great antipathy to me. She was Mr. Roper's wife's cousin. My grandmother used to come to me nearly every day, and bring me something to eat, besides the regular gaol allowance, by which my sufferings were somewhat decreased.

21 Before and after delivery of a baby, nineteenth-century women were often confined to their beds.
22 My mother had seven children living when I last saw her, and the above one was born soon after I left, made the eighth, and they are now all in slavery except myself. [Roper's note]

Whenever the gaoler went out, which he often did, his wife used to come to my dungeon, and shut the wooden door over the grating, by which I was nearly suffocated, the place being very damp and noisome. My master did not hear of my being in gaol for thirty-one days after I had been placed there. He immediately sent his son, and son-in-law, Mr. Anderson, after me. They came in a horse and chaise took me from the gaol to a blacksmith's shop, and got an iron collar fitted round my neck, with a beavy chain attached, then tied my hands, and fastened the other end of the chain on a horse, and put me on its back. Just before we started, my grandmother came to bid me farewell; I gave her my hand as well as I could, and she having given me two or three presents, we parted. I had felt enough, far too much, for the weak state I was in; but how shall I describe my feeling, upon parting with the *last* relative that I *ever saw*. The reader must judge by what would be his own feelings under similar cir-. cumstances. We then went on for fifty miles; I was very weak and could hardly sit on the horse. Having been in prison so long, I had lost the southern tan; and as the people could not see my hair, having my hat on, they thought I was a white man—a criminal—and asked me what crime I had committed. We arrived late at night, at the house of Mr. Britton. I shall never forget the journey that night. The thunder was one continued roar, and the lightning blazing all around. I expected every minute that my iron collar would attract it, and I should be knocked off the horse, and dragged along the ground. This gentleman, a year or two before, had liberated his slaves, and sent them into Ohio, having joined the Society of Friends,[23] which society does not allow the holding of slaves. I was, therefore, treated very well there, and they gave me a very hearty supper, which did me much good in my weak state.

They secured me in the night by locking me to the post of the bed on which they slept. The next morning, we went on to Salisbury. At that place we stopped to water the horses; they chained me to a tree in the yard, by the side of their chaise. On my horse they put the saddle-bags which contained the provisions. As I was in the yard, a black man came and asked me what I had been doing; I told him that I had run away from my master, after which he told me several tales about the slaves, and among them he mentioned the case of a Quaker, who was then in prison, waiting to be hung, for giving a free passage to a slave. I had been considering all the way how I could escape from my horse, and once

23 A religious sect, known as Quakers, founded in England in the seven- teenth century and generally anti- slavery in the United States.

had an idea of cutting his head off, but thought it too cruel: and at last thought of trying to get a rasp and cut the chain by which I was fastened to the horse. As they often let me get on a quarter of a mile before them, I thought I should have a good opportunity of doing this without being seen. The black man procured me a rasp, and I put it into the saddle-bags which contained the provisions. We then went on our journey, and one of the sons asked me if I wanted anything to eat; I answered no, though very hungry at the time, as I was afraid of their going to the bags and discovering the rasp. However, they had not had their own meal at the inn as I had supposed, and went to the bags to supply themselves, where they found the rasp. Upon this, they fastened my horse beside the horse in their chaise, and kept a stricter watch over me. Nothing remarkable occurred till we got within eight miles of Mr. Gooch's, where we stopped a short time; and, taking advantage of their absence, I broke a switch from some boughs above my head, lashed my horse and set off at full speed. I had got about a quarter of a mile before they could get their horse loose from their chaise; one then rode the horse, and the other ran as fast as he could after me. When I caught sight of them, I turned off the main road into the woods, hoping to escape their sight; their horse, however, being much swifter than mine, they soon got within a short distance of me. I then came to a rail fence, which I found it very difficult to get over, but breaking several rails away, I effected my object. They then called me upon to stop more than three times; and I not doing so, they fired after me, but the pistol only snapped.

This is according to law; after three calls they may shoot a runaway slave. Soon after the one on the horse came up with me, and catching hold of the bridle of my horse, pushed the pistol to my side; the other soon came up, and breaking off several stout branches from the trees, they gave me about one hundred blows. This they did very near to a planter's house. The gentleman was not at home, but his wife came out and begged them not to *kill me so near the house*; they took no notice of this, but kept on beating me. They then fastened me to the axle tree of their chaise. One of them got into the chaise, the other took my horse, and they ran me all the eight miles as fast as they could; the one on my horse going behind to guard me.

Mr. Anderson attempting to shoot the author

*(Documenting the American South, <http://docsouth.unc.edu>,
The University of North Carolina at Chapel Hill Libraries,
North Carolina Collection)*

CHAPTER IV

The Author is Flogged and Punished in various ways,
but still perseveres in his attempts to Escape,
till he was sold to Mr. Wilson.

In this way we came to my old master, Mr. Gooch. The first person I saw was himself; he unchained me from the chaise, and at first seemed to treat me very gently, asking me where I had been, &c. The first thing the sons did was to show the rasp which I had got to cut my chain. My master gave me a hearty dinner, the best he ever did give me; but it was to keep me from dying before he had given me all the flogging he intended. After dinner he took me to a log-house, stripped me quite naked, fastened a rail up very high, tied my hands to the rail, fastened my feet together, put a rail between my feet, and stood on one end of it to hold me down; the two sons then gave me fifty lashes each, the son-in-law another fifty, and Mr. Gooch himself fifty more.

While doing this his wife came out, and begged him not to kill me, the first act of sympathy I ever noticed in her. When I called for water, they brought a pail-full and threw it over my back ploughed up by the lashes. After this, they took me to the blacksmith's shop, got *two large bars of iron*, which they bent round my feet, each bar *weighing twenty pounds*, and put a heavy log-chain on my neck. This was on Saturday. On the Monday, he chained me to the same female slave as before. As he had to go out that day, he did not give me the punishment which he intended to give me every day, but at night when he came home, he made us walk round his estate, and by all the houses of the slaves, for them to taunt us; when we came home he told us we must be up very early in the morning, and go to the field before the other slaves. We were up at day-break, but we could not get on fast, on account of the heavy irons on my feet. It may be necessary to state that these irons were first made red hot and bent in a circle, so as just to allow of my feet going through; it having been cooled, and my leg with the iron on lifted up to an anvil, it was made secure round my ankles. When I walked with these irons on, I used to hold them up with my hands by means of a cord. We walked *about a mile in two hours*, but knowing the punishment he was going to inflict on us, we made up our minds to escape into the woods, and secrete ourselves. This we did, and he not being able to find us, which they could not do; and about twelve o'clock, when we thought they would give up looking for us at that time, we went on, and came to the banks of the Catarba. Here I

Mr. Gooch stripping the author to flog him
(Documenting the American South, <http://docsouth.unc.edu>,
The University of North Carolina at Chapel Hill Libraries,
North Carolina Collection)

got a stone, and opened the ring of the chain on her neck, and got it off; and the chain round my neck was only passed through a ring; as soon as I got hers off, I slipped the chain through my ring, and got it off my own neck.[24] We then went on by the banks of the river for some distance, and found a little canoe about two feet wide. I managed to get in, although the irons on my feet made it very dangerous, for if I had upset the canoe, I could not swim. The female got in after me, and gave me the paddles, by which we got some distance down the river. The current being very strong, it drove us against a small island; we paddled round the island to the other side, and then made towards the opposite bank. Here again we were stopped by the current, and made up to a large rock in the river, between the island and the opposite shore. As the weather was very rough we landed on the rock, and secured the canoe, as it was not possible to get back to the island. It was a very dark night and rained tremendously; and, as the water was rising rapidly towards the top of the rock, we gave all up for lost, and sometimes hoped, and sometimes feared to hope, that we should never see the morning. But Providence was moved in our favour; the rain ceased, the water reached the edge of the rock, then receded, and we were out of danger from this cause. We remained all night upon the rock, and in the morning reached the opposite shore, and then made our way through the woods till we came to a field of Indian corn, where we plucked some of the green ears and ate them, having had nothing for two days and nights. We came to the estate of—, where we met with a coloured man who knew me, and having run away himself from a bad master, he gave us some food, and told us we might sleep in the barn that night. Being very fatigued, we overslept ourselves; the proprietor came to the barn, but as I was in one corner under some Indian corn tops, and she in another, he did not perceive us, and we did not leave the barn before night, (Wednesday.) We then went out, got something to eat, and strayed about the estate till Sunday. On that day, I met with some men, one of whom had irons on the same as me; he told me that his master was going out to see his friends, and that he would try and get my feet loose; for this purpose I parted with this female, fearing, that if she were caught with me, she would be forced to tell who took my irons off. The man tried some time without effect, he then gave me a file and I tried myself, but was disappointed on account of their thickness.

24 It may be well to state here, that the ring which fastened the log-chain together round the female's neck, was an open ring, similar to those used at the end of a watch chain. [Roper's note]

On the Monday I went on towards Lancaster,[25] and got within three miles of it that night; and went towards the plantation of Mr. Crockett, as I knew some of his slaves, and hoped to get some food given me. When I got there, however, the dogs smelt me out and barked; upon which, Mr. Crockett came out, followed me with his rifle, and came up with me. He put me on a horse's back, which put me to extreme pain, from the great weight hanging at my feet. We reached Lancaster gaol that night, and he lodged me there. I was placed in the next dungeon to a man who was going to be hung. I shall never forget his cries and groans, as he prayed all night for the mercy of God. Mr. Gooch did not hear of me for several weeks; when he did, he sent his son-in-law, Mr. Anderson, after me. Mr. Gooch himself came within a mile of Lancaster, and waited until Mr. Anderson brought me. At this time I had but one of the irons on my feet, having got so thin round my ankles that I had slipped one off while in gaol. His son-in-law tied my hands, and made me walk along till we came to Mr. Gooch. As soon as we arrived at McDaniel's Ford, two miles above the ferry, on the Catarba river, they made me wade across, themselves going on horseback. The water was very deep, and having irons on one foot and round my neck. I could not keep a footing. They dragged me along by my chain on the top of the water. It was as much as they could do to hold me by the chain, the current being very strong. They then took me home, flogged me, put extra irons on my neck and feet, and put me under the driver, with more work than ever I had before. He did not flog me so severely as before, but continued it every day. Among the instruments of torture employed, I here describe one:—

This is a machine used for packing and pressing cotton. By it he hung me up by the hands at letter a, a horse, and at times, a man moving round the screw[26] e, and carrying it up and down, and pressing the block c into a box d. into which the cotton is put. At this time he hung me up for a quarter of an hour. I was carried up ten feet from the ground, when Mr. Gooch asked me if I was tired? He then let me rest for five minutes, then carried me round again, after which, he let me down and put me into the box d, and shut me down in it for about ten minutes. After this torture, I stayed with him several months, and did my work very well. It was about the beginning of 1832, when he took off my irons, and being in dread of

25 County in north central South Carolina, at the state line and immediately
  north of Kershaw County.
26 This screw is sometimes moved
  round by hand, when there is a
person hanging on it. The screw is
made with wood, a large tree cut
down, and carved the shape of a
screw. [Roper's note]

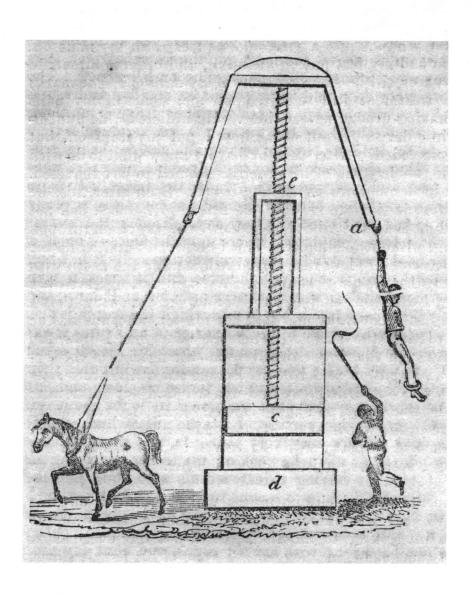

The author hanging by his hands
(Documenting the American South, <http://docsouth.unc.edu>,
The University of North Carolina at Chapel Hill Libraries,
North Carolina Collection)

him, he having threatened me with more punishment, I attempted again to escape from him. At this time I got into North Carolina: but a reward having been offered for me, a Mr. Robinson caught me, and chained me to a chair, upon which he sat up with me all night, and next day proceeded home with me. This was Saturday. Mr. Gooch had gone to church, several miles from his house. When he came back, the first thing he did was to pour some tar upon my head, then rubbed it all over my face, took a torch with pitch on, and set it on fire; he put it out before it did me very great injury, but the pain which I endured was most excruciating, nearly all my hair having been burnt off. On Monday, he put irons on me again, weighing nearly fifty pounds. He threatened me again on the Sunday with another flogging; and on the Monday morning, before daybreak, I got away again, with my irons on, and was about three hours going a distance of two miles.[27] I had gone a good distance, when I met with a coloured man, who got some wedges, and took my irons off. However, I was caught again, and put into prison in Charlotte, where Mr. Gooch came, and took me back to Chester.[28] He asked me how I got my irons off. They having been got off by a slave, I would not answer his question, for fear of getting the man punished. Upon this he put the fingers of my hands into a vice, and squeezed all my nails off. He then had my feet put on an anvil, and ordered a man to beat my toes, till he smashed some of my nails off. The marks of this treatment still remain upon me, some of my nails never having grown perfect since. He inflicted this punishment, in order to get out of me how I got my irons off, but never succeeded. After this, he hardly knew what to do with me; the whole stock of his cruelties seemed to be exhausted. He chained me down in the log-house. Soon after this, he sent a female slave to see if I was safe. Mr. Gooch had not secured me as he thought: but had only run my chain through the ring, without locking it. This I observed; and while the slave was coming, I was employed in loosening the chain with the hand that was not wounded. As soon as I observed her coming, I drew the chain up tight, and she observing that I seemed fast, went away and told her master, who was in the field ordering the slaves. When she was gone, I drew the chain through the ring, escaped under the flooring of the log-house, and went on under it, till I came out at the other side and ran on; but, being sore and weak, I had

27 It must be recollected, that when a person is two miles from a house, in that part of the country, he can hide himself in the woods for weeks, and I knew a slave who was hid for six months without discovery, the trees being so thick. [Roper's note]

28 County in north central South Carolina, immediately west of Lancaster County.

not got a mile before I was caught, and again carried back. He tied me up to a tree in the woods at night, and made his slaves flog me. I cannot say how many lashes I received; but it was the worst flogging I ever had, and the last which Mr. Gooch ever gave me.

There are several circumstances which occurred on this estate while I was there, relative to other slaves, which it may be interesting to mention. Hardly a day ever passed without some one being flogged. To one of his female slaves he had given a doze of castor oil and salts[29] together, as much as she could take;[30] he then got a box, about six feet by two and a half, and one and a half feet deep; he put this slave under the box, and made the men fetch as many logs as they could get; and put them on the top of it; under this she was made to stay all night. I believe, that if he had given this slave one, he had given her three thousand lashes. Mr. Gooch was a member of a Baptist church. His slaves thinking him a very bad sample of what a professing Christian ought to be, would not join the connection he belonged to, thinking they must be a very bad set of people; there were many of them members of the Methodist Church.[31] On Sunday, the slaves can only go to church at the will of their master, when he gives them a pass for the time they are to be out. If they are found by the patrole after the time to which their pass extends, they are severely flogged.

On Sunday nights a slave, named Allen, used to come to Mr. Gooch's estate for the purpose of exhorting and praying with his brother slaves, by whose instrumentality many of them had been converted. One evening, Mr. Gooch caught them all in a room, turned Allen out, and threatened his slaves with one hundred lashes each, if they ever brought him there again. At one time Mr. Gooch was ill and confined to his room; if any of the slaves had done anything which he thought deserved a flogging, he would have them brought into his bed-room and flogged before his eyes.

With respect to food, he used to allow us one peck of Indian meal[32] per week, which, after being sifted and the bran[33] taken from it, would

29 Substances commonly used in medicine of the time to cause purging.
30 The female whom Mr. Gooch chained to me. [Roper's note]
31 In fact, in some of the States, nearly all of the slaves are Methodists; and when in the field at work they may be often heard singing these words,

"I am happy, I am happy, Lord pity poor me.—Me never know what happiness was, until I joined de Methodists. I am happy, Lord pity poor me." [Roper's note]
32 Meal from Indian corn.
33 Broken seed husks.

not be much more than half a peck. Meat we did not get for sometimes several weeks together; however, he was proverbial for giving his slaves more food than any other slave-holder. I stayed with Mr. Gooch a year and a half; during that time the scenes of cruelty I witnessed and experienced, are not at all fitted for these pages. There is much to excite disgust in what has been narrated, but hundreds of other cases might be mentioned.

CHAPTER V

I was not long with Mr. Wilson, who was a Negro trader,
before he exchanged me to Mr. Rowland, who was also a trader,
for another slave, and after being with him about a year, was sold
to Mr. Goodly, who exchanged me again to Mr. Louis.

After this, Mr. Gooch seeing that I was determined to get away from him, chained me, and sent me with another female slave, whom he had treated very cruelly, to Mr. Britton, son of the before-mentioned slave dealer. We were to have gone to Georgia to be sold, but a bargain was struck before we arrived there. Mr. Britton had put chains on me to please Mr. Gooch, but having gone some little distance we came up with a white man, who begged Mr. Britton to unchain me; he then took off my handcuffs. We then went on to Union Court House, where we met a drove of slaves belonging to Mr. Wilson, who ultimately bought me and sent me to his drove: the girl was sold to a planter in the neighbourhood as bad as Mr. Gooch.[34] In court week the negro traders and slaves encamp a little way out of the town. The traders here will often sleep with the best-looking female slaves among them, and they will often have many children in the year, which are said to be slaveholder's children, by which means, through his villainy, he will make an immense profit of this intercourse, by selling the babe with its mother. They often keep an immense stock of slaves on hand; many of them will be with the trader a year or more before they are sold. Mr. Marcus Rowland, the drover, who brought me, then returned with his slaves to his brother's house (Mr. John Rowland), where he kept his drove on his way to Virginia. He kept me as a kind of servant. I had to grease the faces of the blacks every morning with sweet oil, to make them shine, before they are put up to sell. After he had been round several weeks, and sold many slaves, he left me at his brother's

34 As I am often asked "what became of the female I was chained to?" the above is the girl, whom I have seen once since she was last sold, and from what I saw of her then, I do not think she is alive now. [Roper's note]

house, while he went on to Washington, about 600 miles, to buy some more slaves, the drove having got very small. We were treated very well while there, having plenty to eat and little work to do, in order to make us fat. I was brought up as a domestic slave, as they generally prefer slaves of my colour for that purpose. When Mr. Rowland came back, having been absent about five months, he found all the slaves well except one female, who had been grieving very much at being parted from her parents, and at last died of grief. He dressed us very nicely and went on again. I travelled with him for a year, and had to look over the slaves and see that they were dressed well, had plenty of food, and to oil their faces. During this time we stopped once at White House Church, a Baptist Association; a protracted camp meeting was holding there, on the plan of the revival meetings in this country. We got there at the time of the meeting, and sold two female slaves on the Sunday morning, at the time the meeting broke up, to a gentleman who had been attending the meeting the whole of the week. While I was with Mr. Rowland, we were at many such meetings; and the members of the churches are by this means so well influenced towards their fellow-creatures at these meetings for the worship of God, that it becomes a fruitful season for the drover, who carries on an immense traffic with the attendants at these places. This is common to Baptists and Methodists. At the end of the year, he exchanged me to a farmer, Mr. David Goodly, for a female slave in Greenville, about 14 miles from Greenville[35] Court House. This gentleman was going to Missouri to settle, and on his way had to pass through Ohio, a free State. But having learnt after he bought me, that I had before tried to get away to the free States, he was afraid to take me with him, and I was exchanged to a Mr. Louis.

CHAPTER VI

Travel with Mr. Louis to Pendleton Indian Springs,
from thence to Columbus, where I was sold at auction to
Mr. Beveridge. Travels and history with Mr. Beveridge.

Mr. Marvel Louis was in the habit of travelling a great deal, and took me as a domestic slave to wait on him. Mr. Louis boarded at the house of a Mr. Clevelin, a rich planter, at Greenville, South Carolina. Mr. L. was paying his addresses to the daughter of this gentleman, but was surprised and routed in his approaches, by a Colonel Dorkins, of Union

35 Town in Greenville County, in northwest South Carolina.

Court House, who ultimately carried her off in triumph. After this, Mr. Louis took to drinking, to drown his recollection of disappointed love.

One day he went to Pendleton Races, and I waited on the road for him: returning intoxicated he was thrown from his horse into a brook, and was picked up by a gentleman, and taken to an inn, and I went there to take care of him. Next day he went on to Punkintown with Mr. Warren R. Davis,[36] a member of Congress; I went with him. This was at the time of the agitation of the Union and Nullifying party,[37] which was expected to end in a general war. The Nullifying party had a grand dinner on the occasion, after which, they gave their slaves all their refuse, for the purpose of bribing them to fight on the side of their party. The scene on this occasion was humorous, all the slaves scrambling after, bare bones and crumbs, as if they had had nothing for weeks. When Mr. Louis had got over this fit of drunkenness, we returned to Greenville, where I had little to do except in the warehouse. There was preaching in the Courthouse on the Sunday; but scarcely had the sweet savour of the worship of God passed away, when, on Monday, a public auction was held for the sale of slaves, cattle, sugar, iron, &c., by Z. Davis, the high constable and others.

On these days I was generally very busy in handing out the different articles for inspection, and was employed in this way for several months. After which, Mr. Louis left his place for Pendleton; but his health getting worse, and fast approaching consumption, he determined to travel. I went with him over Georgia to the Indian Springs, and from there to Columbus; here he left me with Lawyer Kemp, a member of the State Assembly, to take care of his horse and carriage till he came back from Cuba, where he went for the benefit of his health. I travelled round with Mr. Kemp, waiting until my master came back. I soon after heard, that Mr. Louis had died in Appalachicola,[38] and had been buried at Tennessee Bluff. I was very much attached to the neighbourhood of Pendleton and Greenville, and feared, from Mr. Louis's death, I should not get back there.

As soon as this information arrived, Mr. Kemp put me, the carriage and horses, a gold watch, and cigars, up to auction, on which I was much frightened, knowing there would be some very cruel masters at the sale;

36 Warren Ransom Davis (1793–1835), U.S. congressman, 1827–35.
37 Federal tariffs imposed in 1828 and 1832 were challenged and declared void ("nullified") by the South Caro-lina state legislature in 1832. The South Carolina Ordinance of Nullifi-cation was repealed in 1833.
38 Apalachicola, a town in western Florida on the Gulf coast.

and fearing I should again be disappointed in my attempt to escape from bondage. A Mr. Beveridge, a Scotchman, from Appalachicola, bought me, the horses, and cigars.[39] He was not a cruel master; he had been in America eighteen years, and I believe I was the first slave he ever bought. Mr. Kemp had no right to sell me,[40] which he did, before he had written to Mr. Louis's brother.

Shortly after this, Mr. Kemp having had some altercation with General Woodford, it ended in a duel, in which Mr. W. was killed. A few weeks after, as Mr. Kemp was passing down a street, he was suddenly shot dead by Mr. Milton, a rival lawyer. When I heard this, I considered it a visitation of God on Mr. Kemp for having sold me unjustly, as I did not belong to him. This was soon discovered by me, Mr. Louis's brother having called at Macintosh Hotel, Columbus, to claim me, but which he could not effect. After this, I travelled with Mr. Beveridge through Georgia, to the warm springs, and then back to Columbus, going on to Marianna, his summer house in Florida.

Here I met with better treatment than I had ever experienced before; we travelled on the whole summer; at the fall, Mr. Beveridge went to Appalachicola on business. Mr. Beveridge was contractor for the mail from Columbus to Appalachicola, and owner of three steam-boats, the Versailles, Andrew Jackson, and Van Buren. He made me steward on board of the Versailles, the whole winter. The river then got so low that the boats could not run. At this time Mr. Beveridge went to Mount Vernon.[41] On our way we had to pass through the Indian nation.[42] We arrived at Columbus, where I was taken dangerously ill of a fever. After I got well, Mr. Beveridge returned to Marianna, through the Indian nation. Having gone about twelve miles, he was taken very ill.

I took him out of the carriage to a brook, and washed his hands and face until he got better, when I got him into the carriage again, and drove off till we came to General Irving's, where he stopped several days on account of his health. While there, I observed on the floor of the kitchen

39 How Mr. Beveridge ever became a slave-holder, I cannot account for; for I believe him to be the only kind slave-holder in America: and not only that, I have been in England many years and have never met with a kinder man than Mr. Beveridge; and have often prayed that God would deliver him from that one sin—a sin which he was kept from eighteen years. [Roper's note]

40 As Roper was still part of Louis's estate, he should have been passed on to the nearest family member.

41 Possibly a town in DeKalb County in northeast Alabama, north of Columbus, Georgia.

42 Probably Creek Indian territory in eastern Alabama.

several children, one about three months old, without any body to take care of her; I asked where her mother was, and was told that Mrs. Irving had given her a very hard task to do at washing, in a brook, about a quarter of a mile distant. We heard after, that not being able to get it done, she got some cords, tied them round her neck, climbed up a tree, swung off, and hung herself. Being missed, persons were sent after her, who observed several buzzards flying about a particular spot, to which they directed their steps, and found the poor woman nearly eaten up.

After this we travelled several months without anything remarkable taking place.

CHAPTER VII

The Author's last Attempt and final Escape
from Marianna to Savannah; from thence to New York;
Quarantined at Staten Island.

In the year 1834, Mr. Beveridge, who was now residing in Appalachicola, a town in West Florida, became a bankrupt, when all his property was sold, and I fell into the hands of a very cruel master, Mr. Register, a planter in the same State; of whom, knowing his savage character, I always had a dread. Previously to his purchasing me, he had frequently taunted me, by saying, "You have been a gentleman long enough, and, whatever may be the consequences, I intend to buy you." To which I remarked, that I would on no account live with him if I could help it. Nevertheless, intent upon his purpose, in the month of July, 1834, he bought me; after which I was so exasperated, that I cared not whether I lived or died; in fact, whilst I was on my passage from Appalachicola, I procured a quart bottle of whisky, for the purpose of so intoxicating myself, that I might be able either to plunge myself into the river, or so enrage my master that he should despatch me forth with. I was, however, by a kind Providence, prevented from committing this horrid deed by an old slave on board, who, knowing my intention, secretly took the bottle from me; after which, my hands were tied, and I was led into the town of Ochesa, to a warehouse, where my master was asked by the proprietor of the place the reason of his confining my hands; in answer to which, Mr. Register said that he had purchased me. The proprietor, however, persuaded him to untie me; after which, my master being excessively drunk asked for a cow-hide, intending to flog me, from which the proprietor dissuaded him, saying that he had known me for some time, and he was sure that I did not require to be flogged. From this place we proceeded about mid-day on our way. He placed me on the bare back of a half-starved old horse, which he had purchased, and upon which sharp *surface* he kindly intended I should ride about eighty miles, the distance we were then from his home. In this unpleasant situation I could not help reflecting upon the prospects before me, not forgetting that I had heard my new master had been in the habit of stealing cattle and other property, and among other things a slave woman, and that I had said, as it afterwards turned out, in the hearing of some one who communicated the saying to my master, that I had been accustomed to live with a gentleman and not with a rogue; and, finding that he had been informed of this, I had the additional dread of a few hundred lashes for it on my arrival at my destination.

About two hours after we started it began to rain very heavily, and continued to do so until we arrived at Marianna, about twelve at night, when we were to rest till morning. My master here questioned me as to whether I intended to run away or not; and I not then knowing the sin of lying, at once told him that I would not. He then gave me his clothes to dry. I took them to the kitchen for that purpose, and he retired to bed, taking a bag of clothes belonging to me with him, as a kind of security, I presume, for my safety. In an hour or two afterwards I took his clothes to him dried, and found him fast asleep. I placed them by his side, and said that I would then take my own to dry too, taking care to speak loud enough to ascertain whether he was asleep or not, knowing that he had a dirk and pistol by his side, which he would not have hesitated using against me, if I had attempted secretly to have procured them. I was glad to find that the effects of his drinking the day before had caused his sleeping very soundly, and I immediately resolved on making my escape; and without loss of time started with my few clothes into the woods, which were in the immediate neighbourhood; and after running many miles, I came up to the river Chapoli, which is very deep, and so beset with alligators that I dared not attempt to swim across.

I paced up and down this river, with the hope of finding a conveyance across, for a whole day, the succeeding night, and till noon on the following day, which was Saturday. About twelve o'clock on that day I discovered an Indian canoe, which had not from all appearance been used for some time; this of course, I used to convey myself across, and after being obliged to go a little way down the river, by means of a piece of wood I providentially found in the boat. I landed on the opposite side. Here I found myself surrounded by planters looking for me, in consequence of which, I hid myself in the bushes until night, when I again travelled several miles to the farm of a Mr. Robinson, a large sugar and cotton planter, where I rested till morning in a field. Afterwards I set out, working my way through the woods, about twenty miles towards the east; this I knew by my knowledge of the position of the sun at its rising. Having reached the Chattahoochee river, which divides Florida from Georgia, I was again puzzled to know how to cross; it was about three o'clock in the day, when a number of persons were fishing; having walked for some hours along the banks, I at last, after dark, procured a ferry-boat, which not being able, from the swiftness of the river, to steer direct across, I was carried many miles down the river, landing on the Georgian side, from whence I proceeded on through the woods two or three miles, and came to a little farm-house about twelve o'clock at night; at a short distance from the house I found an old slave hut, into which I went, and informed the old man, who appeared seventy or eighty years old, that I had had a very bad master from whom I run away; and asked him if he could give me something to eat, having had no suitable food for three or four days; he told me he had nothing but a piece of dry Indian bread, which he cheerfully gave me; having eaten it, I went on a short distance from the hut, and laid down in the wood to rest for an hour or two. All the following day (Monday) I continued travelling through the woods, and was greatly distressed for want of water to quench my thirst, it being a very dry country, till I came to Spring Creek, which is a wide, deep stream, and with some of which I gladly quenched my thirst. I then proceeded to cross the same, by a bridge close by, and continued my way until dusk. I came to a gentleman's house in the woods, where I inquired how far it was to the next house, taking care to watch an opportunity to ask some individual whom I could master, and get away from, if any interruption to my progress was attempted. I went on for some time, it being a very fine moonlight night, and was presently alarmed by the howling of a wolf near me; which, I concluded, was calling others to join him in attacking me, having understood that they always assemble in numbers for such a purpose; the howling increased, and I was still pursued, and the numbers were evidently increasing fast; but I was happily rescued from my dreadful fright, by coming to some cattle, which attracted, as I supposed, the wolves, and saved my life; for I could not get up the trees for safety, they being very tall pines, the lowest branches of which were, at least, forty or fifty feet from the ground, and the trunks very large and smooth.

About two o'clock I came to the house of a Mr. Cherry, on the borders of the Flint River; I went up to the house, and called them up to beg something to eat; but having nothing cooked, they kindly allowed me to lie down in the porch, where they made me a bed. In conversation with this Mr. Cherry, I discovered that I had known him before, having been in a steam-boat, the Versailles, some months previous, which sunk very near the house, but which I did not at first discern to be the same. I then thought it would not be prudent for me to stop there, and, therefore, told them, I was in a hurry to get on, and must start very early again, he having no idea who I was; and I gave his son six cents to take me across the river, which he did when the sun was about half an hour high, and unfortunately landed me where there was a man building a boat, who knew me very well, and my former master too,—he calling me by name, asked me where I was going.

I was very much frightened at being discovered, but summoned up courage, and said, that my master had gone to Tallyhassa[43] by the coach, and that there was not room for me, and I had to walk round to meet him. I then asked the man to put me in the best road to get there, which, however, I knew as well as he did, having travelled there before; he directed me the best way; but I, of course, took the contrary direction, wanting to get on to Savannah. By this hasty and wicked deception, I saved myself from going to Bainbridge prison, which was close by, and to which I should certainly have been taken had it been known that I was making my escape.

Leaving Bainbridge, I proceeded about forty miles, travelling all day under a scorching sun, through the woods, in which I saw many deer and serpents, until I reached Thomas Town, in the evening. I there inquired the way to Augusta, of a man whom I met, and also asked where I could obtain lodgings, and was told there was a poor minister about a mile from the place who would give me lodgings. I accordingly went, and found them in a little log-house, where having awakened the family, I found them all lying on the bare boards, where I joined them, for the remainder of the night.

In the morning the old gentleman prayed for me, that I might be preserved on my journey; he had previously asked me where I was going, and knowing, that if I told him the right place, any that inquired of him for me would be able to find me, asked the way to Augusta, instead of Savannah, my real destination. I also told him, that I was partly Indian and partly white, but I am also partly African, but this I omitted to tell him, knowing if I did I should be apprehended. After I had left this hut,

43 Tallahassee, the state capitol of Florida.

I again inquired for Augusta, for the purpose of misleading my pursuers, but I afterwards took my course through the woods, and came into a road, called the Coffee Road,[44] which General Jackson cut down for his troops at the time of the war between the Americans and Spaniards, in Florida; in which road there are but few houses, and which I preferred for the purpose of avoiding detection.

After several days I left this road and took a more direct way to Savannah, where I had to wade through two rivers before I came to the Alatamah, which I crossed in a ferry-boat, about a mile below the place where the rivers Oconee and Ocmulgee run together into one river, called the Alatamah. I here met with some cattle drovers, who were collecting cattle to drive to Savannah. On walking on before them, I began to consider in what way I could obtain a passport[45] for Savannah, and determined on the following plan:—

I called at a cottage, and after I had talked some time with the wife, who began to feel greatly for me, in consequence of my telling her a little of my history (her husband being out hunting), I pretended to show her my passport, feeling for it everywhere about my coat and hat, and not finding it, I went back a little way, pretending to look for it, but came back, saying, I was very sorry, but I did not know where it was. At last, the man came home, carrying a deer upon his shoulders, which he brought into the yard, and began to dress it. The wife then went out to tell him my situation, and after long persuasion, he said he could not write, but that if I could tell his son what was in my passport he would write me one; knowing that I should not be able to pass through Savannah without one, and having heard several free coloured men read theirs, I thought I could tell the boy what to write. The lad sat down and wrote what I told him, nearly filling a large sheet of paper for the passport, and another with recommendations. These being completed, I was invited to partake of the fresh venison, which the woman of the house had prepared for dinner, and having done so, and feeling grateful for their kindness, I proceeded on my way. Going along, I took my papers out of my pocket, and looking at them, although I could not read a word, I perceived that the boy's writing was very unlike other writing that I had seen, and was greatly blotted besides, consequently I was afraid that these documents would not answer my purpose, and began to consider what other plan I could pursue to obtain another pass.

44 Named for General John Coffee, the road ran east-west across southern Georgia.

45 A document authorizing Roper to travel unimpeded to and through Savannah.

I had now to wade through another river to which I came, and which I had great difficulty in crossing, in consequence of the water overflowing the banks of several rivers to the extent of upwards of twenty miles. In the midst of the water, I passed one night upon a small island, and the next day I went through the remainder of the water. On many occasions, I was obliged to walk upon my toes, and consequently found the advantage of being six feet two inches high, (I have grown three inches since,) and at other times was obliged to swim. In the middle of this extremity, I felt it would be imprudent for me to return; for if my master was in pursuit of me, my safest place from him was in the water, if I could keep my head above the surface. I was, however, dreadfully frightened at the crocodiles, and most earnestly prayed that I might be kept from a watery grave, and resolved, that if again I landed, I would spend my life in the service of God.

Having, through mercy, again started on my journey, I met with the drovers; and having, whilst in the waters, taken the pass out of my hat, and so dipped it in the water as to spoil it, I showed it to the men, and asked them where I could get another. They told me that in the neighbourhood, there lived a rich cotton merchant, who would write me one. They took me to him, and gave their word that they saw the passport before it was wet, (for I had previously showed it to them,) upon which, the cotton-planter wrote a free pass and a recommendation, to which the cow-drovers affixed their marks.

The recommendation was as follows:—

"John Roper, a very interesting young lad, whom I have seen and travelled with for eighty or ninety miles on his road from Florida, is a free man, descended from Indian and white. I trust he will be allowed to pass on without interruption, being convinced, from what I have seen, that he is free, and though dark, is not an African. I had seen his papers before they were wetted."

These cow-drovers, who procured me the passport and recommendation from the cotton-planter, could not read; and they were intoxicated when they went with me to him. I am part African, as well as Indian and white, my father being a white man, Henry Roper, Esq. Caswell County, North Carolina, U.S. a very wealthy slave holder, who sold me when quite a child, for the strong resemblance I bore him. My mother is part Indian, part African; but I dared not disclose that, or I should have been taken up. I then had eleven miles to go to Savannah, one of the greatest slaveholding cities in America, and where they are always looking out for run-away slaves. When at this city, I had travelled about five hundred miles.[46] It required great courage to pass through this place. I went through the main street with apparent confidence, though much alarmed; did not stop at any house in the city, but went down immediately to the docks, and inquired for a berth as a steward to a vessel to New York. I had been in this capacity before on the Appalachicola River. The person whom I asked to procure me a berth, was steward of one of the New York Packets; he knew Captain Deckay, of the schooner Fox, and got me a situation on board that vessel in five minutes after I had been at the docks. The schooner Fox was a very old vessel, twenty-seven years old, laden with lumber and cattle for New York; she was rotten, and could not be insured. The sailors were afraid of her; but I ventured on board, and five minutes after, we dropped from the docks into the river. My spirits then began to revive, and I thought I should get to a free country directly. We cast anchor in the stream, to keep the sailors on, as they were so dissatisfied with the vessel, and lay there four days; during which time, I had to go into the city several times, which exposed me to great danger, as my master was after me, and I dreaded meeting him in the city.

Fearing the Fox would not sail before I should be seized, I deserted her, and went on board a brig sailing to Providence, that was towed out by a steam-boat,[47] and got thirty miles from Savannah. During this time I endeavoured to persuade the steward to take me as an assistant, and hoped to have accomplished my purpose; but the captain had examined me attentively, and thought I was a slave; he therefore ordered me, when the steam-boat was sent back, to go on board her to Savannah, as the fine for taking a slave from that city to any of the Free States, is five hundred dollars. I reluctantly went back to Savannah, among slave-holders and slaves. My mind was in a sad state; and I was under strong temptation to throw myself into the river. I had deserted the schooner Fox, and knew that the captain might put me into prison till the vessel was ready to sail; if this happened, and my master had come to jail in search of me, I must have gone back to slavery. But when I reached the docks at Savannah, the first person I met was the captain of the Fox, looking for another steward in my place. He was a very kind man, belonging to the Free States, and

46 The distance between these two places is much less than five hundred miles: but I was obliged to travel round about, in order to avoid being caught. [Roper's note]

47 An iron boat, the first that was ever built in America, belonging to Mr. Lemayor, and this was also the first time she sailed. [Roper's note]. Probably Gazaway Bugg Lamar's *John Randolph*, the first successful American iron steamboat, which made its inaugural voyage from Savannah, July 9, 1834.

MOSES ROPER

inquired if I would go back to his vessel. This usage was very different to what I expected, and I gladly accepted his offer. This captain did not know that I was a slave. In about two days we sailed from Savannah to New York.

I am (August 1834,) unable to express the joy I now felt. I never was at sea before, and after I had been out about an hour, was taken with sea-sickness, which continued five days. I was scarcely able to stand up, and one of the sailors was obliged to take my place. The captain was very kind to me all this time; but even after I recovered, I was not sufficiently well to do my duty properly, and could not give satisfaction to the sailors, who swore at me, and asked me why I shipped as I was not used to the sea? We had a very quick passage; and in six days, after leaving Savannah, we were in the harbour at Staten Island, where the vessel was quarantined for two days, six miles from New York. The captain went to the city, but left me aboard with the sailors, who had most of them been brought up in the slave-holding States, and were very cruel men. One of the sailors was particularly angry with me, because he had to perform the duties of my place; and while the captain was in the city, the sailors called me to the fore-hatch, where they said they would treat me. I went, and while I was talking, they threw a rope round my neck and nearly choked me. The blood streamed from my nose profusely. They also took up ropes with large knots, and knocked me over the head. They said I was a negro; they despised me; and I expected they would have thrown me into the water. When we arrived at the city, these men, who had so ill-treated me, ran away that they might escape the punishment which would otherwise have been inflicted on them.

CHAPTER VIII

Arrived in New York, went on to Poughkeepsie, Albany, Vermont, Boston, and return to New York—Embarked for England.

When I arrived in the city of New York, I thought I was free;[48] but learned I was not, and could be taken there. I went out into the country several miles, and tried to get employment; but failed, as I had no recommendation. I then returned to New York; but finding the same difficulty there to get work as in the country, I went back to the vessel, which was to sail eighty miles up the Hudson river, to Poughkeepsie. When I arrived,

48 Arrival in the North did not confer freedom, since U.S. law allowed any fugitive slave to be captured and returned to his or her owner.

I obtained employment at an inn, and after I had been there about two days, was seized with the cholera,[49] which was at that place. The complaint was, without doubt, brought on by having subsisted on fruit only, for several days, while I was in the slave States. The landlord of the inn came to me when I was in bed, suffering violently from cholera, and told me he knew I had that complaint, and as it had never been in his house, I could not stop there any longer. No one would enter my room, except a young lady, who appeared very pious, and amiable, and had visited persons with the cholera. She immediately procured me some medicine at her own expense, and administered it herself; and whilst I was groaning with agony, the landlord came up and ordered me out of the house directly. Most of the persons in Poughkeepsie had retired for the night, and I lay under a shed on some cotton bales. The medicine relieved me, having been given so promptly; and next morning I went from the shed, and laid on the banks of the river below the city. Towards evening, I felt much better, and went on in a steam-boat, to the city of Albany, about eighty miles. When I reached there, I went into the country, and tried for three or four days to procure employment, but failed.

At that time I had scarcely any money, and lived upon fruit; so I returned to Albany, where I could get no work, as I could not show the recommendations I possessed, which were only from slave States; and I did not wish any one to know I came from them. After a time I went up the western canal as steward in one of the boats. When I had gone about 350 miles up the canal, I found I was going too much towards the slave States, in consequence of which, I returned to Albany, and went up the northern canal, into one of the New England States—Vermont. The distance I had travelled, including the 350 miles I had to return from the west, and the 100 to Vermont, was 2300 miles. When I reached Vermont, I found the people very hospitable and kind; they seemed opposed to slavery, so I told them I was a runaway slave. I hired myself to a firm in Sudbury.[50] After I

49 Cholera is a severe bacterial infection of the small intestine, often caused by ingesting food or water contaminated with feces.

50 During my stay in this town, I thought of the vow I made in the water, (page 129), and I became more thoughtful about the salvation of my soul. I attended the Methodist Chapel, where a Mr. Benton preached, and there I began to feel that I was a great sinner. During the latter part of my stay here, I became more anxious about salvation, and I entertained the absurd notion that religion would come to me in some extraordinary way. With this impression, I used to go into the woods two hours before daylight to pray, and expected something would take place, and I should become religious. [Roper's note]

had been in Sudbury some time, the neighbouring farmers told me, that I had hired myself for much less money than I ought. I mentioned it to my employers, who were very angry about it; I was advised to leave by some of the people around, who thought the gentleman I was with would write to my former master, informing him where I was, and obtain the reward fixed upon me. Fearing I should be taken I immediately left, and went into the town of Ludlow, where I met with a kind friend, Mr.—,[51] who sent me to school for several weeks. At this time I was advertised in the papers, and was obliged to leave. I went a little way out of Ludlow,[52] to a retired place, and lived two weeks with a Mr.—, deacon of a Baptist Church at Ludlow; at this place I could have obtained education, had it been safe to have remained. From there I went to New Hampshire, where I was not safe, so went to Boston, Massachusetts, with the hope of returning to Ludlow, a place to which I was much attached. At Boston, I met with a friend, who kept a shop, and took me to assist him for several weeks. Here I did not consider myself safe, as persons from all parts of the country were continually coming to the shop, and I feared some might come who knew me. I now had my head shaved, and bought a wig, and engaged myself to a Mr. Perkins, of Brookline, three miles from Boston, where I remained about a month. Some of the family discovered that I wore a wig, and said that I was a runaway slave; but the neighbours all around thought I was a white, to prove which I have a document in my possession to call me to military duty. The law is, that no slave or coloured person performs this, but every other person in America, of the age of twenty-one, is called upon to perform military duty once or twice in the year, or pay a fine.

51 It would not be proper to mention any names, as a person in any of the States in America, found harbouring a slave, would have to pay a heavy fine. [Roper's note]

52 Whilst in this neighbourhood, I attended the Baptist Meeting, and trust the preaching of the gospel was much blessed to my soul. As this was the first time I was ever favoured with any education, I was very intent upon learning to read the Bible, and in a few weeks I was able, from my own reading, to repeat by heart the whole of the last chapter of Matthew. I also attended the prayer and inquiry meetings, where the attendants used to relate their experience, and I was requested to do the same. I found these meetings a great blessing, and they were the means, under God, of communicating to my mind a more clear and distinct knowledge of the way of salvation by Jesus Christ. [Roper's note]

"Mr. Moses Roper,

"You being duly enrolled as a soldier in the company, under the command of Captain Benjamin Bradley, are hereby notified and ordered to appear at the Town House, in Brookline, on Friday, 28th instant, at three o'clock, P.M., for the purpose of filling the vacancy in the said company, occasioned by the promotion of Lieut. Nathaniel M. Weeks, and of filling any other vacancy which may then and there occur in the said company, and then wait further orders.

"By order of the Captain.

"F. P. WENTWORTH, Clerk.

"*Brookline, August 14th,* 1835."[53]

I then returned to the city of Boston, to the shop where I was before. Several weeks after I had returned to my situation, two coloured men informed me, that a gentleman had been inquiring for a person, whom, from the description, I knew to be myself, and offered them a considerable sum if they would disclose my place of abode; but they, being much opposed to slavery, came and told me; upon which information, I secreted myself till I could get off. I went into the Green Mountains[54] for several weeks, from thence to the city of New York, and remained in secret several days, till I heard of a ship, the Napoleon, sailing to England, and on the 11th of November, 1835, I sailed, taking my letters of recommendation, to the Drs. Morrison and Raffles, and the Rev. Alexander Fletcher. The time I first started from slavery, was in July, 1834, so that I was nearly sixteen months in making my escape.

CHAPTER IX

The Author arrives at Liverpool, November 29, 1835.—
Manchester.—London.

On the 29th of November, 1835, I reached Liverpool; and my feelings when I first touched the shores of Britain were indescribable, and can only be properly understood by those who have escaped from the cruel bondage of slavery.

---

53 Being very tall, I was taken to be twenty-one; but my correct age, as far as I can tell, is stated in page 98. [Roper's note]

54 A mountain range located in southwest Vermont.

"'Tis liberty alone that gives the flower of fleeting life its lustre
     and perfume;
And we are weeds without it."

"Slaves cannot breathe in England;
If their lungs receive our air, that moment they are free;
They touch our country, and their shackles fall."—*Cowper*.[55]

When I reached Liverpool, I proceeded to Dr. Raffles, and handed my letters of recommendation to him. He received me very kindly, and introduced me to a member of his church, with whom I stayed the night.—Here I met with the greatest attention and kindness. The next day I went to Manchester, where I met with many kind friends; among others, Mr. Ads-head, of that town, to whom I desire, through this medium, to return my most sincere thanks for the many great services which he rendered me, adding both to my spiritual and temporal comfort. I would not, however, forget to remember here Mr. Leese, Mr. Giles, Mr. Crewdson, and Mr. Clare, the latter of whom gave me a letter to Mr. Scoble,[56] the secretary of the Anti-slavery Society. I remained here several days, and then proceeded to London, December 12th, 1835, and immediately called on Mr. Scoble, to whom I delivered my letter. This gentleman procured me a lodging. I then lost no time in delivering my letters to Dr. Morrison and the Rev. Alexander Fletcher, who received me with the greatest kindness; and shortly after this, Dr. Morrison sent my letter from New York, with another from himself, to the *Patriot* newspaper, in which he kindly implored the sympathy of the public in my behalf. The appeal was read by Mr. Christopherson, a member of Dr. Morrison's church, of which gentleman I express but little of my feelings and gratitude, when I say, that throughout he has been towards me a parent, for whose tenderness and sympathy I desire ever to feel that attachment which I do not know how to express.

I stayed at his house several weeks, being treated as one of the family. The appeal in the *Patriot* referred to getting a suitable academy for me, which the Rev. Dr. Cox[57] recommended, at Hackney, where I remained

---

55 From "The Task" (1785), by William Cowper (1731–1800). The first excerpt is from book 5, lines 446–48 ("The Winter Morning's Walk"), and the second is from book 2, lines 40–42 ("The Timepiece").

56 Rev. John Scoble (1799–1867?)

helped found the British and Foreign Antislavery Society in 1839.

57 Francis Augustus Cox, D.D. (1783–1853), Baptist pastor at Hackney, who helped finance Roper's education.

half a year, going through the rudiments of an English education. At this time, I attended the ministry of Dr. Cox, which I enjoyed very much, and to which I ascribe the attainment of clearer views of divine grace than I had before. I had attended here several months, when I expressed my wish to Dr. Cox to become a member of his church. I was proposed; and after stating my experience, was admitted, March 31, 1846.

Here it is necessary that I should draw this narrative to a close, not that my materials are exhausted, but that I am unwilling to extend it to a size which might preclude many well-wishers from the possession of it.

But I must remark, that my feelings of happiness at having escaped from cruel bondage, are not unmixed with sorrow of a very touching kind. *"The Land of the Free"* still contains the mother,[58] the brothers, and the sister of Moses Roper, not enjoying liberty, not the possessors of like feelings with me, not having even a distant glimpse of advancing towards freedom, but still slaves! This is a weight which hangs heavy on me. As circumstances at present stand, there is not much prospect of ever again seeing those dear ones, from whom, on the Sunday night, I was torn away by armed slaveholders and carried into cruel bondage.[59] And nothing would contribute so much to my entire happiness, if the kindness of gracious Providence should ever place me in such favourable circumstances as to be able to purchase their freedom. But I desire to express my entire resignation to the will of God. Should that Divine Being who made of one flesh all the kindreds of the earth, see fit that I should again clasp them to my breast, and see in them the reality of free men and free women, how shall I, a poor mortal, be enabled to sing a strain of praise sufficiently appropriate to such a boon from heaven.

But if the All-wise Disposer of all things should see fit to keep them still in suffering and bondage, it is a mercy to know that he orders all things well, that he is still the judge of all the earth, and that under such

---

58 About five months ago the Author wrote to Dr. Gallon, his mother's master, to know what sum would be sufficient to purchase her freedom, and he has received the following painful answer:—
"Milton, North Carolina, Aug. 28, 1839.
"Your mother and her family were transferred from this place, two or three years ago, to Grunsburgh, in the State of Alabama, and I regret to inform you that your mother is since dead."
The Author has since ascertained that the above is untrue, and sent merely to annoy him. April, 1843. [Roper's note]

59 See page 109. [Roper's note]

dispensations of his providence, he is working out that which shall be most for the advantage of his creatures.

Whatever I may have experienced in America at the hands of cruel taskmasters, yet I am unwilling to speak in any but respectful terms of the land of my birth. It is far from my wish to attempt to degrade America in the eyes of Britons. I love her institutions in the Free States, her zeal for Christ; I bear no enmity to the slave-holders, but regret their delusions; many, I am aware, are deeply sensible of the fault, but some I regret to say are not, and I could wish to open their eyes to their sin; may the period come, when God shall wipe off this deep stain from her constitution, and may America soon be indeed the land of the free.

In conclusion, I thank my dear friends in England for their affectionate attentions, and may God help me to show by my future walk in life, that I am not wanting in my acknowledgments of their kindness. But above all, to the God of all grace, I desire here before his people, that all the way in which he has led me has been the right way, and as in his mercy and wisdom, he has led me to this country, where I am allowed to go free, may all my actions tend to lead me on, through the mercy of God in Christ, in the right way, to a city of habitation.

Appendix

BERWICK, MARCH, 1846.

Soon after my arrival in England, I went to a boarding-school at Hackney, near London, and afterwards to another boarding-school at Wallingford, and after learning to read and write and some other branches, I entered as student at University College, London, which place, I very much regret, however, I was obliged to leave, in consequence of bad health; and during the time I was at school I lectured in different towns and sold my Narrative or book to pay for my education. On the 29th of December, 1839, I was married to a lady of Bristol, and, after travelling tens of thousands of miles, and lecturing in nearly every town and hundreds of villages in England, at the commencement of 1844, I left England with my family for British North America, and have taken up my future residence in Canada West, it being as near as I can get to my relations (who are still in bondage) without being again taken. Having some matters of a private nature to settle in this country, I left Canada in December, 1845, for England, and arrived at Liverpool, on the 25th of January, 1846, in the ship Orphan. I intend now, before I return to Canada, to visit Scotland

and Ireland, and deliver lectures, as I have not been in many towns in those countries. I shall then bid farewell once more to dear and happy Old England, not expecting again ever to return, but hoping to meet many thousands of her inhabitants (whom I have seen and addressed) in Heaven. My dear and kind friends, throughout Great Britain and Ireland, farewell!

Lunsford Lane (from William G. Hawkins's *Lunsford Lane*, 1863)

(Documenting the American South, <http://docsouth.unc.edu>, The University of North Carolina at Chapel Hill Libraries, North Carolina Collection)

THE FIRST-PERSON ACCOUNT of a remarkable slave entrepreneur, *The Narrative of Lunsford Lane*, published in Boston 1842, stands out among many slave narratives of the period because of its central irony: its relatively mild portrayal of slavery followed by its disturbing depiction of freedom as Lane experienced it in antebellum Raleigh, North Carolina. Unlike more famous slave narrators, Lane never claims to have been beaten, separated from his family, or sold by his southern masters. Equally striking, Lane never seems to have considered running away, although he longed for freedom. A dedicated family man rather than the isolated individual usually featured in slave narratives, Lane focuses on the preservation of his family and his personal economic advancement in slavery. Working within the system, establishing businesses but comporting himself humbly, and purchasing himself and his family according to the laws of the slaveocracy, Lane seems to have believed that Raleigh, the town of his birth, would accommodate his ambitions, despite his color and once-enslaved condition. As the conclusion of his narrative demonstrates, Lane's experiences following his acquisition of his freedom proved him naive and almost cost him his life.

Lane's narrative is framed by class and economic concerns—from his desire for freedom, always couched within the idea of making and saving money, to his marriage, which he describes as a "bargain" between him and his wife. Politic and restrained in slavery, his *Narrative* expresses a bitterness that derides lower-class whites and those who forced him to leave Raleigh, along with a stinging commentary on the inability of prejudiced whites to appreciate African American feelings, such as the desire for freedom.

Unlike many less fortunate slaves, Lunsford Lane was raised by both his mother and father, Clarissa Haywood and Edward Lane. From selling peaches as a child to becoming a successful tobacconist as an adult, Lane was diligent enough to purchase the freedom of himself, his wife, and their seven children. To rise to this level of class and economic security while still enslaved, Lane depended on the simultaneous goodwill and acquisitiveness of whites. In addition to hiring his time from his owner, Lane worked in the office of the governor, which seems to have confirmed his class allegiance with those he termed the "first men and the more wealthy" whom he considered his "friends." However, Lane's economic success as a black man, reflected in his ability to buy his own freedom and negotiate the terms of purchase for his wife and children, did not exempt him from North Carolina laws restricting free blacks. Ultimately he was forced to leave Raleigh and take up residence in Boston. There, through donations and speeches, Lane raised the money he needed to free his family and bring them to the North.

Lane states in the introduction to his narrative that he "employ[ed] the services of a friend" in helping him prepare the book. Evidence suggests that Lane's "friend" was engaged in the role of editing Lane's text, much as nonprofessional writers depend on editors today. Aside from his autobiography, the only known source of information about Lane during his lifetime comes from an 1863 biography written by William G. Hawkins, an antislavery minister. In addition to a continuing interest in entrepreneurial ventures, Lane lectured for the American Anti-Slavery Society after moving to Boston. That *The Narrative of Lunsford Lane* went through four printings in both American and British editions testifies to the popularity of Lane as a public figure. Nevertheless, his fate after 1862, when he was employed as head steward in a Worcester, Massachusetts, hospital, remains unknown.

Suggested Readings

Andrews, William L. *To Tell a Free Story: The First Century of Afro-American Autobiography, 1760–1865.* Urbana: University of Illinois Press, 1986.

Bassett, John Spencer. *Anti-Slavery Leaders of North Carolina.* Baltimore: Johns Hopkins University Press, 1898. [Partly devoted to the biography of Lunsford Lane, whom Bassett refers to as an "exceptional negro".]

Blassingame, John W., ed. *Slave Testimony: Two Centuries of Letters, Speeches, Interviews, and Autobiographies.* Baton Rouge: Louisiana State University Press, 1977. [Contains a speech given by Lunsford Lane in 1842.]

Evans, Tampathia, ed. "The Narrative of Lunsford Lane." In *North Carolina Slave Narratives: The Lives of Moses Roper, Lunsford Lane, Moses Grandy, and Thomas H. Jones,* edited by William L. Andrews, 93–130. Chapel Hill: University of North Carolina Press, 2003.

Hawkins, William G. *Lunsford Lane: Another Helper from North Carolina.* 1863. Miami, Fla.: Mnemosyne Pub. Co., 1969. [A biography of Lane drawn mostly from Lane's autobiography and concerned with expressing the antislavery views of the Reverend Hawkins.]

Note on the Text

The abridged version of Lunsford Lane's *Narrative* printed here incorporates all the events of Lane's life as recounted in *The Narrative of Lunsford Lane,*

Formerly of Raleigh, N.C., Embracing an Account of His Early Life, the Redemption By Purchase of Himself and Family from Slavery, and His Banishment from the Place of His Birth for the Crime of Wearing a Colored Skin, first published in Boston in 1842. Introductory matter, bills of sale for slaves, and some of the author's commentary on slave life have been omitted. A complete edition of *The Narrative of Lunsford Lane* can be found in Andrews, ed., *North Carolina Slave Narratives*.

The state capital in Raleigh during Lunsford Lane's lifetime;
painting by Jacob Marling (1774–1833)
*(North Carolina Department of Cultural Resources,
Office of Archives and History, Raleigh)*

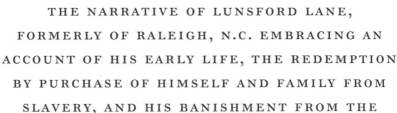

THE NARRATIVE OF LUNSFORD LANE,

FORMERLY OF RALEIGH, N.C. EMBRACING AN

ACCOUNT OF HIS EARLY LIFE, THE REDEMPTION

BY PURCHASE OF HIMSELF AND FAMILY FROM

SLAVERY, AND HIS BANISHMENT FROM THE

PLACE OF HIS BIRTH FOR THE CRIME OF

WEARING A COLORED SKIN.

The small city of Raleigh, North Carolina, it is known, is the capital of the State, situated in the interior, and containing about thirty-six hundred inhabitants. Here lived Mr. SHERWOOD HAYWOOD,[1] a man of considerable respectability, a planter, and the cashier of a bank. He owned three plantations, at the distances respectively of seventy-five, thirty, and three miles from his residence in Raleigh. He owned in all about two hundred and fifty slaves, among the rest my mother,[2] who was a house servant to her master, and of course a resident in the city. My father[3] was a slave to a near neighbor. The apartment where I was born and where I spent my childhood and youth was called "the kitchen," situated some fifteen or twenty rods from the "great house." Here the house servants lodged and lived, and here the meals were prepared for the people in the mansion. The "field hands," of course, reside upon the plantation.

On the 30th of May, 1803, I was ushered into the world but I did not begin to see the rising of its dark clouds, nor fancy how they might be broken and dispersed, until some time afterwards. My infancy was spent upon the floor, in a rough cradle, or sometimes in my mother's arms. My

1 Mr. Sherwood Haywood (1762–1829) was an agent for the Bank of New Bern in Raleigh, and clerk of the North Carolina State Senate from 1786 to 1798.

2 Clarissa Haywood (?–1859) was manumitted by Eleanor Hawkins Haywood in 1842 and moved to Boston with her son Lunsford. She later settled in Wrentham, Massachusetts, with her husband, Edward.

3 Edward Lane belonged to John Haywood, the brother of Sherwood Haywood. At John Haywood's death around 1830, Edward was manumitted. He worked as a steward for the Haywood family for fourteen years before reuniting with his family in Massachusetts. He died in Wrentham.

early boyhood in playing with the other boys and girls, colored and white, in the yard, and occasionally doing such little matters of labor as one of so young years could. I knew no difference between myself and the white children nor did they seem to know any in turn. Sometimes my master would come out and give a biscuit to me, and another to one of his own white boys but I did not perceive the difference between us. I had no brothers or sisters, but there were other colored families living in the same kitchen, and the children playing in the same yard, with me and my mother.

When I was ten or eleven years old, my master set me regularly to cutting wood, in the yard in the winter, and working in the garden in the summer. And when I was fifteen years of age, he gave me the care of the pleasure horses, and made me his carriage driver; but this did not exempt me from other labor, especially in the summer. Early in the morning I used to take his three horses to the plantation, and turn them into the pasture to graze, and myself into the cotton or cornfield, with a hoe in my hand, to work through the day and after sunset I would take these horses back to the city, a distance of three miles, feed them, and then attend to any other business my master or any of his family had for me to do, until bed time, when with my blanket in my hand, I would go into the dining room to rest through the night. The next day the same round of labor would be repeated, unless some of the family wished to ride out, in which case I must be on hand with the horses to wait upon them, and in the meantime to work about the yard. On Sunday I had to drive to Church twice, which with other things necessary to be done, took the whole day. So my life went wearily on from day to day, from night to night, and from week to week.

When I began to work, I discovered the difference between myself and my master's white children. They began to order me about, and were told to do so by my master and mistress. I found, too, that they had learned to read, while I was not permitted to have a book in my hand. To be in the possession of anything written or printed, was regarded as an offence. And then there was the fear that I might be sold away from those who were dear to me, and conveyed to the far South. I had learned that being a slave I was subject to this worst (to us) of all calamities and I knew of others in similar situations to myself, thus sold away. My friends were not numerous but in proportion as they were few they were dear and the thought that I might be separated from them forever, was like that of having the heart torn from its socket; while the idea of being conveyed to the far South, seemed infinitely worse than the terrors of death. To know, also, that I was never to consult my own will, but was, while I lived, to be entirely under the control of another, was another state of mind hard for me to bear. Indeed all things now made me *feel*, what I had before known only in words, that *I was a slave*. Deep was this feeling, and it preyed upon my heart like a never-dying worm. I saw no prospect that my condition would ever be changed. Yet I used to plan in my mind from day to day, and from night to night, how I might be free.

One day, while I was in this state of mind, my father gave me a small basket of peaches. I sold them for thirty cents, which was the first money I ever had in my life. Afterwards I won some marbles, and sold them for sixty cents, and some weeks after Mr. Hog from Fayetteville,[4] came to visit my master, and on leaving gave me one dollar. After that Mr. Bennahan[5] from Orange county,[6] gave me a dollar, and a son of my master fifty cents. These sums, and the hope that then entered my mind of purchasing at some future time my freedom, made me long for money; and plans for money-making took the principal possession of my thoughts. At night I would steal away with my axe, get a load of wood to cut for twenty-five cents, and the next morning hardly escape a whipping for the offence. But I persevered until I had obtained twenty dollars. Now I began to think seriously of becoming able to buy myself; and cheered by this hope, I went on from one thing to another, laboring "at dead of night," after the long weary day's toil for my master was over, till I found I had collected one hundred dollars. This sum I kept hid, first in one place and then in another, as I dare not put it out, for fear I should lose it.

After this I lit upon a plan which proved of great advantage to me. My father suggested a mode of preparing smoking tobacco, different from any then or since employed. It had the double advantage of giving the tobacco a peculiarly pleasant flavor, and of enabling me to manufacture a good article out of a very indifferent material. I improved somewhat upon his suggestion, and commenced the manufacture, doing as I have before said, all my work in the night. The tobacco I put up in papers of about a quarter of a pound each, and sold them at fifteen cents.[7] But

4 Fayetteville is located in Cumberland County, North Carolina.

5 Richard Bennahan (1743–1825) was a merchant, planter, and builder in 1799 of a house that became Stagville Plantation, which covered over 4,000 acres in 1800.

6 Orange County is in the central piedmont area of North Carolina.

7 A 1788 North Carolina statute required slaves to possess written permission from their owners for each act of trading in order to discourage slaves from trading in stolen goods from their owners. In 1826, the legislature created a specific list of articles that slaves could not sell without written permission. These included cotton, tobacco, corn, pork, farming utensils, meal, and liquor.

the tobacco could not be smoked without a pipe, and as I had given the former a flavor peculiarly grateful, it occurred to me that I might so construct a pipe as to cool the smoke in passing through it, and thus meet the wishes of those who are more fond of smoke than heat. This I effected by means of a reed, which grows plentifully in that region; I made a passage through the reed with a hot wire, polished it, and attached a clay pipe to the end, so that the smoke should be cooled in flowing through the stem like whiskey or rum in passing from the boiler through the worm of the still. These pipes I sold at ten cents apiece. In the early part of the night I would sell my tobacco and pipes, and manufacture them in the latter part. As the Legislature sit in Raleigh every year, I sold these articles considerably to the members, so that I became known not only in the city, but in many parts of the State, as a *tobacconist*.[8]

Perceiving that I was getting along so well, I began, slave as I was, to think about taking a wife. So I fixed my mind upon Miss Lucy Williams, a slave of Thomas Devereaux, Esq.,[9] an eminent lawyer in the place; but failed in my undertaking. Then I thought I never would marry; but at the end of two or three years my resolution began to slide away, till finding I could not keep it longer I set out once more in pursuit of a wife. So I fell in with her to whom I am now united, Miss MARTHA CURTIS, and the bargain between *us* was completed. I next went to her master, Mr. Boylan,[10] and asked him, according to the custom, if I might "marry his woman." His reply was, "Yes, if you will behave yourself." I told him I would. "And make her behave herself?" To this I also assented; and then proceeded to ask the approbation of my master, which was granted. So in May, 1828, I was bound as fast in wedlock as a slave can be. God may at any time sunder that band in a freeman; either master may do the same at pleasure in a slave. The bond is not recognized in law. But in my case it has never been broken; and now it cannot be, except by a higher power.

When we had been married nine months and one day, we were blessed with a son, and two years afterwards with a daughter. My wife also passed from the hands of Mr. Boylan, into those of Mr. BENJAMIN B. SMITH,[11]

8 A tobacconist is a dealer in tobacco, especially in retail.

9 Thomas Pollock Devereux (1793–1869) was the owner of several plantations in North Carolina and served as U.S. attorney for North Carolina, as well as a justice of the peace and presiding justice of the Halifax, North Carolina, County Court.

10 William Boylan was the editor of the *North Carolina Minerva* and publisher of *Boylan's Almanac*. He was also one of the owners and a president of the Raleigh and Gaston Railroad Company.

11 Benjamin B. Smith was a Raleigh merchant.

a merchant, a member and class-leader in the Methodist church, and in much repute for his deep piety and devotion to religion. But grace (of course) had not wrought in the same *manner* upon the heart of Mr. Smith, as nature had done upon that of Mr. Boylan, who made no religious profession. This latter gentleman used to give my wife, who was a favorite slave, (her mother nursed every one of his own children,) sufficient food and clothing to render her comfortable, so that I had to spend for her but little, except to procure such small articles of extra comfort as I was prompted to from time to time. Indeed Mr. Boylan was regarded as a very kind master to all the slaves about him; that is, to his house servants; nor did he personally inflict much cruelty, if any, upon his field hands. The overseer on his nearest plantation (I know but little about the rest) was a very cruel man; in one instance, as it was said among the slaves, he whipped a man *to death*; but of course denied that the man died in consequence of the whipping. Still it was the choice of my wife to pass into the hands of Mr. Smith, as she had become attached to him in consequence of belonging to the same church, and receiving his religious instruction and counsel as her class-leader, and in consequence of the peculiar devotedness to the cause of religion for which he was noted, and which he always seemed to manifest. — But when she became his slave, he withheld both from her and her children, the needful food and clothing, while he exacted from them to the uttermost all the labor they were able to perform. Almost every article of clothing worn either by my wife or children, especially every article of much value, I had to purchase; while the food he furnished the family amounted to less than a meal a day, and that of the coarser kind. I have no remembrance that he ever gave us a blanket or any other article of bedding, although it is considered a rule at the South that the master shall furnish each of his slaves with one blanket a year. So that, both as to food and clothing, I had in fact to support both my wife and the children, while he claimed them as his property, and received all their labor. She was a house servant to Mr. Smith, sometimes cooked the food for his family, and usually took it from the table, but her mistress was so particular in giving it out to be cooked, or so watched it, that she always knew whether it was all returned; and when the table was cleared away, the stern old lady would sit by and see that every dish (except the very little she would send into the kitchen) was put away, and then she would turn the key upon it, so as to be sure her slaves should not die of gluttony. . . . [B]y the expense of providing for my wife and children, all the money I had earned and could earn by my night labor was consumed, till I found myself reduced to five dollars, and this I lost one day in going to the plantation. My light of hope now went out. My prop seemed to have given way from under me. Sunk in the very night or despair respecting my freedom, I discovered myself, as though I had never known it before, a husband, the father of two children, a family looking up to me for bread, and I a slave, penniless, and well watched by my master, his wife and his children, lest I should, perchance, catch the friendly light of the stars to make something in order to supply the cravings of nature in those with whom my soul was bound up; or lest some plan of freedom might lead me to trim the light of diligence after the day's labor was over, while the rest of the world were enjoying the hours in pleasure or sleep.

At this time an event occurred, which, while it cast a cloud over the prospects of some of my fellow slaves, was a rainbow over mine. My master died; and his widow,[12] by the will, became sole executrix of his property. To the surprise of all, the bank of which he had been cashier presented a claim against the estate for forty thousand dollars. By a compromise, this sum was reduced to twenty thousand dollars; and my mistress, to meet the amount, sold some of her slaves, and hired out others. I hired my time of her,[13] for which I paid her a price varying from one hundred dollars to one hundred and twenty dollars per year. This was a privilege which comparatively few slaves at the South enjoy; and in this I felt truly blessed.

I commenced the manufacture of pipes and tobacco on an enlarged scale. I opened a regular place of business, labelled my tobacco in a conspicuous manner with the names of "*Edward and Lunsford Lane*," and of some of the persons who sold it for me,—established agencies for the sale in various parts of the State, one at Fayetteville, one at Salisbury,[14] one at Chapel Hill,[15] and so on,—sold my articles from my place of business, and about town, also deposited them in stores on commission, and thus, after paying my mistress for my time, and rendering such support as necessary to my family, I found in the space of some six or eight years, that I had collected the sum of one thousand dollars. During this time I had

12 Eleanor Hawkins Haywood.
13 It is contrary to the laws of the State, for a slave to have command of his own time in this way, but in Raleigh it is sometimes winked at. I knew one slave-man who was doing well for himself, taken up by the public authorities and hired out for the public good, three times in succession for this offence. The time of hiring in such a case is one year. The master is subject to a fine. But generally as I have said, if the slave is orderly and appears to be making nothing, neither he nor the master is interfered with. [Lane's note]
14 Salisbury is in Rowan County, in central North Carolina.
15 Chapel Hill is in Orange County, North Carolina.

found it politic to go shabbily dressed, and to appear to be very poor, but to pay my mistress for my services promptly. I kept my money hid, never venturing to put out a penny, nor to let any body but my wife know that I was making any. The thousand dollars was what I supposed my mistress would ask for me, and so I determined now what I would do.

I went to my mistress and inquired what was her price for me. She said a thousand dollars. I then told her that I wanted to be free, and asked her if she would sell me to be made free. She said she would; and accordingly I arranged with her, and with the master of my wife, Mr. Smith, already spoken of, for the latter to take my money[16] and buy of her my freedom, as I could not legally purchase it, and as the laws forbid emancipation except, for "meritorious services."[17] This done, Mr. Smith endeavored to emancipate me formally, and to get my manumission recorded; I tried also; but the court judged that I had done nothing "meritorious," and so I remained, nominally only, the slave of Mr. Smith for a year; when, feeling unsafe in that relation, I accompanied him to New York whither he was going to purchase goods, and was there regularly and formally made a freeman, and there my manumission was recorded. I returned to my family in Raleigh, and endeavored to do by them as a freeman should. I had known what it was to be a slave, and I knew what it was to be free. . . .

I had endured what a freeman would indeed call hard fare; but my lot, on the whole, had been a favored one for a slave. It is known that there is a wide difference in the situations of what are termed house servants, and plantation hands. I, though sometimes employed upon the plantation, belonged to the former, which is the favored class. My master, too, was esteemed a kind and humane man; and altogether I fared quite differently from many poor fellows whom it makes my blood run chill to think of, confined to the plantation, with not enough of food and that little of the coarsest kind, to satisfy the gnawings of hunger,—compelled oftentimes, to hie[18] away in the night-time, when worn down with work, and *steal*, (if it be stealing,) and privately devour such things as they

16 *Legally*, my money belonged to my mistress; and she could have taken it and refused to grant me my freedom. But she was a very kind woman for a slave owner; and she would under the circumstances, scorn to do such a thing. I have known of slaves, however, served in this way. [Lane's note]

17 A 1715 North Carolina statute per-mitted slave owners to manumit slaves as a reward for faithful service. In 1741, the state legislature allowed a master to legally emancipate a slave in North Carolina but required him or her to prove to the county court that the slave had performed "meritorious services."

18 To hasten.

can lay their hands upon,—made to feel the rigors of bondage with no cessation,—torn away sometimes from the few friends they love, friends doubly dear because they are few, and transported to a climate where in a few hard years they die,—or at best conducted heavily and sadly to their resting place under the sod, upon their old master's plantation,—sometimes, perhaps, enlivening the air with merriment, but a forced merriment, that comes from a stagnant or a stupified heart. Such as this is the fate of the plantation slaves generally, but such was not my lot. My way was comparatively light, and what is better, it conducted to freedom. And my wife and children were with me. After my master died, my mistress sold a number of her slaves from their families and friends—but not me. She sold several children from their parents—but my children were with me still. She sold two husbands from their wives—but I was still with mine. She sold one wife from her husband—but mine had not been sold from me. The master of my wife, Mr. Smith, had separated members of families by sale—but not of mine. With me and my house, the tenderer tendrils of the heart still clung to where the vine had entwined; pleasant was its shade and delicious our fruits to our taste, though we knew, and what is more, we *felt* that we were slaves. But all around I could see where the vine had been torn down, and its bleeding branches told of vanished joys, and of new wrought sorrows, such as, slave though I was, had never entered into my practical experience. . . .

My manumission, as I shall call it; that is, the bill of sale conveying me to Mr. Smith, was dated Sept. 9th, 1835. I continued in the tobacco and pipe business, as already described, to which I added a small trade in a variety of articles; and some two years before I left Raleigh, I entered also into a considerable business in wood, which I used to purchase by the acre standing, cut it, haul it into the city, deposit it in a yard and sell it out as I advantageously could. Also I was employed about the office of the Governor as I shall hereafter relate. I used to keep one or two horses, and various vehicles, by which I did a variety of work at hauling about town. Of course I had to hire more or less help, to carry on my business. . . .

Not long after obtaining my own freedom, I began seriously to think about purchasing the freedom of my family. The first proposition was that I should buy my wife, and that we should jointly labor to obtain the freedom of the children afterwards as we were able. But that idea was abandoned, when her master, Mr. Smith, refused to sell her to me for less than one thousand dollars, a sum which then appeared too much for me to raise.

Afterwards, however, I conceived the idea of purchasing at once the entire family. I went to Mr. Smith to learn his price, which he put at *three thousand dollars* for my wife and six children, the number we then had. This seemed a large sum, both because it was a great deal for me to raise; and also because Mr. Smith, when he bought my wife and *two* children, had actually paid but five hundred and sixty dollars for them, and had received, ever since, their labor, while I had almost entirely supported them, both as to food and clothing. Altogether, therefore, the case seemed a hard one, but as I was entirely in his power I must do the best I could. At length he concluded, perhaps partly of his own motion, and partly through the persuasion of a friend, to sell the family for $2,500, as I wished to free them, though he contended still that they were worth three thousand dollars. Perhaps they would at that time have brought this larger sum, if sold for the Southern market. The arrangement with Mr. Smith was made in December, 1838. I gave him five notes of five hundred dollars each, the first due in January, 1840, and one in January each succeeding year; for which he transferred my family into my own possession, with a *bond* to give me a bill of sale when I should pay the notes. With this arrangement, we found ourselves living in our own house—a house which I had previously purchased—in January, 1839. . . .

In this new and joyful situation, we found ourselves getting along very well, until September, 1840, when to my surprise, as I was passing the street one day, engaged in my business, the following note was handed me. "Read it," said the officer, "or if you cannot read, get some white man to read it to you." Here it is, *verbatim*:

> *To Lunsford Lane, a free man of Colour*
> Take notice that whereas complaint has been made to us two Justices of the Peace for the county of Wake and state of North Carolina that you are a free negro from another state who has migrated into this state contrary to the provisions of the act of assembly concerning free negros and mulattoes now notice is given you that unless you leave and remove out of this state within twenty days that you will be proceeded against for the penalty porscribed by said act of assembly and be otherwise dealt with as the law directs given under our hands and seals this the 5th Sept. 1840.
>
> WILLIS SCOTT JP (Seal)
JORDAN WOMBLE JP (Seal)

This was a terrible blow to me; for it prostrated at once all my hopes in my cherished object of obtaining the freedom of my family, and led me to expect nothing but a separation from them forever.

In order that the reader may understand the full force of the foregoing notice, I will copy the Law of the State[19] under which it was issued:

SEC. 65. It shall not be lawful for any free negro or mulatto to migrate into this State: and if he or she shall do so, contrary to the provisions of this act, and being thereof informed, shall not, within twenty days thereafter, remove out of the State, he or she being thereof convicted in the manner hereafter directed, shall be liable to a penalty of five hundred dollars; and upon failure to pay the same, within the time prescribed in the judgment awarded against such person or persons, he or she shall be liable to be held in servitude and at labor a term of time not exceeding ten years, in such manner and upon such terms as may be provided by the court awarding such sentence, and the proceeds arising therefrom shall be paid over to the county trustee for county purposes: Provided, that in case any free negro or mulatto shall pay the penalty of five hundred dollars, according to the provisions of this act, it shall be the duty of such free negro or mulatto to remove him or herself out of this State within twenty days thereafter, and for every such failure, he or she shall be subject to the like penalty, as is prescribed for a failure to remove in the first instance.—*Revised Statutes, North Carolina, chap.* III.

The next section provides that if the free person of color so notified, does not leave within the twenty days after receiving the notice, he may be arrested on a warrant from any Justice, and be held to bail for his appearance at the next county court, when he will be subject to the penalties specified above; or in case of his failure to give bonds, he may be sent to jail.

I made known my situation to my friends, and after taking legal counsel it was determined to induce, if possible, the complainants to prosecute no farther at present, and then as the Legislature of the State was to sit in about two months, to petition that body for permission to remain in the State until I could complete the purchase of my family; after which I was willing, if necessary, to leave.

From January 1st, 1837, I had been employed as I have mentioned, in the office of the Governor of the State,[20] principally under the direction of his private Secretary, in keeping the office in order, taking the letters to

19 This act was passed by the North Carolina legislature in 1715.
20 Edward Bishop Dudley (1789–1855) was a leader in the formation of the Whig Party in North Carolina and a two-term governor of the state from 1836 to 1840.

the Post Office, and doing such other duties of the sort as occurred from time to time. This circumstance, with the fact of the high standing in the city of the family of my former master, and of the former masters of my wife, had given me the friendship of the first people in the place generally, who from that time forward acted towards me the friendly part.

Mr. BATTLE, then private Secretary to Governor Dudley, addressed the following letter to the prosecuting attorney in my behalf:

RALEIGH, Nov. 3, 1840.

DEAR SIR:—Lunsford Lane, a free man of Color, has been in the employ of the State under me since my entering on my present situation. I understand that under a law of the State, he has been notified to leave, and that the time is now at hand.

In the discharge of the duties I had from him, I have found him prompt, obedient, and faithful. At this particular time, his absence to me would be much regretted, as I am now just fixing up my books and other papers in the new office, and I shall not have time to learn another what he can already do so well. With me the period of the Legislature is a very busy one, and I am compelled to have a servant who understands the business I want done, and one I can trust. I would not wish to be an obstacle in the execution of any law, but the enforcing of the one against him, will be doing me a serious inconvenience, and the object of this letter is to ascertain whether I could not procure a suspension of the sentence till after the adjournment of the Legislature, say about 1st January, 1841.

I should feel no hesitation in giving my word that he will conduct himself orderly and obediently.

I am most respectfully,

Your obedient servant,

C. C. BATTLE.

G. W. HAYWOOD, ESQ.[21]

Attorney at Law, Raleigh, N.C.

To the above letter, the following reply was made:

RALEIGH, Nov. 3, 1840.

MY DEAR SIR:—I have no objection so far as I am concerned, that all further proceedings against Lunsford should be postponed until after the adjournment of the Legislature.

21 George Washington Haywood (1802–90) was a lawyer in Raleigh, North Carolina.

The process now out against him is one issued by two magistrates, Messrs. Willis Scott and Jordan Womble, over which I have no control. You had better see them to-day, and perhaps, at your request, they will delay further action on the subject. Respectfully yours,

GEO. W. HAYWOOD.

Mr. Battle then enclosed the foregoing correspondence to Messrs. Scott and Womble, requesting their "favorable consideration." They returned the correspondence, but neglected to make any reply.

In consequence, however, of this action on the part of my friends, I was permitted to remain without further interruption, until the day the Legislature commenced its session. On that day a warrant was served upon me, to appear before the county court, to answer for the sin of having remained in the place of my birth for the space of twenty days and more after being warned out. I escaped going to jail through the kindness of Mr. Haywood, a son of my former master, and Mr. Smith, who jointly became security for my appearance at court.

This was on Monday; and on Wednesday I appeared before the court; but as my prosecutors were not ready for the trial, the case was laid over three months, to the next term.

I then proceeded to get up a petition to the Legislature. It required much hard labor and persuasion on my part to start it; but after that, I readily obtained the signatures of the principal men in the place. Then I went round to the members, many of whom were known to me, calling upon them at their rooms, and urging them for my sake, for humanity's sake, for the sake of my wife and little ones, whose hopes had been excited by the idea that they were even now free; I appealed to them as husbands, fathers, brothers, sons, to vote in favor of my petition, and allow me to remain in the State long enough to purchase my family. I was doing well in business, and it would be but a short time before I could accomplish the object. Then, if it was desired, I and my wife and children, redeemed from bondage, would together seek a more friendly home, beyond the dominion of slavery. The following is the petition presented, endorsed as the reader will see:

To the Hon. General Assembly of the State of North Carolina.
GENTLEMEN:—The petition of Lunsford Lane humbly shews[22]
—That about five years ago, he purchased his freedom from his mis-

---

22 An English variant of "shows."

tress, Mrs. Sherwood Haywood and by great economy and industry has paid the purchase money; that he has a wife and seven children whom he has agreed to purchase, and for whom he has paid a part of the purchase money; but not having paid in full, is not yet able to leave the State, without parting with his wife and children.

Your petitioner prays your Honorable Body to pass a law allowing him to remain a limited time within the State, until he can remove his family also. Your petitioner will give bond and good security for his good behaviour while he remains.

Your petitioner will ever pray, &c.

LUNSFORD LANE.

The undersigned are well acquainted with Lunsford Lane, the petitioner, and join in his petition to the Assembly for relief.

· Charles Manly,[23]
· R. W. Haywood,
· Eleanor Haywood,
· Wm. Hill,[24]
· R. Smith,
· Wm. Peace,[25]
· Jos. Peace,[26]
· Wm. M'Pheeters,[27]
· Wm. Boylan,
· Fabius J. Haywood,[28]
· D. W. Stone,[29]
· T. Meredith,[30]

23 Charles Manly (1795–1871) was governor of North Carolina from 1849 to 1851.

24 William Hill was North Carolina secretary of state in 1812.

25 William Peace (1773–1865) was director of the Bank of North Carolina and one of the founders of what is now Peace College in Raleigh.

26 Joseph Peace (1776–1842) was brother and business partner of William Peace.

27 William McPheeters was minister of the First Presbyterian Church in Raleigh and principal of the Raleigh Academy.

28 Fabius J. Haywood was a Raleigh physician and surgeon. He was also owner of Hannah Stanley, the mother of Anna Julia Cooper, whose writing also appears in this volume.

29 David Williamson Stone (1800–?), the son of David Stone, a former North Carolina governor and congressman, was a lawyer and the president of the branch of the Bank of Cape Fear in Raleigh.

30 Thomas Meredith (1795–1850) was a minister, editor, and one of the fourteen founders of the North Carolina Baptist State Convention in 1830. Meredith College in Raleigh was named after him.

- A. J. Battle,[31]
- Drury Lacy,[32]
- Will. Peck,[33]
- W. A. Stith,
- A. B. Stith,
- J. Brown,
- William White,
- Geo. Simpson,
- Jno. I. Christophers,
- John Primrose,
- Hugh M'Queen,[34]
- Alex. J. Lawrence,
- C. L. Hinton.[35]

Lunsford Lane, the petitioner herein, has been servant to the Executive Office since the 1st of January, 1837, and it gives me pleasure to state that, during the whole time, without exception, I have found him faithful and obedient, in keeping every thing committed to his care in good condition. From what I have seen of his conduct and demeanor, I cheerfully join in the petition for his relief.

C. C. BATTLE,
P. Secretary to Gov. Dudley.
Raleigh, Nov. 20, 1840.

[Lane's petition was denied.[36] He was obliged to leave North Carolina.]

31 Amos Johnston Battle (1805–70) was the pastor of the Baptist Church in Raleigh.

32 Drury Lacy (1802–84) was a Presbyterian minister in Raleigh and a president of Davidson College in Davidson, North Carolina.

33 William Peck (ca. 1837–?) was president of the Raleigh Society around 1840.

34 Hugh McQueen was the attorney general of North Carolina from 1840 to 1842.

35 Charles Lewis Hinton (1793–1861) was a planter, legislator, and state treasurer.

36 The wording of the failed resolution is as follows: "Resolved by the General Assembly of the State of North Carolina—That Lunsford Lane aledging [*sic*] himself to be a free man of colour now of the City of Raleigh, who has migrated into this state from the State of New York, be And he is hereby licencsed [*sic*] and allowed to remain and reside in this state for twelve months from and after the first day of January next. Any provision in the law of this State to the contrary notwithstanding. And that each and every—the provisions of any final statute prohibiting his residence be so far as he is concerned suspended—provided nevertheless that after the expiration of this said twelve months the said Lunsford

And why must I be banished? Ever after I entertained the first idea of being free, I had endeavored so to conduct myself as not to become obnoxious to the white inhabitants, knowing as I did their power, and their hostility to the colored people. The two points necessary in such a case I had kept constantly in mind. First, I had made no display of the little property or money I possessed, but in every way I wore as much as possible the aspect of poverty. Second, I had never appeared to be even so intelligent as I really was. This all colored people at the south, free and slaves, find it peculiarly necessary to their own comfort and safety to observe. . . .

On the 18th of May, 1841, three days after the court commenced its session, I bid adieu to my friends in Raleigh, and set out for the city of New York. . . .

My success in New York was at first small; but at length I fell in with two friends who engaged to raise for me three hundred dollars, provided I should first obtain from other sources the balance of the sum required, which balance would be one thousand and eighty dollars. Thus encouraged, I proceeded to Boston; and in the city and vicinity the needful sum was contributed by about the 1st of April, 1842. My thanks I have endeavored to express in my poor way to the many friends who so kindly and liberally assisted me. I cannot reward them; I hope they will receive their reward in another world. If the limits of this publication would permit, I should like to record the names of many to whom I am very especially indebted for their kindness and aid, not only in contributing, but in introducing me, and opening various ways of access to others.

On the 5th of February, 1842, finding that I should soon have in my

Lane if he shall not remove from this state, shall be subject to all the pains and penalties, prescribed for free persons of colour migrating into this state, by the provisions of an act entitled an act concerning slaves and free person of colour" (North Carolina State Archives, General Assembly, *Sessions Records*, November 1840–January 1841, Senate Bills, [Nov. 20–Jan. 11], House Resolutions, [Nov. 20–Jan. 9 and unnumbered], Box 2: Nov., 1840–Jan., 1841, House Resolutions, [Dec. 10–31]). Though the bill to allow Lane to remain in the state was indeed "killed," the following resolution was passed to compensate Lane for his services to the Office of the Governor: "Resolution in favor of Lunsford Lane. *Resolved*, That the Public Treasurer pay to Lunsford Lane, a free man of colour, twenty-four dollars, for six months attendance on the Executive Office, from the first day of July one thousand eight hundred and forty, to the first day of January one thousand eight hundred and forty-one. [Ratified, the 12th day of January, 1841]" (*Laws of the State of North Carolina, Passed by the General Assembly, at the Session of 1840–41* [Raleigh: Printed by W. R. Gales, Office of the Raleigh Register, 1841], p. 204).

possession the sum necessary to procure my family, and fearing that there might be danger in visiting Raleigh for that purpose, in consequence of the strong opposition of many of the citizens against colored people, their opposition to me, and their previously persecuting me from the city, I wrote to Mr. Smith, requesting him to see the Governor,[37] and obtain under his hand a permit to visit the State for a sufficient time to accomplish this business. I requested Mr. Smith to publish the permit in one or two of the city papers, and then to enclose the original to me. This letter he answered, under date of Raleigh, 19th Feb. 1841, as follows:

> LUNSFORD:—Your letter of the 5th inst. came duly to hand, and in reply I have to inform you, that owing to the absence of Gov. Morehead, I cannot send you the permit you requested, but this will make no difference, for you can come home, and after your arrival you may obtain one to remain long enough to settle up your affairs. You ought of course to apply to the Governor immediately on your arrival, before any malicious person would have time to inform against you; I don't think by pursuing this course you need apprehend any danger.
>
> We are all alive at present in Raleigh on the subjects of temperance and religion. We have taken into the temperance societies, about five hundred members, and about fifty persons have been happily converted. The work seems still to be spreading, and such a time I have never seen before in my life. Glorious times truly.
>
> Do try and get all the religion in your heart you possibly can, for it is the only thing worth having after all.
> Your, &c.
>
> B. B. SMITH.

The way now appeared to be in a measure open; also I thought that the religious and temperance interest mentioned in the latter portion of Mr. Smith's letter, augured a state of feeling which would be a protection to me. But fearing still that there might be danger in visiting Raleigh without the permit from the Governor, or at least wishing to take every possible precaution, I addressed another letter to Mr. Smith, and received under date of March 12th, a reply, from which I copy as follows:

"The Governor has just returned, and I called upon him to get the permit as you requested, but he said he had no authority by law to grant one;

---

37 John Motley Morehead (1796–1866) was a two-term governor of the state from 1840 to 1844.

and *he told me to say to you, that you might in perfect safety come home* in a quiet manner, and remain twenty days without being interrupted. I also consulted Mr. Manly [a lawyer] and he *told me the same thing. Surely you need not fear any thing under these circumstances. You had therefore better come on just as soon as possible.*"

I need not say, what the reader has already seen, that my life so far had been one of joy succeeding sorrow, and sorrow following joy; of hope, of despair, of bright prospects, of gloom; and of as many hues as ever appear on the varied sky, from the black of midnight, or the deep brown of a tempest, to the bright warm glow of a clear noon day. On the 11th of April, it was noon with me; I left Boston on my way for Raleigh with high hopes, intending to pay over the money for my family and return with them to Boston, which I designed should be my future home; for there I had found friends, and there I would find a grave. The visit I was making to the South was to be a farewell one; and I did not dream that my old cradle, hard as it once had jostled me, would refuse to rock me a pleasant, or even an affectionate good bye. I thought, too, that the assurances I had received from the Governor, through Mr. Smith, and the assurances of other friends, were a sufficient guaranty that I might visit the home of my boyhood, of my youth, of my manhood, in peace, especially as I was to stay but for a few days and then to return. With these thoughts, and with the thoughts of my family and freedom, I pursued my way to Raleigh, and arrived there on the 23d of the month. It was Saturday about four o'clock, P.M. when I found myself once more in the midst of my family. With them I remained over the Sabbath, as it was sweet to spend a little time with them after so long an absence, an absence filled with so much of interest to us, and as I could not do any business until the beginning of the week. On Monday morning between eight and nine o'clock, while I was making ready to leave the house for the first time after my arrival, to go the store of Mr. Smith, where I was to transact my business with him, two constables, Messrs. Murray and Scott, entered, accompanied by two other men, and summoned me to appear immediately before the police. I accordingly accompanied them to the City Hall, but as it was locked and the officers could not at once find the key, we were told that the court would be held in Mr. Smith's store, a large and commodious room. This was what is termed in common phrase, in Raleigh, a "call court." The Mayor, Mr. Loring,[38] presided, assisted by William Boylan and Jonathan

38 Thomas Loring was a native of Massachusetts and the editor of the *North Carolina Standard*.

Busbye, Esqs. Justices of the Peace. There were a large number of people together—more than could obtain admission to the room, and a large company of mobocratic[39] spirits crowded around the door. Mr. Loring read the writ, setting forth that I had been guilty of *delivering abolition lectures in the State of Massachusetts*. He asked me whether I was guilty or not guilty. I told him I did not know whether I had given abolition lectures or not, but if it pleased the court, I would relate the course I had pursued during my absence from Raleigh. He then said that I was at liberty to speak.

The circumstances under which I left Raleigh, said I, are perfectly familiar to you. It is known that I had no disposition to remove from this city, but resorted to every lawful means to remain. After I found that I could not be permitted to stay, I went away leaving behind everything I held dear, with the exception of one child, whom I took with me, after paying two hundred and fifty dollars for her. It is also known to you and to many other persons here present, that I had engaged to purchase my wife and children of their master, Mr. Smith, for the sum of twenty-five hundred dollars, and that I had paid of this sum (including my house and lot) eleven hundred and twenty dollars, leaving a balance to be made up of thirteen hundred and eighty dollars. I had previously to that lived in Raleigh, a slave, the property of Mr. Sherwood Haywood, and had purchased my freedom by paying the sum of one thousand dollars. But being driven away, no longer permitted to live in this city, to raise the balance of the money due on my family, my last resort was to call upon the friends of humanity in other places, to assist me.

I went to the city of Boston, and there I related the story of my persecutions here, the same as I have now stated to you. The people gave ear to my statements; and one of them, Rev. Mr. Neale, wrote back, unknown to me, to Mr. Smith, inquiring of him whether the statements made by me were correct. After Mr. Neale received the answer, he sent for me, informed me of his having written, and read to me the reply. The letter fully satisfied Mr. Neale and his friends. He placed it in my hands, remarking that it would, in a great measure, do away the necessity of using the other documents in my possession. I then with that letter in my hands went out from house to house, from place of business to place of business, and from church to church, relating, where I could gain an ear, the same heart-rending and soul-trying story which I am now repeating to you. In pursuing that course, the people, first one and then another contributed,

39 Control of public affairs by mob action rather than by law.

until I had succeeded in raising the amount alluded to, namely, thirteen hundred and eighty dollars. I may have had contributions from abolitionists, but I did not stop to ask those who assisted me whether they were anti-slavery or pro-slavery, for I considered that the money coming from either, would accomplish the object I had in view. These are the facts; and now, sir, it remains for you to say, whether I have been giving abolition lectures or not.

In the course of my remarks I presented the letter of Mr. Smith to Mr. Neale, showing that I had acted the open part while in Massachusetts; also I referred to my having written to Mr. Smith requesting him to obtain for me the permit of the Governor; and I showed to the court, Mr. Smith's letters in reply, in order to satisfy them that I had reason to believe I should be unmolested in my return.

Mr. Loring then whispered to some of the leading men; after which he remarked that he saw nothing in what I had done, according to my statements, implicating me in a manner worthy of notice. He called upon any present who might be in possession of information tending to disprove what I had said, or to show any wrong on my part, to produce it, otherwise I should be set at liberty. No person appeared against me; so I was discharged.

I started to leave the house; but just before I got to the door I met Mr. James Litchford, who touched me on the shoulder, and I followed him back. He observed to me that if I went out of that room I should in less than five minutes be a dead man; for there was a mob outside waiting to drink my life. Mr. Loring then spoke to me again, and said that notwithstanding I had been found guilty of nothing, yet public opinion was law; and he advised me to leave the place the next day, otherwise he was convinced I should have to suffer death. I replied, "not to-morrow, but to-day." He answered that I could not go that day, because I had not done my business. I told him that I would leave my business in his hands and in those of other such gentlemen as himself, who might settle it for me and send my family to meet me at Philadelphia. This was concluded upon, and a guard appointed to conduct me to the depot. I took my seat in the cars, when the mob that had followed us surrounded me, and declared that the cars should not go, if I were permitted to go in them. Mr. Loring inquired what they wanted of me; he told them that there had been an examination, and nothing had been found against me; that they were at the examination invited to speak if they knew aught to condemn me, but they had remained silent, and that now it was but right I should be permitted to leave in peace. They replied that they wanted a more thorough investigation, that they wished to search my trunks (I had but one trunk) and see if I was not in possession of abolition papers. It now became evident that I should be unable to get off in the cars; and my friends advised me to go the shortest way possible to jail, for my safety. They said they were persuaded that what the rabble wanted was to get me into their possession, and then to murder me. The mob looked dreadfully enraged, and seemed to lap for blood. The whole city was in an uproar. But the first men and the more wealthy were my friends: and they did everything in their power to protect me. Mr. Boylan, whose name has repeatedly occurred in this publication, was more than a father to me; and Mr. Smith and Mr. Loring, and many other gentlemen, whose names it would give me pleasure to mention, were exceedingly kind.

The guard then conducted me through the mob to the prison; and I felt joyful that even a prison could protect me. Looking out from the prison window, I saw my trunk in the hands of Messrs. Johnson, Scott, and others, who were taking it to the City Hall for examination. I understood afterwards that they opened my trunk; and as the lid flew up, Lo! a paper! a paper!! Those about seized it, three or four at once, as hungry dogs would a piece of meat after forty days famine. But the meat quickly turned to a stone; for the paper it happened, was one *printed in Raleigh*, and edited by Weston R. Gales, a nice man to be sure, but no abolitionist. The only other printed or written things in the trunk were some business cards of a firm in Raleigh—not incendiary.

Afterwards I saw from the window Mr. Scott, accompanied by Mr. Johnson, lugging my carpet-bag in the same direction my trunk had gone. It was opened at the City Hall, and found actually to contain a pair of old shoes, and a pair of old boots!—but they did not conclude that these were incendiary.

Mr. Smith now came to the prison and told me that the examination had been completed, and nothing found against me; but that it would not be safe for me to leave the prison immediately. It was agreed that I should remain in prison until after night-fall, and then steal secretly away, being let out by the keeper, and pass unnoticed to the house of my old and tried friend Mr. Boylan. Accordingly I was discharged between nine and ten o'clock. I went by the back way leading to Mr. Boylan's; but soon and suddenly a large company of men sprang upon me, and instantly I found myself in their possession. They conducted me sometimes high above ground and sometimes dragging me along, but as silently as possible, in the direction of the gallows, which is always kept standing upon the

Common,[40] or as it is called "the pines," or "piny old field." I now expected to pass speedily into the world of spirits; I thought of that unseen region to which I seemed to be hastening; and then my mind would return to my wife and children, and the labors I had made to redeem them from bondage. Although I had the money to pay for them according to a bargain already made, it seemed to me some white man would get it, and they would die in slavery, without benefit from my exertions and the contributions of my friends. Then the thought of my own death, to occur in a few brief moments, would rush over me, and I seemed to bid adieu in spirit to all earthly things, and to hold communion already with eternity. But at length I observed those who were carrying me away, changed their course a little from the direct line to the gallows, and hope, a faint beaming, sprung up within me; but then as they were taking me to the woods, I thought they intended to murder me there, in a place where they would be less likely to be interrupted than in so public a spot as where the gallows stood. They conducted me to a rising ground among the trees, and set me down. "Now," said they, "tell us the truth about those abolition lectures you have been giving at the North." I replied that I had related the circumstances before the court in the morning; and could only repeat what I had then said. "But that was not the truth—tell us the truth." I again said that any different story would be false, and as I supposed I was in a few minutes to die, I would not, whatever they might think I would say under other circumstances, pass into the other world with a lie upon my lips. Said one, "you were always, Lunsford, when you were here, a clever fellow, and I did not think you would be engaged in such business as giving abolition lectures." To this and similar remarks, I replied that the people of Raleigh had always said the abolitionists did not believe in buying slaves, but contended that their masters ought to free them without pay. I had been laboring to buy my family; and how then could they suppose me to be in league with the abolitionists?

After other conversation of this kind, and after they seemed to have become tired of questioning me, they held a consultation in a low whisper among themselves. Then a bucket was brought and set down by my side; but what it contained or for what it was intended, I could not divine. But soon, one of the number came forward with a pillow, and then hope sprung up, a flood of light and joy within me. The heavy weight on my heart rolled off; death had passed by and I unharmed. They commenced

40 A tract of land belonging to or used by a community as a whole.

stripping me till every rag of clothes was removed; and then the bucket was set near, and I discovered it to contain tar. One man, I will do him the honor to record his name, Mr. WILLIAM ANDRES, a journeyman printer, when he is any thing, except a tar-and-featherer, put his hands the first into the bucket, and was about passing them to my face. "Don't put any in his face or eyes," said one.[41] So he desisted; but he, with three other "gentlemen," whose names I should be happy to record if I could recall them, gave me as nice a coat of tar all over, face only excepted, as any one would wish to see. Then they took the pillow and ripped it open at one end, and with the open end commenced the operation at the head and so worked downwards, of putting a coat of its contents over that of the contents of the bucket. A fine escape from the hanging this will be, thought I, provided they do not with a match set fire to the feathers. I had some fear they would. But when the work was completed they gave me my clothes, and one of them handed me my watch which he had carefully kept in his hands; they all expressed great interest in my welfare, advised me how to proceed with my business the next day, told me to stay in the place as long as I wished, and with other such words of consolation they bid me good night.

After I had returned to my family, to their inexpressible joy, as they had become greatly alarmed for my safety, some of the persons who had participated in this outrage, came in (probably influenced by a curiosity to see how the tar and feathers would be got off) and expressed great sympathy for me. They said they regretted that the affair had happened—that they had no objections to my living in Raleigh—I might feel perfectly safe to go out and transact my business preparatory to leaving—I should not be molested.

Meanwhile, my friends understanding that I had been discharged from prison, and perceiving I did not come to them, had commenced a regular search for me, on foot and on horseback, every where; and Mr. Smith called upon the Governor to obtain his official interference; and after my return, a guard came to protect me; but I chose not to risk myself at my own house, and so went to Mr. Smith's, where this guard kept me safely until morning. They seemed friendly indeed, and were regaled with a supper during the night by Mr. Smith. My friend, Mr. Battle, (late Private Secretary to the Governor,) was with them; and he made a speech

41 I think this was Mr. Burns, a black-smith in the place, but I am not certain. At any rate, this man was my *friend* (if so he may be called) on this occasion; and it was fortunate for me that the company generally seemed to look up to him for wisdom. [Lane's note]

to them setting forth the good qualities I had exhibited in my past life, particularly in my connection with the Governor's office.

In the morning Mr. Boylan, true as ever, and unflinching in his friendship, assisted me in arranging my business,[42] so that I should start with my family *that day* for the north. He furnished us with provisions more than sufficient to sustain the family to Philadelphia, where we intended to make a halt; and sent his own baggage wagon to convey our baggage to the depot, offering also to send his carriage for my family. But my friend, Mr. Malone, had been before him in this kind offer, which I had agreed to accept.

Brief and sorrowful was the parting from my kind friends; but the worst was the thought of leaving my mother. The cars were to start at ten o'clock in the morning. I called upon my old mistress, Mrs. Haywood, who was affected to weeping by the considerations that naturally came to her mind. She had been kind to me; the day before she and her daughter, Mrs. Hogg, now present, had jointly transmitted a communication to the court representing that in consequence of my good conduct from my youth, I could not be supposed to be guilty of any offence. And now, "with tears that ceased not flowing," they gave me their parting blessing. My mother was still Mrs. Haywood's slave, and I her only child. Our old mistress could not witness the sorrow that would attend the parting with my mother. She told her to go with me; and said that if I ever became able to pay two hundred dollars for her, I might; otherwise it should be her loss. She gave her the following paper, which is in the ordinary form of a *pass*:

RALEIGH, N.C. April 26, 1842.

Know all persons by these presents, that the bearer of this, Clarissa, a slave, belonging to me, hath my permission to visit the city of New York with her relations, who are in company with her; and it is my desire that she may be protected and permitted to pass without molestation or hindrance, on good behavior. Witness my hand this 26th April, 1842.

ELEANOR HAYWOOD.
Witness—J. A. Campbell.

42 Of course I was obliged to sacrifice much on my property, leaving in this hurried manner. And while I was in the North, a kind *friend* had removed from the wood-lot, wood that I had cut and corded, for which I expected to receive over one hundred dollars; thus saving me the trouble of making sale of it, or of being burdened with the money it would bring. I suppose I have no redress. I might add other things as bad. [Lane's note]

On leaving Mrs. Haywood's, I called upon Mrs. Badger, another daughter, and wife of Judge Badger, previously mentioned. She seemed equally affected; she wept as she gave me her parting counsel. She and Mrs. Hogg and I had been children together, playing in the same yard, while yet none of us had learned that they were of a superior and I of a subject race. And in those infant years there were pencillings made upon the heart, which time and opposite fortunes could not all efface.—May these friends never be slaves as I have been; nor their bosom companions and their little ones be slaves like mine.

When the cars were about to start, the whole city seemed to be gathered at the depot; and among the rest the mobocratic portion, who appeared to be determined still that I should not go peaceably away. Apprehending this, it had been arranged with my friends and the conductor, that my family should be put in the cars and that I should go a distance from the city on foot, and be taken up as they passed. The mob, therefore, supposing that I was left behind, allowed the cars to start. . . .

On reaching Philadelphia we found that our money had all been expended, but kind friends furnished us with the means of proceeding as far as New-York; and thence we were with equal kindness aided on to Boston.

In Boston and in the vicinity, are persons almost without number, who have done me favors more than I can express. The thought that I was now in my loved, though recently acquired home—that my family were with me where the stern, cruel, hated hand of slavery could never reach us more—the greetings of friends—the interchange of feeling and sympathy—the kindness bestowed upon us, more grateful than rain to the thirsty earth—the reflections of the past that would rush into my mind,—these and more almost overwhelmed me with emotion, and I had deep and strange communion with my own soul. Next to God from whom every good gift proceeds, I feel under the greatest obligations to my kind friends in Massachusetts. To be rocked in their cradle of Liberty,—oh, how unlike being stretched on the pillory of slavery! May that cradle rock forever; may many a poor care-worn child of sorrow, many a spirit-bruised (worse than lash-mangled) victim of oppression, there sweetly sleep to the lullaby of Freedom, sung by Massachusetts' sons and daughters.

A number of meetings have been held at which friends have contributed to our temporal wants, and individuals have sent us various articles of provision and furniture and apparel, so that our souls have been truly made glad. There are now ten of us in the family, my wife, my mother, and myself, with seven children, and we expect soon to be joined by my father, who several years ago received his freedom by legacy. The wine fresh from the clustering grapes never filled so sweet a cup as mine. May I and my family be permitted to drink it, remembering whence it came!

SARAH H. FICKE

ANDREÁ N. WILLIAMS

Harriet Jacobs in 1894
(from Yellin, ed., Incidents in the Life of a Slave Girl*)*

HARRIET JACOBS'S *Incidents in the Life of a Slave Girl* (1861) is the first autobiography authored by an American female slave. Prior to Jacobs, male fugitives, including Moses Roper and Frederick Douglass, had written their own autobiographies, and a few slave women, such as Louisa Picquet, had dictated their stories for sympathetic collaborators to write. But as its subtitle, "Written by Herself," proclaims, *Incidents* is exceptional as the work of a literate, formerly enslaved woman responsible for her own narrative's publication.

Jacobs supplies the details of her life in *Incidents*, though she uses pseudonyms to conceal the people and places of her history. Born in 1813, she grew up in Edenton, along the Albemarle Sound of eastern North Carolina. Her enslaved parents, Delilah and Elijah, were privileged to live in a home of their own, providing a sheltered life for Jacobs and her brother, John S. Jacobs. Only after their mother's death, when Harriet was six, did she realize that she was a slave. Her indulgent mistress, Margaret Horniblow, taught her to read, write, and sew, leading Jacobs to believe that Horniblow would free her before dying. Instead, she willed twelve-year-old Jacobs to Mary Matilda Norcom, the young daughter of Dr. James Norcom. As an adolescent, Jacobs became the target of Norcom's persistent sexual harassment and his wife's jealousy. In a defensive move to thwart her master's unwanted advances, she engaged in a sexual liaison and had two children with Samuel Tredwell Sawyer, a neighboring white lawyer who later served as a North Carolina congressman.

As Norcom's threats to Jacobs and her family intensified, she determined in 1835 to hide away, supposing that with her gone, Norcom would lose interest in her children and sell them to their father. Her neighbors, both black and white, concealed her until she retreated to a more secure refuge in the home of her free grandmother, Molly Horniblow. In a crawlspace too small to stand up in, Jacobs practiced her writing skills, sewed, read the Bible, and observed her growing children, who were sold to Sawyer as she had hoped. After remaining hidden for seven years, Jacobs escaped on a boat to Philadelphia and made her way to New York City in 1842.

In the North, Jacobs remained at risk of being reclaimed since, under the Fugitive Slave Law of 1850, runaways in the North could be captured and returned to slavery. She worked as a nursemaid for the family of writer Nathaniel Parker Willis in New York and moved periodically to evade her pursuers. Jacobs lived briefly in Brooklyn and Boston, reuniting with her children and brother, who had arrived in the North. In 1849, while working in Rochester, New York, where her brother was an abolitionist lecturer, Jacobs met Amy Post, a Quaker feminist, who proposed that Jacobs write her autobiography to contribute to the national antislavery agitation.

After determining to make her story public, Jacobs encountered multiple obstacles to drafting and marketing her narrative. She initially requested the aid of Harriet Beecher Stowe in writing her story, but when the famed author of *Uncle Tom's Cabin* (1852) offered to incorporate Jacobs's story into one of her own literary projects, Jacobs refused, preferring to maintain independent possession of her autobiography. Deciding in 1853 to produce her autobiography herself, Jacobs spent the next seven years writing it. White abolitionist author Lydia Maria Child collaborated as editor, but written correspondence between the two women indicates that Child's influence was limited to advice and minor revisions. Jacobs was solely responsible for the subject matter and voice of the text. Yet Jacobs maintained her anonymity so that when the forty-one-chapter narrative appeared in 1861, the book's title page did not identify her as the author.

Incidents received favorable but modest attention after its publication. The narrative did not appear in a second edition in the United States but was reprinted in 1862 in England as *The Deeper Wrong*. Meanwhile, a month after the release of *Incidents*, John S. Jacobs's autobiography, *A True Tale of Slavery*, appeared serially in the British periodical *The Leisure Hour*. His narrative reiterates several details of the enslavement he and his sister shared in North Carolina. Yet his more concise account skims over the details of his sister's sexual history that she dares to expose in *Incidents*.

Considered shocking in 1861, *Incidents* gives readers unprecedented insight into the sexual exploitation of enslaved women, a topic that previous slave narratives neglected and polite discourse deliberately avoided. Although careful not to offend her genteel white female readers, Jacobs insists that "Slavery is terrible for men; but it is far more terrible for women." Using the pseudonymous first-person narrator Linda Brent, Jacobs situates herself not as the helpless victim of sexual abuse—as black women were often depicted in male-authored slave narratives—but as a determined model of resistance to slavery's physical and psychological oppressions. While confessing to having children out of wedlock, the narrator portrays herself as a heroic mother who, by seeking freedom for herself and her children, exemplifies the domestic values of self-sacrifice, devotion, and piety promoted in the nineteenth century.

Incidents recounts Jacobs's biography through 1852, the year in which she received her freedom. She spent the remaining years of her life striving for social reform. During and after the Civil War, she volunteered as a nurse and teacher with slave refugees in Virginia and Georgia, corresponding with northern newspapers to report the progress of the freed people. Jacobs was also involved with the black women's club movement in Washington, D.C., where she spent her last years and died in 1897.

Though the record of Jacobs's sexual harassment, confinement, and eventual freedom seemed incredible to early readers, extensive research, especially by Jacobs's biographer, Jean Fagan Yellin, confirms that *Incidents* is an authentic autobiography. Jacobs's only book-length work, *Incidents in the Life of a Slave Girl* is now recognized as a seminal text in the American and African American literary traditions because of its innovative female voice, its frank discussion of sexuality, and its skillful blending of the genres of slave narrative and sentimental fiction.

Suggested Readings

Andrews, William L. "The Changing Moral Discourse of Nineteenth-Century African American Women's Autobiography: Harriet Jacobs and Elizabeth Keckley." In *De/Colonizing the Subject: The Politics of Gender in Women's Autobiography*, edited by Sidonie Smith and Julia Watson, 225–41. Minneapolis: University of Minnesota Press, 1992.

Fleishner, Jennifer. *Mastering Slavery: Memory, Family and Identity in Women's Slave Narratives*. New York: New York University Press, 1996.

Foster, Frances Smith. *Written by Herself: Literary Production by African American Women, 1746–1892*. Bloomington: Indiana University Press, 1993.

Garfield, Deborah, and Rafia Zafar, eds. *Harriet Jacobs and Incidents in the Life of a Slave Girl: New Critical Essays*. New York: Cambridge University Press, 1996.

Jacobs, Harriet A. *Incidents in the Life of a Slave Girl: Written by Herself.* Edited by Jean Fagan Yellin. Cambridge, Mass.: Harvard University Press, 2000. Original edition also available in electronic form through Documenting the American South, an electronic database sponsored by The Academic Affairs Library at the University of North Carolina at Chapel Hill, <http://docsouth.unc.edu/jacobs/menu.html>.

Jacobs, John S. "A True Tale of Slavery." *The Leisure Hour: A Family Journal of Instruction and Recreation* 10 (February 7, 14, 21, and 28, 1861): 476–79. In Yellin, ed., *Incidents in the Life of a Slave Girl.*

McKay, Nellie, and Frances Smith Foster, eds. *Incidents in the Life of a Slave Girl: Contexts and Criticism*. New York: Norton, 2001.

Mills, Bruce. "Lydia Maria Child and the Endings to Harriet Jacobs' *Incidents in the Life of a Slave Girl*." *American Literature* 64, no. 2 (1992): 255–72.

Yellin, Jean Fagan. *Harriet Jacobs: A Life*. New York: Basic Civitas, 2004.

——. *Women and Sisters: The Anti-Slavery Feminists in American Culture*. New Haven, Conn.: Yale University Press, 1989.

Note on the Text

The following text, based on the first edition of *Incidents in the Life of a Slave Girl* (1861), condenses Harriet Jacobs's lengthy narrative for brevity. Where chapters have been abbreviated or omitted, bracketed summaries detail the narrative's intervening development. The selected excerpts present the most pivotal events of Jacobs's life and highlight her infrequent observations of race relations and folk customs in North Carolina.

INCIDENTS

IN THE

LIFE OF A SLAVE GIRL.

WRITTEN BY HERSELF.

"Northerners know nothing at all about Slavery. They think it is perpetual bondage only. They have no conception of the depth of *degradation* involved in that word, SLAVERY; if they had, they would never cease their efforts until so horrible a system was overthrown."

A WOMAN OF NORTH CAROLINA.

"Rise up, ye women that are at ease! Hear my voice, ye careless daughters! Give ear unto my speech."

ISAIAH xxxii. 9.

EDITED BY L. MARIA CHILD.

BOSTON:
PUBLISHED FOR THE AUTHOR.
1861.

Title page of the 1861 edition of *Incidents in the Life of a Slave Girl*
(Documenting the American South, <http://docsouth.unc.edu>, The University of North Carolina at Chapel Hill Libraries, North Carolina Collection)

❖

From INCIDENTS IN THE LIFE OF A SLAVE GIRL

Preface by the Author

READER, be assured this narrative is no fiction. I am aware that some of my adventures may seem incredible; but they are, nevertheless, strictly true. I have not exaggerated the wrongs inflicted by Slavery; on the contrary, my descriptions fall far short of the facts. I have concealed the names of places, and given persons fictitious names. I had no motive for secrecy on my own account, but I deemed it kind and considerate towards others to pursue this course.

I wish I were more competent to the task I have undertaken. But I trust my readers will excuse deficiencies in consideration of circumstances. I was born and reared in Slavery; and I remained in a Slave State twenty-seven years. Since I have been at the North, it has been necessary for me to work diligently for my own support, and the education of my children. This has not left me much leisure to make up for the loss of early opportunities to improve myself; and it has compelled me to write these pages at irregular intervals, whenever I could snatch an hour from household duties.

When I first arrived in Philadelphia, Bishop Paine[1] advised me to publish a sketch of my life, but I told him I was altogether incompetent to such an undertaking. Though I have improved my mind somewhat since that time, I still remain of the same opinion; but I trust my motives will excuse what might otherwise seem presumptuous. I have not written my experiences in order to attract attention to myself; on the contrary, it would have been more pleasant to me to have been silent about my own history. Neither do I care to excite sympathy for my own sufferings. But I do earnestly desire to arouse the women of the North to a realizing sense of the condition of two millions of women at the South, still in bondage, suffering what I suffered, and most of them far worse. I want to add my testimony to that of abler pens to convince the people of the Free States what Slavery really is. Only by experience can any one realize how deep,

1 Daniel A. Payne (1811–93), prominent bishop in the African Methodist Episcopal Church.

HARRIET JACOBS

and dark, and foul is that pit of abominations. May the blessing of God rest on this imperfect effort in behalf of my persecuted people!

LINDA BRENT.[2]

[Brent is born into what she terms "unusually fortunate circumstances," including an intact, though enslaved, family and a kind mistress who teaches her to read and to sew. But when the mistress dies, twelve-year-old Brent is bequeathed to the daughter of Dr. Flint.]

11. *The New Master and Mistress*

DR. FLINT,[3] a physician in the neighborhood, had married the sister of my mistress, and I was now the property of their little daughter.[4] It was not without murmuring that I prepared for my new home; and what added to my unhappiness, was the fact that my brother William[5] was purchased by the same family. My father, by his nature, as well as by the habit of transacting business as a skilful mechanic, had more of the feelings of a freeman than is common among slaves. My brother was a spirited boy; and being brought up under such influences, he early detested the name of master and mistress. One day, when his father and his mistress both happened to call him at the same time, he hesitated between the two; being perplexed to know which had the strongest claim upon his obedience. He finally concluded to go to his mistress. When my father reproved him for it, he said, "You both called me, and I didn't know which I ought to go to first."

"You are *my* child," replied our father, "and when I call you, you should come immediately, if you have to pass through fire and water."

Poor Willie! He was now to learn his first lesson of obedience to a master. Grandmother[6] tried to cheer us with hopeful words, and they found an echo in the credulous hearts of youth.

When we entered our new home we encountered cold looks, cold words, and cold treatment. We were glad when the night came. On my narrow bed I moaned and wept, I felt so desolate and alone.

I had been there nearly a year, when a dear little friend of mine was buried. I heard her mother sob, as the clods fell on the coffin of her only child, and I turned away from the grave, feeling thankful that I still had

2 Pen name used by Harriet Jacobs.

3 Dr. James Norcom (1778–1850), local physician.

4 Mary Matilda Norcom (1822–?).

5 John S. Jacobs (1815?–73).

6 Molly Horniblow (c. 1771–1853).

something left to love. I met my grandmother, who said, "Come with me, Linda;" and from her tone I knew that something sad had happened. She led me apart from the people, and then said, "My child, your father is dead." Dead! How could I believe it? He had died so suddenly I had not even heard that he was sick. I went home with my grandmother. My heart rebelled against God, who had taken from me mother, father, mistress, and friend.[7] The good grandmother tried to comfort me. "Who knows the ways of God?" said she. "Perhaps they have been kindly taken from the evil days to come." Years afterwards I often thought of this. She promised to be a mother to her grandchildren, so far as she might be permitted to do so; and strengthened by her love, I returned to my master's. I thought I should be allowed to go to my father's house the next morning; but I was ordered to go for flowers, that my mistress's house might be decorated for an evening party. I spent the day gathering flowers and weaving them into festoons, while the dead body of my father was lying within a mile of me. What cared my owners for that? he was merely a piece of property. Moreover, they thought he had spoiled his children, by teaching them to feel that they were human beings. This was blasphemous doctrine for a slave to teach; presumptuous in him, and dangerous to the masters.

The next day I followed his remains to a humble grave beside that of my dear mother. There were those who knew my father's worth, and respected his memory.

My home now seemed more dreary than ever. The laugh of the little slave-children sounded harsh and cruel. It was selfish to feel so about the joy of others. My brother moved about with a very grave face. I tried to comfort him, by saying, "Take courage, Willie; brighter days will come by and by."

"You don't know any thing about it, Linda," he replied. "We shall have to stay here all our days; we shall never be free."

I argued that we were growing older and stronger, and that perhaps we might, before long, be allowed to hire our own time, and then we could earn money to buy our freedom. William declared this was much easier to say than to do; moreover, he did not intend to *buy* his freedom. We held daily controversies upon this subject.

Little attention was paid to the slaves' meals in Dr. Flint's house. If

7 By 1826, when Jacobs is thirteen, her mother, Delilah (1797?–c. 1819), her father, Elijah (?–c. 1826), and her first mistress, Margaret Horniblow (1797–1825), have died.

they could catch a bit of food while it was going, well and good. I gave myself no trouble on that score, for on my various errands I passed my grandmother's house, where there was always something to spare for me. I was frequently threatened with punishment if I stopped there; and my grandmother, to avoid detaining me, often stood at the gate with something for my breakfast or dinner. I was indebted to *her* for all my comforts, spiritual or temporal. It was *her* labor that supplied my scanty wardrobe. I have a vivid recollection of the linsey-woolsey[8] dress given me every winter by Mrs. Flint.[9] How I hated it! It was one of the badges of slavery.

While my grandmother was thus helping to support me from her hard earnings, the three hundred dollars she had lent her mistress were never repaid. When her mistress died, her son-in-law, Dr. Flint, was appointed executor. When grandmother applied to him for payment, he said the estate was insolvent, and the law prohibited payment. It did not, however, prohibit him from retaining the silver candelabra, which had been purchased with that money. I presume they will be handed down in the family, from generation to generation.

My grandmother's mistress had always promised her that, at her death, she should be free; and it was said that in her will she made good the promise. But when the estate was settled, Dr. Flint told the faithful old servant that, under existing circumstances, it was necessary she should be sold.

On the appointed day, the customary advertisement was posted up, proclaiming that there would be "a public sale of negroes, horses, &c." Dr. Flint called to tell my grandmother that he was unwilling to wound her feelings by putting her up at auction, and that he would prefer to dispose of her at private sale. My grandmother saw through his hypocrisy; she understood very well that he was ashamed of the job. She was a very spirited woman, and if he was base enough to sell her, when her mistress intended she should be free, she was determined the public should know it. She had for a long time supplied many families with crackers and preserves; consequently, "Aunt Marthy," as she was called, was generally known, and every body who knew her respected her intelligence and good character. Her long and faithful service in the family was also well known, and the intention of her mistress to leave her free. When the day of sale came, she took her place among the chattels, and at the first call

8 A coarse fabric made of wool and linen.

9 Mary Norcom (1794–1868), second wife of Dr. James Norcom.

she sprang upon the auction-block. Many voices called out, "Shame! Shame! Who is going to sell *you*, aunt Marthy? Don't stand there! That is no place for *you*." Without saying a word, she quietly awaited her fate. No one bid for her. At last, a feeble voice said, "Fifty dollars." It came from a maiden lady, seventy years old, the sister of my grandmother's deceased mistress. She had lived forty years under the same roof with my grandmother; she knew how faithfully she had served her owners, and how cruelly she had been defrauded of her rights; and she resolved to protect her. The auctioneer waited for a higher bid; but her wishes were respected; no one bid above her. She could neither read nor write; and when the bill of sale was made out, she signed it with a cross. But what consequence was that, when she had a big heart overflowing with human kindness? She gave the old servant her freedom.

At that time, my grandmother was just fifty years old. Laborious years had passed since then; and now my brother and I were slaves to the man who had defrauded her of her money, and tried to defraud her of her freedom. One of my mother's sisters, called Aunt Nancy, was also a slave in his family. She was a kind, good aunt to me; and supplied the place of both housekeeper and waiting maid to her mistress. She was, in fact, at the beginning and end of every thing.

Mrs. Flint, like many southern women, was totally deficient in energy. She had not strength to superintend her household affairs; but her nerves were so strong, that she could sit in her easy chair and see a woman whipped, till the blood trickled from every stroke of the lash. She was a member of the church; but partaking of the Lord's supper did not seem to put her in a Christian frame of mind. If dinner was not served at the exact time on that particular Sunday, she would station herself in the kitchen, and wait till it was dished, and then spit in all the kettles and pans that had been used for cooking. She did this to prevent the cook and her children from eking out their meagre fare with the remains of the gravy and other scrapings. The slaves could get nothing to eat except what she chose to give them. Provisions were weighed out by the pound and ounce, three times a day. I can assure you she gave them no chance to eat wheat bread from her flour barrel. She knew how many biscuits a quart of flour would make, and exactly what size they ought to be.

Dr. Flint was an epicure.[10] The cook never sent a dinner to his table without fear and trembling; for if there happened to be a dish not to his liking, he would either order her to be whipped, or compel her to eat

10 Someone with discriminating tastes, especially in food or drink.

every mouthful of it in his presence. The poor, hungry creature might not have objected to eating it; but she did object to having her master cram it down her throat till she choked.

They had a pet dog, that was a nuisance in the house. The cook was ordered to make some Indian mush[11] for him. He refused to eat, and when his head was held over it, the froth flowed from his mouth into the basin. He died a few minutes after. When Dr. Flint came in, he said the mush had not been well cooked, and that was the reason the animal would not eat it. He sent for the cook, and compelled her to eat it. He thought that the woman's stomach was stronger than the dog's; but her sufferings afterwards proved that he was mistaken. This poor woman endured many cruelties from her master and mistress; sometimes she was locked up, away from her nursing baby, for a whole day and night.

When I had been in the family a few weeks, one of the plantation slaves was brought to town, by order of his master. It was near night when he arrived, and Dr. Flint ordered him to be taken to the work house, and tied up to the joist, so that his feet would just escape the ground. In that situation he was to wait till the doctor had taken his tea. I shall never forget that night. Never before, in my life, had I heard hundreds of blows fall, in succession, on a human being. His piteous groans, and his "O, pray don't, massa," rang in my ear for months afterwards. There were many conjectures as to the cause of this terrible punishment. Some said master accused him of stealing corn; others said the slave had quarrelled with his wife, in presence of the overseer, and had accused his master of being the father of her child. They were both black, and the child was very fair.

I went into the work house next morning, and saw the cowhide still wet with blood, and the boards all covered with gore. The poor man lived, and continued to quarrel with his wife. A few months afterwards Dr. Flint handed them both over to a slave-trader. The guilty man put their value into his pocket, and had the satisfaction of knowing that they were out of sight and hearing. When the mother was delivered into the trader's hands, she said, "You *promised* to treat me well." To which he replied, "You have let your tongue run too far; damn you!" She had forgotten that it was a crime for a slave to tell who was the father of her child.

From others than the master persecution also comes in such cases. I once saw a young slave girl dying soon after the birth of a child nearly white. In her agony she cried out, "O Lord, come and take me!" Her mistress stood by, and mocked at her like an incarnate fiend. "You suffer,

11 A mush made of cornmeal or maize.

do you?" she exclaimed. "I am glad of it. You deserve it all, and more too."

The girl's mother said, "The baby is dead, thank God; and I hope my poor child will soon be in heaven, too."

"Heaven!" retorted the mistress. "There is no such place for the like of her and her bastard."

The poor mother turned away, sobbing. Her dying daughter called her, feebly, and as she bent over her, I heard her say, "Don't grieve so, mother; God knows all about it; and HE will have mercy upon me."

Her sufferings, afterwards, became so intense, that her mistress felt unable to stay; but when she left the room, the scornful smile was still on her lips. Seven children called her mother. The poor black woman had but the one child, whose eyes she saw closing in death, while she thanked God for taking her away from the greater bitterness of life.

[Dr. Flint begins to harass Brent sexually, though she resists his advances. Determined to make her his concubine, Flint refuses to sell her to a free black man who wants to buy her freedom and marry her.]

x. *A Perilous Passage in the Slave Girl's Life*

AFTER my lover went away, Dr. Flint contrived a new plan. He seemed to have an idea that my fear of my mistress was his greatest obstacle. In the blandest tones, he told me that he was going to build a small house for me, in a secluded place, four miles away from the town. I shuddered; but I was constrained to listen, while he talked of his intention to give me a home of my own, and to make a lady of me. Hitherto, I had escaped my dreaded fate, by being in the midst of people. My grandmother had already had high words with my master about me. She had told him pretty plainly what she thought of his character, and there was considerable gossip in the neighborhood about our affairs, to which the open-mouthed jealousy of Mrs. Flint contributed not a little. When my master said he was going to build a house for me, and that he could do it with little trouble and expense, I was in hopes something would happen to frustrate his scheme; but I soon heard that the house was actually begun. I vowed before my Maker that I would never enter it. I had rather toil on the plantation from dawn till dark; I had rather live and die in jail, than drag on, from day to day, through such a living death. I was determined that the master, whom I so hated and loathed, who had blighted the prospects of my youth, and made my life a desert, should not, after my long struggle with him, succeed at last in trampling his victim under his feet. I would do any thing, every thing, for the sake of defeating him. What *could* I do? I thought and thought, till I became desperate, and made a plunge into the abyss.

And now, reader, I come to a period in my unhappy life, which I would gladly forget if I could. The remembrance fills me with sorrow and shame. It pains me to tell you of it; but I have promised to tell you the truth, and I will do it honestly, let it cost me what it may. I will not try to screen myself behind the plea of compulsion from a master; for it was not so. Neither can I plead ignorance or thoughtlessness. For years, my master had done his utmost to pollute my mind with foul images, and to destroy the pure principles inculcated by my grandmother, and the good mistress of my childhood. The influences of slavery had had the same effect on me that they had on other young girls; they had made me prematurely knowing, concerning the evil ways of the world. I know what I did, and I did it with deliberate calculation.

But, O, ye happy women, whose purity has been sheltered from childhood, who have been free to choose the objects of your affection, whose homes are protected by law, do not judge the poor desolate slave girl too severely! If slavery had been abolished, I, also, could have married the man of my choice; I could have had a home shielded by the laws; and I should have been spared the painful task of confessing what I am now about to relate; but all my prospects had been blighted by slavery. I wanted to keep myself pure; and, under the most adverse circumstances, I tried hard to preserve my self-respect; but I was struggling alone in the powerful grasp of the demon Slavery; and the monster proved too strong for me. I felt as if I was forsaken by God and man; as if all my efforts must be frustrated; and I became reckless in my despair.

I have told you that Dr. Flint's persecutions and his wife's jealousy had given rise to some gossip in the neighborhood. Among others, it chanced that a white unmarried gentleman[12] had obtained some knowledge of the circumstances in which I was placed. He knew my grandmother, and often spoke to me in the street. He became interested for me, and asked questions about my master, which I answered in part. He expressed a great deal of sympathy, and a wish to aid me. He constantly sought opportunities to see me, and wrote to me frequently. I was a poor slave girl, only fifteen years old.

So much attention from a superior person was, of course, flattering; for human nature is the same in all. I also felt grateful for his sympathy,

12 Samuel Tredwell Sawyer (c. 1800–1865), called Mr. Sands in the text.

and encouraged by his kind words. It seemed to me a great thing to have such a friend. By degrees, a more tender feeling crept into my heart. He was an educated and eloquent gentleman; too eloquent, alas, for the poor slave girl who trusted in him. Of course I saw whither all this was tending. I knew the impassable gulf between us; but to be an object of interest to a man who is not married, and who is not her master, is agreeable to the pride and feelings of a slave, if her miserable situation has left her any pride or sentiment. It seems less degrading to give one's self, than to submit to compulsion. There is something akin to freedom in having a lover who has no control over you, except that which he gains by kindness and attachment. A master may treat you as rudely as he pleases, and you dare not speak; moreover, the wrong does not seem so great with an unmarried man, as with one who has a wife to be made unhappy. There may be sophistry in all this; but the condition of a slave confuses all principles of morality, and, in fact, renders the practice of them impossible.

When I found that my master had actually begun to build the lonely cottage, other feelings mixed with those I have described. Revenge, and calculations of interest, were added to flattered vanity and sincere gratitude for kindness. I knew nothing would enrage Dr. Flint so much as to know that I favored another; and it was something to triumph over my tyrant even in that small way. I thought he would revenge himself by selling me, and I was sure my friend, Mr. Sands, would buy me. He was a man of more generosity and feeling than my master, and I thought my freedom could be easily obtained from him. The crisis of my fate now came so near that I was desperate. I shuddered to think of being the mother of children that should be owned by my old tyrant. I knew that as soon as a new fancy took him, his victims were sold far off to get rid of them; especially if they had children. I had seen several women sold, with his babies at the breast. He never allowed his offspring by slaves to remain long in sight of himself and his wife. Of a man who was not my master I could ask to have my children well supported; and in this case, I felt confident I should obtain the boon.[13] I also felt quite sure that they would be made free. With all these thoughts revolving in my mind, and seeing no other way of escaping the doom I so much dreaded, I made a headlong plunge. Pity me, and pardon me, O virtuous reader! You never knew what it is to be a slave; to be entirely unprotected by law or custom; to have the laws reduce you to the condition of a chattel, entirely subject to the will of another. You never exhausted your ingenuity in avoiding

13 Favor.

the snares, and eluding the power of a hated tyrant; you never shuddered at the sound of his footsteps, and trembled within hearing of his voice. I know I did wrong. No one can feel it more sensibly than I do. The painful and humiliating memory will haunt me to my dying day. Still, in looking back, calmly, on the events of my life, I feel that the slave woman ought not to be judged by the same standard as others.

The months passed on. I had many unhappy hours. I secretly mourned over the sorrow I was bringing on my grandmother, who had so tried to shield me from harm. I knew that I was the greatest comfort of her old age, and that it was a source of pride to her that I had not degraded myself, like most of the slaves. I wanted to confess to her that I was no longer worthy of her love; but I could not utter the dreaded words.

As for Dr. Flint, I had a feeling of satisfaction and triumph in the thought of telling *him*. From time to time he told me of his intended arrangements, and I was silent. At last, he came and told me the cottage was completed, and ordered me to go to it. I told him I would never enter it. He said, "I have heard enough of such talk as that. You shall go, if you are carried by force; and you shall remain there." I replied, "I will never go there. In a few months I shall be a mother."

He stood and looked at me in dumb amazement, and left the house without a word. I thought I should be happy in my triumph over him. But now that the truth was out, and my relatives would hear of it, I felt wretched. Humble as were their circumstances, they had pride in my good character. Now, how could I look them in the face? My self-respect was gone! I had resolved that I would be virtuous, though I was a slave. I had said, "Let the storm beat! I will brave it till I die." And now, how humiliated I felt!

I went to my grandmother. My lips moved to make confession, but the words stuck in my throat. I sat down in the shade of a tree at her door and began to sew. I think she saw something unusual was the matter with me. The mother of slaves is very watchful. She knows there is no security for her children. After they have entered their teens she lives in daily expectation of trouble. This leads to many questions. If the girl is of a sensitive nature, timidity keeps her from answering truthfully, and this well-meant course has a tendency to drive her from maternal counsels. Presently, in came my mistress, like a mad woman, and accused me concerning her husband. My grandmother, whose suspicions had been previously awakened, believed what she said. She exclaimed, "O Linda! has it come to this? I had rather see you dead than to see you as you now are. You are a disgrace to your dead mother." She tore from my fingers my mother's wedding ring and her silver thimble. "Go away!" she exclaimed, "and never come to my house, again." Her reproaches fell so hot and heavy, that they left me no chance to answer. Bitter tears, such as the eyes never shed but once, were my only answer. I rose from my seat, but fell back again, sobbing. She did not speak to me; but the tears were running down her furrowed cheeks, and they scorched me like fire. She had always been so kind to me! *So* kind! How I longed to throw myself at her feet, and tell her all the truth! But she had ordered me to go, and never to come there again. After a few minutes, I mustered strength, and started to obey her. With what feelings did I now close that little gate, which I used to open with such an eager hand in my childhood! It closed upon me with a sound I never heard before.

Where could I go? I was afraid to return to my master's. I walked on recklessly, not caring where I went, or what would become of me. When I had gone four or five miles, fatigue compelled me to stop. I sat down on the stump of an old tree. The stars were shining through the boughs above me. How they mocked me, with their bright, calm light! The hours passed by, and as I sat there alone a chilliness and deadly sickness came over me. I sank on the ground. My mind was full of horrid thoughts. I prayed to die; but the prayer was not answered. At last, with great effort I roused myself, and walked some distance further, to the house of a woman who had been a friend of my mother. When I told her why I was there, she spoke soothingly to me; but I could not be comforted. I thought I could bear my shame if I could only be reconciled to my grandmother. I longed to open my heart to her. I thought if she could know the real state of the case, and all I had been bearing for years, she would perhaps judge me less harshly. My friend advised me to send for her. I did so; but days of agonizing suspense passed before she came. Had she utterly forsaken me? No. She came at last. I knelt before her, and told her the things that had poisoned my life; how long I had been persecuted; that I saw no way of escape; and in an hour of extremity I had become desperate. She listened in silence. I told her I would bear any thing and do any thing, if in time I had hopes of obtaining her forgiveness. I begged of her to pity me, for my dead mother's sake. And she did pity me. She did not say, "I forgive you;" but she looked at me lovingly, with her eyes full of tears. She laid her old hand gently on my head, and murmured, "Poor child! Poor child!"

[Brent's jealous mistress forbids her to return to the Norcom household, and Brent moves into her grandmother's home. She gives birth to a son, Benjamin. Norcom continues his intimidations.]

NOT far from this time Nat Turner's insurrection broke out; and the news threw our town into great commotion.[14] Strange that they should be alarmed when their slaves were so "contented and happy"! But so it was.

It was always the custom to have a muster every year. On that occasion every white man shouldered his musket. The citizens and the so-called country gentlemen wore military uniforms. The poor whites took their places in the ranks in every-day dress, some without shoes, some without hats. This grand occasion had already passed; and when the slaves were told there was to be another muster, they were surprised and rejoiced. Poor creatures! They thought it was going to be a holiday. I was informed of the true state of affairs, and imparted it to the few I could trust. Most gladly would I have proclaimed it to every slave; but I dared not. All could not be relied on. Mighty is the power of the torturing lash.

By sunrise, people were pouring in from every quarter within twenty miles of the town. I knew the houses were to be searched; and I expected it would be done by country bullies and the poor whites. I knew nothing annoyed them so much as to see colored people living in comfort and respectability; so I made arrangements for them with especial care. I arranged every thing in my grandmother's house as neatly as possible. I put white quilts on the beds, and decorated some of the rooms with flowers. When all was arranged, I sat down at the window to watch. Far as my eye could reach, it rested on a motley crowd of soldiers. Drums and fifes were discoursing martial music. The men were divided into companies of sixteen, each headed by a captain. Orders were given, and the wild scouts rushed in every direction, wherever a colored face was to be found.

It was a grand opportunity for the low whites, who had no negroes of their own to scourge. They exulted in such a chance to exercise a little brief authority, and show their subserviency to the slaveholders; not reflecting that the power which trampled on the colored people also kept themselves in poverty, ignorance, and moral degradation. Those who never witnessed such scenes can hardly believe what I know was inflicted at this time on innocent men, women, and children, against whom there was not the slightest ground for suspicion. Colored people and slaves who lived in remote parts of the town suffered in an especial manner. In some

14. Nat Turner and his fellow slaves killed more than fifty whites on August 21 and 22, 1831. The insurrection, which took place in Southampton County, Virginia, just forty miles from Edenton, ignited white terrorist retaliation throughout North Carolina and the South.

cases the searchers scattered powder and shot among their clothes, and then sent other parties to find them, and bring them forward as proof that they were plotting insurrection. Every where men, women, and children were whipped till the blood stood in puddles at their feet. Some received five hundred lashes; others were tied hands and feet, and tortured with a bucking paddle, which blisters the skin terribly. The dwellings of the colored people, unless they happened to be protected by some influential white person, who was nigh at hand, were robbed of clothing and every thing else the marauders thought worth carrying away. All day long these unfeeling wretches went round, like a troop of demons, terrifying and tormenting the helpless. At night, they formed themselves into patrol bands, and went wherever they chose among the colored people, acting out their brutal will. Many women hid themselves in woods and swamps, to keep out of their way. If any of the husbands or fathers told of these outrages, they were tied up to the public whipping post, and cruelly scourged for telling lies about white men. The consternation was universal. No two people that had the slightest tinge of color in their faces dared to be seen talking together.

I entertained no positive fears about our household, because we were in the midst of white families who would protect us. We were ready to receive the soldiers whenever they came. It was not long before we heard the tramp of feet and the sound of voices. The door was rudely pushed open; and in they tumbled, like a pack of hungry wolves. They snatched at every thing within their reach. Every box, trunk, closet, and corner underwent a thorough examination. A box in one of the drawers containing some silver change was eagerly pounced upon. When I stepped forward to take it from them, one of the soldiers turned and said angrily, "What d'ye foller us fur? D'ye s'pose white folks is come to steal?"

I replied, "You have come to search; but you have searched that box, and I will take it, if you please."

At that moment I saw a white gentleman who was friendly to us; and I called to him, and asked him to have the goodness to come in and stay till the search was over. He readily complied. His entrance into the house brought in the captain of the company, whose business it was to guard the outside of the house, and see that none of the inmates left it. This officer was Mr. Litch, the wealthy slaveholder whom I mentioned, in the account of neighboring planters, as being notorious for his cruelty. He felt above soiling his hands with the search. He merely gave orders; and, if a bit of writing was discovered, it was carried to him by his ignorant followers, who were unable to read.

My grandmother had a large trunk of bedding and table cloths. When that was opened, there was a great shout of surprise; and one exclaimed, "Where'd the damned niggers git all dis sheet an' table clarf?"

My grandmother, emboldened by the presence of our white protector, said, "You may be sure we didn't pilfer 'em from *your* houses."

"Look here, mammy," said a grim-looking fellow without any coat, "you seem to feel mighty gran' 'cause you got all them 'ere fixens. White folks oughter have 'em all."

His remarks were interrupted by a chorus of voices shouting, "We's got 'em! We's got 'em! Dis 'ere yaller gal's got letters!"

There was a general rush for the supposed letter, which, upon examination, proved to be some verses written to me by a friend. In packing away my things, I had overlooked them. When their captain informed them of their contents, they seemed much disappointed. He inquired of me who wrote them. I told him it was one of my friends. "Can you read them?" he asked. When I told him I could, he swore, and raved, and tore the paper into bits. "Bring me all your letters!" said he, in a commanding tone. I told him I had none. "Don't be afraid," he continued, in an insinuating way. "Bring them all to me. Nobody shall do you any harm." Seeing I did not move to obey him, his pleasant tone changed to oaths and threats. "Who writes to you? half free niggers?" inquired he. I replied, "O, no; most of my letters are from white people. Some request me to burn them after they are read, and some I destroy without reading."

An exclamation of surprise from some of the company put a stop to our conversation. Some silver spoons which ornamented an old-fashioned buffet had just been discovered. My grandmother was in the habit of preserving fruit for many ladies in the town, and of preparing suppers for parties; consequently she had many jars of preserves. The closet that contained these was next invaded, and the contents tasted. One of them, who was helping himself freely, tapped his neighbor on the shoulder, and said, "Wal done! Don't wonder de niggers want to kill all de white folks, when dey live on 'sarves" [meaning preserves]. I stretched out my hand to take the jar, saying, "You were not sent here to search for sweetmeats."

"And what *were* we sent for?" said the captain, bristling up to me. I evaded the question.

The search of the house was completed, and nothing found to condemn us. They next proceeded to the garden, and knocked about every bush and vine, with no better success. The captain called his men together, and, after a short consultation, the order to march was given. As they passed out of the gate, the captain turned back, and pronounced a malediction on the house. He said it ought to be burned to the ground, and each of its inmates receive thirty-nine lashes. We came out of this affair very fortunately; not losing any thing except some wearing apparel.

Towards evening the turbulence increased. The soldiers, stimulated by drink, committed still greater cruelties. Shrieks and shouts continually rent the air. Not daring to go to the door, I peeped under the window curtain. I saw a mob dragging along a number of colored people, each white man, with his musket upraised, threatening instant death if they did not stop their shrieks. Among the prisoners was a respectable old colored minister. They had found a few parcels of shot in his house, which his wife had for years used to balance her scales. For this they were going to shoot him on Court House Green. What a spectacle was that for a civilized country! A rabble, staggering under intoxication, assuming to be the administrators of justice!

The better class of the community exerted their influence to save the innocent, persecuted people; and in several instances they succeeded, by keeping them shut up in jail till the excitement abated. At last the white citizens found that their own property was not safe from the lawless rabble they had summoned to protect them. They rallied the drunken swarm, drove them back into the country, and set a guard over the town.

The next day, the town patrols were commissioned to search colored people that lived out of the city; and the most shocking outrages were committed with perfect impunity. Every day for a fortnight, if I looked out, I saw horsemen with some poor panting negro tied to their saddles, and compelled by the lash to keep up with their speed, till they arrived at the jail yard. Those who had been whipped too unmercifully to walk were washed with brine, tossed into a cart, and carried to jail. One black man, who had not fortitude to endure scourging, promised to give information about the conspiracy. But it turned out that he knew nothing at all. He had not even heard the name of Nat Turner. The poor fellow had, however, made up a story, which augmented his own sufferings and those of the colored people.

The day patrol continued for some weeks, and at sundown a night guard was substituted. Nothing at all was proved against the colored people, bond or free. The wrath of the slaveholders was somewhat appeased by the capture of Nat Turner. The imprisoned were released. The slaves were sent to their masters, and the free were permitted to return to their ravaged homes. Visiting was strictly forbidden on the plantations. The slaves begged the privilege of again meeting at their little church in the woods, with their burying ground around it. It was built by the colored people, and they had no higher happiness than to meet there and sing hymns together, and pour out their hearts in spontaneous prayer. Their request was denied, and the church was demolished. They were permitted to attend the white churches, a certain portion of the galleries being appropriated to their use. There, when every body else had partaken of the communion, and the benediction had been pronounced, the minister said, "Come down, now, my colored friends." They obeyed the summons, and partook of the bread and wine, in commemoration of the meek and lowly Jesus, who said, "God is your Father, and all ye are brethren."[15]

XIV. *Another Link to Life*

I HAD NOT returned to my master's house since the birth of my child. The old man raved to have me thus removed from his immediate power; but his wife vowed, by all that was good and great, she would kill me if I came back; and he did not doubt her word. Sometimes he would stay away for a season. Then he would come and renew the old threadbare discourse about his forbearance and my ingratitude. He labored, most unnecessarily, to convince me that I had lowered myself. The venomous old reprobate[16] had no need of descanting on that theme. I felt humiliated enough. My unconscious babe was the ever-present witness of my shame. I listened with silent contempt when he talked about my having forfeited *his* good opinion; but I shed bitter tears that I was no longer worthy of being respected by the good and pure. Alas! slavery still held me in its poisonous grasp. There was no chance for me to be respectable. There was no prospect of being able to lead a better life.

Sometimes, when my master found that I still refused to accept what he called his kind offers, he would threaten to sell my child. "Perhaps that will humble you," said he.

Humble *me*! Was I not already in the dust?[17] But his threat lacerated my heart. I knew the law gave him power to fulfil it; for slaveholders have been cunning enough to enact that "the child shall follow the condition of the *mother*," not of the *father*; thus taking care that licentiousness shall not interfere with avarice. This reflection made me clasp my innocent babe all the more firmly to my heart. Horrid visions passed through my mind when I thought of his liability to fall into the slave trader's hands. I wept over him, and said, "O my child! perhaps they will leave you in

15 Matthew 23:8. 17 Job 42:6.
16 A depraved, vicious, or unprincipled person.

some cold cabin to die, and then throw you into a hole, as if you were a dog."

When Dr. Flint learned that I was again to be a mother, he was exasperated beyond measure. He rushed from the house, and returned with a pair of shears. I had a fine head of hair; and he often railed about my pride of arranging it nicely. He cut every hair close to my head,[18] storming and swearing all the time. I replied to some of his abuse, and he struck me. Some months before, he had pitched me down stairs in a fit of passion; and the injury I received was so serious that I was unable to turn myself in bed for many days. He then said, "Linda, I swear by God I will never raise my hand against you again;" but I knew that he would forget his promise.

After he discovered my situation, he was like a restless spirit from the pit. He came every day; and I was subjected to such insults as no pen can describe. I would not describe them if I could; they were too low, too revolting. I tried to keep them from my grandmother's knowledge as much as I could. I knew she had enough to sadden her life, without having my troubles to bear. When she saw the doctor treat me with violence, and heard him utter oaths terrible enough to palsy a man's tongue, she could not always hold her peace. It was natural and motherlike that she should try to defend me; but it only made matters worse.

When they told me my new-born babe was a girl, my heart was heavier than it had ever been before.[19] Slavery is terrible for men; but it is far more terrible for women. Superadded to the burden common to all, *they* have wrongs, and sufferings, and mortifications peculiarly their own.

Dr. Flint had sworn that he would make me suffer, to my last day, for this new crime against *him*, as he called it; and as long as he had me in his power he kept his word. On the fourth day after the birth of my babe, he entered my room suddenly, and commanded me to rise and bring my baby to him. The nurse who took care of me had gone out of the room to prepare some nourishment, and I was alone. There was no alternative. I rose, took up my babe, and crossed the room to where he sat. "Now stand there," said he, "till I tell you to go back!" My child bore a strong resemblance to her father, and to the deceased Mrs. Sands, her grandmother. He noticed this; and while I stood before him, trembling with weakness, he heaped upon me and my little one every vile epithet he could think

18 An Old Testament practice meant to humiliate a woman by indicating her sexual impurity.

19 Louisa Matilda Jacobs (1833–1917), called Ellen in the narrative.

of. Even the grandmother in her grave did not escape his curses. In the midst of his vituperations[20] I fainted at his feet. This recalled him to his senses. He took the baby from my arms, laid it on the bed, dashed cold water on my face, took me up, and shook me violently, to restore my consciousness before any one entered the room. Just then my grandmother came in, and he hurried out of the house. I suffered in consequence of this treatment; but I begged my friends to let me die, rather than send for the doctor. There was nothing I dreaded so much as his presence. My life was spared; and I was glad for the sake of my little ones. Had it not been for these ties to life, I should have been glad to be released by death, though I had lived only nineteen years.

Always it gave me a pang that my children had no lawful claim to a name. Their father offered his; but, if I had wished to accept the offer, I dared not while my master lived. Moreover, I knew it would not be accepted at their baptism. A Christian name they were at least entitled to; and we resolved to call my boy for our dear good Benjamin,[21] who had gone far away from us.

My grandmother belonged to the church; and she was very desirous of having the children christened. I knew Dr. Flint would forbid it, and I did not venture to attempt it. But chance favored me. He was called to visit a patient out of town, and was obliged to be absent during Sunday. "Now is the time," said my grandmother; "we will take the children to church, and have them christened."

When I entered the church, recollections of my mother came over me, and I felt subdued in spirit. There she had presented me for baptism, without any reason to feel ashamed. She had been married, and had such legal rights as slavery allows to a slave. The vows had at least been sacred to *her*, and she had never violated them. I was glad she was not alive, to know under what different circumstances her grandchildren were presented for baptism. Why had my lot been so different from my mother's? *Her* master had died when she was a child; and she remained with her mistress till she married. She was never in the power of any master; and thus she escaped one class of the evils that generally fall upon slaves.

When my baby was about to be christened, the former mistress of my father stepped up to me, and proposed to give it her Christian name. To this I added the surname of my father, who had himself no legal right to it; for my grandfather on the paternal side was a white gentleman. What

20 Abusive and bitter language.
21 Joseph Jacobs (c. 1829–63?) was named after Harriet's uncle Joseph.

tangled skeins are the genealogies of slavery! I loved my father; but it mortified me to be obliged to bestow his name on my children.

When we left the church, my father's old mistress invited me to go home with her. She clasped a gold chain round my baby's neck. I thanked her for this kindness; but I did not like the emblem. I wanted no chain to be fastened on my daughter, not even if its links were of gold. How earnestly I prayed that she might never feel the weight of slavery's chain, whose iron entereth into the soul!

[Flint gives Brent an ultimatum either to move into a cottage where she will live as his mistress, or be punished by working on his son's plantation. Brent moves to the plantation, leaving Benny and Ellen with Aunt Martha. When Flint threatens the children, Brent plans to hide so as to manipulate him into selling the children to their father, Mr. Sands.]

XVII. *The Flight*

MR. FLINT[22] was hard pushed for house servants, and rather than lose me he had restrained his malice. I did my work faithfully, though not, of course, with a willing mind. They were evidently afraid I should leave them. Mr. Flint wished that I should sleep in the great house instead of the servants' quarters. His wife agreed to the proposition, but said I mustn't bring my bed into the house, because it would scatter feathers on her carpet. I knew when I went there that they would never think of such a thing as furnishing a bed of any kind for me and my little one. I therefore carried my own bed, and now I was forbidden to use it. I did as I was ordered. But now that I was certain my children were to be put in their power, in order to give them a stronger hold on me, I resolved to leave them that night. I remembered the grief this step would bring upon my dear old grandmother; and nothing less than the freedom of my children would have induced me to disregard her advice. I went about my evening work with trembling steps. Mr. Flint twice called from his chamber door to inquire why the house was not locked up. I replied that I had not done my work. "You have had time enough to do it," said he. "Take care how you answer me!"

I shut all the windows, locked all the doors, and went up to the third story, to wait till midnight. How long those hours seemed, and how fervently I prayed that God would not forsake me in this hour of utmost need! I was about to risk every thing on the throw of a die; and if I failed,

22 Dr. Flint's son.

O what would become of me and my poor children? They would be made to suffer for my fault.

At half past twelve I stole softly down stairs. I stopped on the second floor, thinking I heard a noise. I felt my way down into the parlor, and looked out of the window. The night was so intensely dark that I could see nothing. I raised the window very softly and jumped out. Large drops of rain were falling, and the darkness bewildered me. I dropped on my knees, and breathed a short prayer to God for guidance and protection. I groped my way to the road, and rushed towards the town with almost lightning speed. I arrived at my grandmother's house, but dared not see her. She would say, "Linda, you are killing me;" and I knew that would unnerve me. I tapped softly at the window of a room, occupied by a woman, who had lived in the house several years. I knew she was a faithful friend, and could be trusted with my secret. I tapped several times before she heard me. At last she raised the window, and I whispered, "Sally, I have run away. Let me in, quick." She opened the door softly, and said in low tones, "For God's sake, don't. Your grandmother is trying to buy you and de chillern. Mr. Sands was here last week. He tole her he was going away on business, but he wanted her to go ahead about buying you and de chillern, and he would help her all he could. Don't run away, Linda. Your grandmother is all bowed down wid trouble now."

I replied, "Sally, they are going to carry my children to the plantation to-morrow; and they will never sell them to any body so long as they have me in their power. Now, would you advise me to go back?"

"No, chile, no," answered she. "When dey finds you is gone, dey won't want de plague ob de chillern; but where is you going to hide? Dey knows ebery inch ob dis house."

I told her I had a hiding-place, and that was all it was best for her to know. I asked her to go into my room as soon as it was light, and take all my clothes out of my trunk, and pack them in hers; for I knew Mr. Flint and the constable would be there early to search my room. I feared the sight of my children would be too much for my full heart; but I could not go out into the uncertain future without one last look. I bent over the bed where lay my little Benny and baby Ellen. Poor little ones! fatherless and motherless! Memories of their father came over me. He wanted to be kind to them; but they were not all to him, as they were to my womanly heart. I knelt and prayed for the innocent little sleepers. I kissed them lightly, and turned away.

As I was about to open the street door, Sally laid her hand on my shoulder, and said, "Linda, is you gwine all alone? Let me call your uncle."

"No Sally," I replied, "I want no one to be brought into trouble on my account."

I went forth into the darkness and rain. I ran on till I came to the house of the friend who was to conceal me.

Early the next morning Mr. Flint was at my grandmother's inquiring for me. She told him she had not seen me, and supposed I was at the plantation. He watched her face narrowly, and said, "Don't you know any thing about her running off?" She assured him that she did not. He went on to say, "Last night she ran off without the least provocation. We had treated her very kindly. My wife liked her. She will soon be found and brought back. Are her children with you?" When told that they were, he said, "I am very glad to hear that. If they are here, she cannot be far off. If I find out that any of my niggers have had any thing to do with this damned business, I'll give 'em five hundred lashes." As he started to go to his father's, he turned round and added, persuasively, "Let her be brought back, and she shall have her children to live with her."

The tidings made the old doctor rave and storm at a furious rate. It was a busy day for them. My grandmother's house was searched from top to bottom. As my trunk was empty, they concluded I had taken my clothes with me. Before ten o'clock every vessel northward bound was thoroughly examined, and the law against harboring fugitives was read to all on board. At night a watch was set over the town. Knowing how distressed my grandmother would be, I wanted to send her a message; but it could not be done. Every one who went in or out of her house was closely watched. The doctor said he would take my children, unless she became responsible for them; which of course she willingly did. The next day was spent in searching. Before night, the following advertisement was posted at every corner, and in every public place for miles round:—

"$300 REWARD! Ran away from the subscriber, an intelligent, bright, mulatto girl, named Linda, 21 years of age. Five feet four inches high. Dark eyes, and black hair inclined to curl; but it can be made straight. Has a decayed spot on a front tooth. She can read and write, and in all probability will try to get to the Free States. All persons are forbidden, under penalty of the law, to harbor or employ said slave. $150 will be given to whoever takes her in the state, and $300 if taken out of the state and delivered to me, or lodged in jail.

DR. FLINT

HARRIET JACOBS

A SMALL shed had been added to my grandmother's house years ago. Some boards were laid across the joists at the top, and between these boards and the roof was a very small garret, never occupied by any thing but rats and mice. It was a pent roof, covered with nothing but shingles, according to the southern custom for such buildings. The garret was only nine feet long and seven wide. The highest part was three feet high, and sloped down abruptly to the loose board floor. There was no admission for either light or air. My uncle Philip, who was a carpenter, had very skilfully made a concealed trap-door, which communicated with the store-room. He had been doing this while I was waiting in the swamp. The storeroom opened upon a piazza.[24] To this hole I was conveyed as soon as I entered the house. The air was stifling; the darkness total. A bed had been spread on the floor. I could sleep quite comfortably on one side; but the slope was so sudden that I could not turn on the other without hitting the roof. The rats and mice ran over my bed; but I was weary, and I slept such sleep as the wretched may, when a tempest has passed over them. Morning came. I knew it only by the noises I heard; for in my small den day and night were all the same. I suffered for air even more than for light. But I was not comfortless. I heard the voices of my children. There was joy and there was sadness in the sound. It made my tears flow. How I longed to speak to them! I was eager to look on their faces; but there was no hole, no crack, through which I could peep. This continued darkness was oppressive. It seemed horrible to sit or lie in a cramped position day after day, without one gleam of light. Yet I would have chosen this, rather than my lot as a slave, though white people considered it an easy one; and it was so compared with the fate of others. I was never cruelly over-worked; I was never lacerated with the whip from head to foot; I was never so beaten and bruised that I could not turn from one side to the other; I never had my heel-strings cut to prevent my running away; I was never chained to a log and forced to drag it about, while I toiled in the fields from morning till night; I was never branded with hot iron, or torn by bloodhounds. On the contrary, I had always been kindly treated, and tenderly cared for, until I came into the hands of Dr. Flint. I had never wished for freedom till then. But though my life in slavery was compara-

---

23 The title derives from the poem "The Task" (book 4, lines 88–90) by William Cowper (1731–1800): "'Tis pleasant, through the loopholes of retreat / To peep at such a world, to see the stir."

24 A verandah or porch.

tively devoid of hardships, God pity the woman who is compelled to lead such a life!

My food was passed up to me through the trap-door my uncle had contrived; and my grandmother, my uncle Phillip, and aunt Nancy would seize such opportunities as they could, to mount up there and chat with me at the opening. But of course this was not safe in the daytime. It must all be done in darkness. It was impossible for me to move in an erect position, but I crawled about my den for exercise. One day I hit my head against something, and found it was a gimlet.[25] My uncle had left it sticking there when he made the trap-door. I was as rejoiced as Robinson Crusoe[26] could have been in finding such a treasure. It put a lucky thought into my head. I said to myself, "Now I will have some light. Now I will see my children." I did not dare to begin my work during the daytime, for fear of attracting attention. But I groped round; and having found the side next the street, where I could frequently see my children, I stuck the gimlet in and waited for evening. I bored three rows of holes, one above another; then I bored out the interstices between. I thus succeeded in making one hole about an inch long and an inch broad. I sat by it till late into the night, to enjoy the little whiff of air that floated in. In the morning I watched for my children. The first person I saw in the street was Dr. Flint. I had a shuddering, superstitious feeling that it was a bad omen. Several familiar faces passed by. At last I heard the merry laughing of children, and presently two sweet little faces were looking up at me, as though they knew I was there, and were conscious of the joy they imparted. How I longed to *tell* them I was there!

My condition was now a little improved. But for weeks I was tormented by hundreds of little red insects, fine as a needle's point, that pierced through my skin, and produced an intolerable burning. The good grandmother gave me herb teas and cooling medicines, and finally I got rid of them. The heat of my den was intense, for nothing but thin shingles protected me from the scorching summer's sun. But I had my consolations. Through my peeping-hole I could watch the children, and when they were near enough, I could hear their talk. Aunt Nancy brought me all the news she could hear at Dr. Flint's. From her I learned that the doctor had written to New York to a colored woman, who had been born and raised in our neighborhood, and had breathed his contaminating atmosphere. He offered her a reward if she could find out any thing

25 Tool for boring holes.
26 Crusoe, the title character of Daniel Defoe's 1719 novel, survives a ship-wreck and lives on a secluded island for years before being rescued.

HARRIET JACOBS

about me. I know not what was the nature of her reply; but he soon after started for New York in haste, saying to his family that he had business of importance to transact. I peeped at him as he passed on his way to the steamboat. It was a satisfaction to have miles of land and water between us, even for a little while; and it was a still greater satisfaction to know that he believed me to be in the Free States. My little den seemed less dreary than it had done. He returned, as he did from his former journey to New York, without obtaining any satisfactory information. When he passed our house next morning, Benny was standing at the gate. He had heard them say that he had gone to find me, and he called out, "Dr. Flint, did you bring my mother home? I want to see her." The doctor stamped his foot at him in a rage, and exclaimed, "Get out of the way, you little damned rascal! If you don't, I'll cut off your head."

Benny ran terrified into the house, saying, "You can't put me in jail again. I don't belong to you now." It was well that the wind carried the words away from the doctor's ear. I told my grandmother of it, when we had our next conference at the trap-door; and begged of her not to allow the children to be impertinent to the irascible old man.

Autumn came, with a pleasant abatement of heat. My eyes had become accustomed to the dim light, and by holding my book or work in a certain position near the aperture I contrived to read and sew. That was a great relief to the tedious monotony of my life. But when winter came, the cold penetrated through the thin shingle roof, and I was dreadfully chilled. The winters there are not so long, or so severe, as in northern latitudes; but the houses are not built to shelter from cold, and my little den was peculiarly comfortless. The kind grandmother brought me bed-clothes and warm drinks. Often I was obliged to lie in bed all day to keep comfortable; but with all my precautions, my shoulders and feet were frostbitten. O, those long, gloomy days, with no object for my eye to rest upon, and no thoughts to occupy my mind, except the dreary past and the uncertain future! I was thankful when there came a day sufficiently mild for me to wrap myself up and sit at the loophole to watch the passers by. Southerners have the habit of stopping and talking in the streets, and I heard many conversations not intended to meet my ears. I heard slave-hunters planning how to catch some poor fugitive. Several times I heard allusions to Dr. Flint, myself, and the history of my children, who, perhaps, were playing near the gate. One would say, "I wouldn't move my little finger to catch her, as old Flint's property." Another would say, "I'll catch *any* nigger for the reward. A man ought to have what belongs to him, if he *is* a damned brute." The opinion was often expressed that I was in the Free

States. Very rarely did any one suggest that I might be in the vicinity. Had the least suspicion rested on my grandmother's house, it would have been burned to the ground. But it was the last place they thought of. Yet there was no place, where slavery existed, that could have afforded me so good a place of concealment.

Dr. Flint and his family repeatedly tried to coax and bribe my children to tell something they had heard said about me. One day the doctor took them into a shop, and offered them some bright little silver pieces and gay handkerchiefs if they would tell where their mother was. Ellen shrank away from him, and would not speak; but Benny spoke up, and said, "Dr. Flint, I don't know where my mother is. I guess she's in New York; and when you go there again, I wish you'd ask her to come home, for I want to see her; but if you put her in jail, or tell her you'll cut her head off, I'll tell her to go right back."

XXII. *Christmas Festivities*

CHRISTMAS was approaching. Grandmother brought me materials, and I busied myself making some new garments and little playthings for my children. Were it not that hiring day[27] is near at hand, and many families are fearfully looking forward to the probability of separation in a few days, Christmas might be a happy season for the poor slaves. Even slave mothers try to gladden the hearts of their little ones on that occasion. Benny and Ellen had their Christmas stockings filled. Their imprisoned mother could not have the privilege of witnessing their surprise and joy. But I had the pleasure of peeping at them as they went into the street with their new suits on. I heard Benny ask a little playmate whether Santa Claus brought him any thing. "Yes," replied the boy; "but Santa Claus ain't a real man. It's the children's mothers that put things into the stockings." "No, that can't be," replied Benny, "for Santa Claus brought Ellen and me these new clothes, and my mother has been gone this long time."

How I longed to tell him that his mother made those garments, and that many a tear fell on them while she worked!

Every child rises early on Christmas morning to see the Johnkannaus.[28] Without them, Christmas would be shorn of its greatest attraction. They

27 January 1 was the annual auction day on which slaves were contracted for hire by neighboring slaveholders.
28 Folk festival involving masquerades and music observed by people of African descent in the West Indies, New Orleans, and along the Atlantic coast in the Carolinas.

consist of companies of slaves from the plantations, generally of the lower class. Two athletic men, in calico wrappers, have a net thrown over them, covered with all manner of bright-colored stripes. Cows' tails are fastened to their backs, and their heads are decorated with horns. A box, covered with sheepskin, is called the gumbo box. A dozen beat on this, while others strike triangles and jawbones, to which bands of dancers keep time. For a month previous they are composing songs, which are sung on this occasion. These companies, of a hundred each, turn out early in the morning, and are allowed to go round till twelve o'clock, begging for contributions. Not a door is left unvisited where there is the least chance of obtaining a penny or a glass of rum. They do not drink while they are out, but carry the rum home in jugs, to have a carousal.[29] These Christmas donations frequently amount to twenty or thirty dollars. It is seldom that any white man or child refuses to give them a trifle. If he does, they regale his ears with the following song:—

> "Poor massa, so dey say;
> Down in de heel, so dey say;
> Got no money, so dey say;
> Not one shillin, so dey say;
> God A'mighty bress you, so dey say."

Christmas is a day of feasting, both with white and colored people. Slaves, who are lucky enough to have a few shillings, are sure to spend them for good eating; and many a turkey and pig is captured, without saying "By your leave, sir." Those who cannot obtain these, cook a 'possum, or a raccoon, from which savory dishes can be made. My grandmother raised poultry and pigs for sale; and it was her established custom to have both a turkey and a pig roasted for Christmas dinner.

On this occasion, I was warned to keep extremely quiet, because two guests had been invited. One was the town constable, and the other was a free colored man, who tried to pass himself off for white, and who was always ready to do any mean work for the sake of currying favor with white people. My grandmother had a motive for inviting them. She managed to take them all over the house. All the rooms on the lower floor were thrown open for them to pass in and out; and after dinner, they were invited up stairs to look at a fine mocking bird my uncle had just brought home. There, too, the rooms were all thrown open, that they might look in. When I heard them talking on the piazza, my heart almost stood still.

29 Loud, drunken celebration.

I knew this colored man had spent many nights hunting for me. Every body knew he had the blood of a slave father in his veins; but for the sake of passing himself off for white, he was ready to kiss the slaveholders' feet. How I despised him! As for the constable, he wore no false colors. The duties of his office were despicable, but he was superior to his companion, inasmuch as he did not pretend to be what he was not. Any white man, who could raise money enough to buy a slave, would have considered himself degraded by being a constable; but the office enabled its possessor to exercise authority. If he found any slave out after nine o'clock, he could whip him as much as he liked; and that was a privilege to be coveted. When the guests were ready to depart, my grandmother gave each of them some of her nice pudding, as a present for their wives. Through my peep-hole I saw them go out of the gate, and I was glad when it closed after them. So passed the first Christmas in my den.

XXIX. *Preparations for Escape*

I HARDLY expect that the reader will credit me, when I affirm that I lived in that little dismal hole, almost deprived of light and air, and with no space to move my limbs, for nearly seven years. But it is a fact; and to me a sad one, even now; for my body still suffers from the effects of that long imprisonment, to say nothing of my soul. Members of my family, now living in New York and Boston, can testify to the truth of what I say.

Countless were the nights that I sat late at the little loophole scarcely large enough to give me a glimpse of one twinkling star. There, I heard the patrols and slave-hunters conferring together about the capture of runaways, well knowing how rejoiced they would be to catch me.

Season after season, year after year, I peeped at my children's faces, and heard their sweet voices, with a heart yearning all the while to say, "Your mother is here." Sometimes it appeared to me as if ages had rolled away since I entered upon that gloomy, monotonous existence. At times, I was stupefied and listless; at other times I became very impatient to know when these dark years would end, and I should again be allowed to feel the sunshine, and breathe the pure air.

After Ellen left us,[30] this feeling increased. Mr. Sands had agreed that Benny might go to the north whenever his uncle Phillip could go with

30 Sands sent Ellen to live with his relatives in Brooklyn, New York, claiming that she would be educated and treated better in the North.

him; and I was anxious to be there also, to watch over my children, and protect them so far as I was able. Moreover, I was likely to be drowned out of my den, if I remained much longer; for the slight roof was getting badly out of repair, and uncle Phillip was afraid to remove the shingles, lest some one should get a glimpse of me. When storms occurred in the night, they spread mats and bits of carpet, which in the morning appeared to have been laid out to dry; but to cover the roof in the daytime might have attracted attention. Consequently, my clothes and bedding were often drenched; a process by which the pains and aches in my cramped and stiffened limbs were greatly increased. I revolved various plans of escape in my mind, which I sometimes imparted to my grandmother, when she came to whisper with me at the trap-door. The kind-hearted old woman had an intense sympathy for runaways. She had known too much of the cruelties inflicted on those who were captured. Her memory always flew back at once to the sufferings of her bright and handsome son, Benjamin, the youngest and dearest of her flock. So, whenever I alluded to the subject, she would groan out, "O, don't think of it, child. You'll break my heart." I had no good old aunt Nancy now to encourage me; but my brother William and my children were continually beckoning me to the north.

And now I must go back a few months in my story. I have stated that the first of January was the time for selling slaves, or leasing them out to new masters. If time were counted by heart-throbs, the poor slaves might reckon years of suffering during that festival so joyous to the free. On the New Year's day preceding my aunt's death, one of my friends, named Fanny, was to be sold at auction, to pay her master's debts. My thoughts were with her during all the day, and at night I anxiously inquired what had been her fate. I was told that she had been sold to one master, and her four little girls to another master, far distant; that she had escaped from her purchaser, and was not to be found. Her mother was the old Aggie I have spoken of. She lived in a small tenement belonging to my grandmother, and built on the same lot with her own house. Her dwelling was searched and watched, and that brought the patrols so near me that I was obliged to keep very close in my den. The hunters were somehow eluded; and not long afterwards Benny accidentally caught sight of Fanny in her mother's hut. He told his grandmother, who charged him never to speak of it, explaining to him the frightful consequences; and he never betrayed the trust. Aggie little dreamed that my grandmother knew where her daughter was concealed, and that the stooping form of her old neighbor was bending under a similar burden of anxiety and fear; but these dangerous secrets deepened the sympathy between the two old persecuted mothers.

My friend Fanny and I remained many weeks hidden within call of each other; but she was unconscious of the fact. I longed to have her share my den, which seemed a more secure retreat than her own; but I had brought so much trouble on my grandmother, that it seemed wrong to ask her to incur greater risks. My restlessness increased. I had lived too long in bodily pain and anguish of spirit. Always I was in dread that by some accident, or some contrivance, slavery would succeed in snatching my children from me. This thought drove me nearly frantic, and I determined to steer for the North Star[31] at all hazards. At this crisis, Providence opened an unexpected way for me to escape. My friend Peter came one evening, and asked to speak with me. "Your day has come, Linda," said he. "I have found a chance for you to go to the Free States. You have a fortnight to decide." The news seemed too good to be true; but Peter explained his arrangements, and told me all that was necessary was for me to say I would go. I was going to answer him with a joyful yes, when the thought of Benny came to my mind. I told him the temptation was exceedingly strong, but I was terribly afraid of Dr. Flint's alleged power over my child, and that I could not go and leave him behind. Peter remonstrated earnestly. He said such a good chance might never occur again; that Benny was free, and could be sent to me; and that for the sake of my children's welfare I ought not to hesitate a moment. I told him I would consult with uncle Phillip. My uncle rejoiced in the plan, and bade me to go by all means. He promised, if his life was spared, that he would either bring or send my son to me as soon as I reached a place of safety. I resolved to go, but thought nothing had better be said to my grandmother till very near the time of departure. But my uncle thought she would feel it more keenly if I left her so suddenly. "I will reason with her," said he, "and convince her how necessary it is, not only for your sake, but for hers also. You cannot be blind to the fact that she is sinking under her burdens." I was not blind to it. I knew that my concealment was an ever-present source of anxiety, and that the older she grew the more nervously fearful she was of discovery. My uncle talked with her, and finally succeeded in persuading her that it was absolutely necessary for me to seize the chance so unexpectedly offered.

31 Bright star in the Little Dipper constellation used by fugitive slaves as a navigational point when escaping to the North.

HARRIET JACOBS

The anticipation of being a free woman proved almost too much for my weak frame. The excitement stimulated me, and at the same time bewildered me. I made busy preparations for my journey, and for my son to follow me. I resolved to have an interview with him before I went, that I might give him cautions and advice, and tell him how anxiously I should be waiting for him at the north. Grandmother stole up to me as often as possible to whisper words of counsel. She insisted upon my writing to Dr. Flint, as soon as I arrived in the Free States, and asking him to sell me to her. She said she would sacrifice her house, and all she had in the world, for the sake of having me safe with my children in any part of the world. If she could only live to know *that* she could die in peace. I promised the dear old faithful friend that I would write to her as soon as I arrived, and put the letter in a safe way to reach her; but in my own mind I resolved that not another cent of her hard earnings should be spent to pay rapacious slaveholders for what they called their property. And even if I had not been unwilling to buy what I had already a right to possess, common humanity would have prevented me from accepting the generous offer, at the expense of turning my aged relative out of house and home, when she was trembling on the brink of the grave.

I was to escape in a vessel; but I forbear to mention any further particulars.

I made all my arrangements to go on board as soon as it was dusk. The intervening time I resolved to spend with my son. I had not spoken to him for seven years, though I had been under the same roof, and seen him every day, when I was well enough to sit at the loophole. I did not dare to venture beyond the storeroom; so they brought him there, and locked us up together, in a place concealed from the piazza door. It was an agitating interview for both of us. After we had talked and wept together for a little while, he said, "Mother, I'm glad you're going away. I wish I could go with you. I knew you was here; and I have been *so* afraid they would come and catch you!"

I was greatly surprised, and asked him how he had found it out.

He replied, "I was standing under the eaves, one day, before Ellen went away, and I heard somebody cough up over the wood shed. I don't know what made me think it was you, but I did think so. I missed Ellen, the night before she went away; and grandmother brought her back into the room in the night; and I thought maybe she'd been to see *you*, before she went, for I heard grandmother whisper to her, 'Now go to sleep; and remember never to tell.'"

I asked him if he ever mentioned his suspicions to his sister. He said he never did; but after he heard the cough, if he saw her playing with other children on that side of the house, he always tried to coax her round to the other side, for fear they would hear me cough, too. He said he had kept a close lookout for Dr. Flint, and if he saw him speak to a constable, or a patrol, he always told grandmother. I now recollected that I had seen him manifest uneasiness, when people were on that side of the house, and I had at the time been puzzled to conjecture a motive for his actions. Such prudence may seem extraordinary in a boy of twelve years, but slaves, being surrounded by mysteries, deceptions, and dangers, early learn to be suspicious and watchful, and prematurely cautious and cunning. He had never asked a question of grandmother, or uncle Phillip, and I had often heard him chime in with other children, when they spoke of my being at the north.

I told him I was now really going to the Free States, and if he was a good, honest boy, and a loving child to his dear old grandmother, the Lord would bless him, and bring him to me, and we and Ellen would live together. He began to tell me that grandmother had not eaten any thing all day. While he was speaking, the door was unlocked, and she came in with a small bag of money, which she wanted me to take. I begged her to keep a part of it, at least, to pay for Benny's being sent to the north; but she insisted, while her tears were falling fast, that I should take the whole. "You may be sick among strangers," she said, "and they would send you to the poorhouse to die." Ah, that good grandmother!

For the last time I went up to my nook. Its desolate appearance no longer chilled me, for the light of hope had risen in my soul. Yet, even with the blessed prospect of freedom before me, I felt very sad at leaving forever that old homestead, where I had been sheltered so long by the dear old grandmother; where I had dreamed my first young dream of love; and where, after that had faded away, my children came to twine themselves so closely round my desolate heart. As the hour approached for me to leave, I again descended to the storeroom. My grandmother and Benny were there. She took me by the hand, and said, "Linda, let us pray." We knelt down together, with my child pressed to my heart, and my other arm round the faithful, loving old friend I was about to leave forever. On no other occasion has it ever been my lot to listen to so fervent a supplication for mercy and protection. It thrilled through my heart, and inspired me with trust in God.

Peter was waiting for me in the street. I was soon by his side, faint in body, but strong of purpose. I did not look back upon the old place, though I felt that I should never see it again.

[Finding that Sands has not kept his promise to educate Ellen, Brent reclaims her daughter and sends her to school. Benny is sent north, Brent arranging for him to live with William in Boston. Brent lives for ten years as a fugitive slave, moving frequently and supporting herself as a nanny and seamstress for the Bruce family.]

XLI. *Free at Last* [32]

MRS. BRUCE,[33] and every member of her family, were exceedingly kind to me. I was thankful for the blessings of my lot, yet I could not always wear a cheerful countenance. I was doing harm to no one; on the contrary, I was doing all the good I could in my small way; yet I could never go out to breathe God's free air without trepidation at my heart. This seemed hard; and I could not think it was a right state of things in any civilized country.

From time to time I received news from my good old grandmother. She could not write; but she employed others to write for her. The following is an extract from one of her last letters:—

"Dear Daughter: I cannot hope to see you again on earth; but I pray to God to unite us above, where pain will no more rack this feeble body of mine; where sorrow and parting from my children will be no more.[34] God has promised these things if we are faithful unto the end. My age and feeble health deprive me of going to church now; but God is with me here at home. Thank your brother for his kindness. Give much love to him, and tell him to remember the Creator in the days of his youth,[35] and strive to meet me in the Father's kingdom. Love to Ellen and Benjamin. Don't neglect him.

32 The chapter title derives from the refrain of a spiritual: "Oh, free at last, free at last / I thank God, I'm free at last."

33 Cornelia Grinnell Willis (1825–1904), Jacobs's employer and the second wife of writer Nathaniel Parker Willis.

34 Compare Revelation 21:4: "And God shall wipe away all tears from their eyes; and there shall be no more death, neither sorrow, nor crying, neither shall there be any more pain: for the former things are passed away."

35 Ecclesiastes 12:1: "Remember now thy Creator in the days of thy youth, while the evil days come not, nor the years draw nigh, when though shalt say, I have no pleasure in them."

Tell him for me, to be a good boy. Strive, my child, to train them for God's children. May he protect and provide for you, is the prayer of your loving old mother."

These letters both cheered and saddened me. I was always glad to have tidings from the kind, faithful old friend of my unhappy youth; but her messages of love made my heart yearn to see her before she died, and I mourned over the fact that it was impossible. Some months after I returned from my flight to New England, I received a letter from her, in which she wrote, "Dr. Flint is dead.[36] He has left a distressed family. Poor old man! I hope he made his peace with God."

I remembered how he had defrauded my grandmother of the hard earnings she had loaned; how he had tried to cheat her out of the freedom her mistress had promised her, and how he had persecuted her children; and I thought to myself that she was a better Christian than I was, if she could entirely forgive him. I cannot say, with truth, that the news of my old master's death softened my feelings towards him. There are wrongs which even the grave does not bury. The man was odious to me while he lived, and his memory is odious now.

His departure from this world did not diminish my danger. He had threatened my grandmother that his heirs should hold me in slavery after he was gone; that I never should be free so long as a child of his survived. As for Mrs. Flint, I had seen her in deeper afflictions than I supposed the loss of her husband would be, for she had buried several children; yet I never saw any signs of softening in her heart. The doctor had died in embarrassed circumstances, and had little to will to his heirs, except such property as he was unable to grasp. I was well aware what I had to expect from the family of Flints; and my fears were confirmed by a letter from the south, warning me to be on my guard, because Mrs. Flint openly declared that her daughter could not afford to lose so valuable a slave as I was.

I kept close watch of the newspapers for arrivals; but one Saturday night, being much occupied, I forgot to examine the Evening Express as usual. I went down into the parlor for it, early in the morning, and found the boy about to kindle a fire with it. I took it from him and examined the list of arrivals. Reader, if you have never been a slave, you cannot imagine the acute sensation of suffering at my heart, when I read the names of Mr. and Mrs. Dodge,[37] at a hotel in Courtland Street. It was a third-rate hotel,

36 Dr. James Norcom died on November 9, 1850.

37 Jacobs's young mistress Mary Matilda Norcom Messmore and her husband Daniel Messmore.

and that circumstance convinced me of the truth of what I had heard, that they were short of funds and had need of my value, as *they* valued me; and that was by dollars and cents. I hastened with the paper to Mrs. Bruce. Her heart and hand were always open to every one in distress, and she always warmly sympathized with mine. It was impossible to tell how near the enemy was. He might have passed and repassed the house while we were sleeping. He might at that moment be waiting to pounce upon me if I ventured out of doors. I had never seen the husband of my young mistress, and therefore I could not distinguish him from any other stranger. A carriage was hastily ordered; and, closely veiled, I followed Mrs. Bruce, taking the baby again with me into exile.[38] After various turnings and crossings, and returnings, the carriage stopped at the house of one of Mrs. Bruce's friends, where I was kindly received. Mrs. Bruce returned immediately, to instruct the domestics what to say if any one came to inquire for me.

It was lucky for me that the evening paper was not burned up before I had a chance to examine the list of arrivals. It was not long after Mrs. Bruce's return to her house, before several people came to inquire for me. One inquired for me, another asked for my daughter Ellen, and another said he had a letter from my grandmother, which he was requested to deliver in person.

They were told, "She *has* lived here, but she has left."

"How long ago?"

"I don't know, sir."

"Do you know where she went?"

"I do not, sir." And the door was closed.

This Mr. Dodge, who claimed me as his property, was originally a Yankee pedler in the south; then he became a merchant, and finally a slaveholder. He managed to get introduced into what was called the first society, and married Miss Emily Flint. A quarrel arose between him and her brother, and the brother cowhided him. This led to a family feud, and he proposed to remove to Virginia. Dr. Flint left him no property, and his own means had become circumscribed, while a wife and children depended upon him for support. Under these circumstances, it was very natural that he should make an effort to put me into his pocket.

I had a colored friend, a man from my native place, in whom I had the

38 Jacobs previously evaded recapture by taking the baby, Lilian Willis (b. 1850), to visit Cornelia Grinnell Willis's family in New Bedford, Massachusetts.

most implicit confidence. I sent for him, and told him that Mr. and Mrs. Dodge had arrived in New York. I proposed that he should call upon them to make inquiries about his friends at the south, with whom Dr. Flint's family were well acquainted. He thought there was no impropriety in his doing so, and he consented. He went to the hotel, and knocked at the door of Mr. Dodge's room, which was opened by the gentleman himself, who gruffly inquired, "What brought you here? How came you to know I was in the city?"

"Your arrival was published in the evening papers, sir; and I called to ask Mrs. Dodge about my friends at home. I didn't suppose it would give any offence."

"Where's that negro girl, that belongs to my wife?"

"What girl, sir?"

"You know well enough. I mean Linda, that ran away from Dr. Flint's plantation, some years ago. I dare say you've seen her, and know where she is."

"Yes, sir, I've seen her, and know where she is. She is out of your reach, sir."

"Tell me where she is, or bring her to me, and I will give her a chance to buy her freedom."

"I don't think it would be of any use, sir. I have heard her say she would go to the ends of the earth, rather than pay any man or woman for her freedom, because she thinks she has a right to it. Besides, she couldn't do it, if she would, for she has spent her earnings to educate her children."

This made Mr. Dodge very angry, and some high words passed between them. My friend was afraid to come where I was; but in the course of the day I received a note from him. I supposed they had not come from the south, in the winter, for a pleasure excursion; and now the nature of their business was very plain.

Mrs. Bruce came to me and entreated me to leave the city the next morning. She said her house was watched, and it was possible that some clew to me might be obtained. I refused to take her advice. She pleaded with an earnest tenderness, that ought to have moved me; but I was in a bitter, disheartened mood. I was weary of flying from pillar to post. I had been chased during half my life, and it seemed as if the chase was never to end. There I sat, in that great city, guiltless of crime, yet not daring to worship God in any of the churches. I heard the bells ringing for afternoon service, and, with contemptuous sarcasm, I said, "Will the preachers take for their text, 'Proclaim liberty to the captive, and the opening of prison doors to them that are bound'?[39] or will they preach from the text, 'Do unto others as ye would they should do unto you'?"[40] Oppressed Poles and Hungarians could find a safe refuge in that city; John Mitchell[41] was free to proclaim in the City Hall his desire for "a plantation well stocked with slaves;" but there I sat, an oppressed American, not daring to show my face. God forgive the black and bitter thoughts I indulged on that Sabbath day! The Scripture says, "Oppression makes even a wise man mad;"[42] and I was not wise.

I had been told that Mr. Dodge said his wife had never signed away her right to my children, and if he could not get me, he would take them. This it was, more than any thing else, that roused such a tempest in my soul. Benjamin was with his uncle William in California, but my innocent young daughter had come to spend a vacation with me. I thought of what I had suffered in slavery at her age, and my heart was like a tiger's when a hunter tries to seize her young.

Dear Mrs. Bruce! I seem to see the expression of her face, as she turned away discouraged by my obstinate mood. Finding her expostulations[43] unavailing, she sent Ellen to entreat me. When ten o'clock in the evening arrived and Ellen had not returned, this watchful and unwearied friend became anxious. She came to us in a carriage, bringing a well-filled trunk for my journey—trusting that by this time I would listen to reason. I yielded to her, as I ought to have done before.

The next day, baby and I set out in a heavy snow storm, bound for New England again. I received letters from the City of Iniquity,[44] addressed to me under an assumed name. In a few days one came from Mrs. Bruce, informing me that my new master was still searching for me, and that she intended to put an end to this persecution by buying my freedom. I felt grateful for the kindness that prompted this offer, but the idea was not so pleasant to me as might have been expected. The more my mind had become enlightened, the more difficult it was for me to consider myself an article of property; and to pay money to those who had so grievously oppressed me seemed like taking from my sufferings the glory of triumph.

39 Isaiah 61:1.

40 Compare Matthew 7:12: "Therefore all things whatsoever ye would that men should do to you, do ye even so to them."

41 Jacobs refers to John Mitchel (1815–75), Irish nationalist and proslavery newspaper editor in New York.

42 Ecclesiastes 7:7.

43 Speech intended to dissuade.

44 Biblical epithet, referring here to New York City. Compare Habakkuk 2:12: "Woe to him that buildeth a town with blood, and stablisheth a city by iniquity."

I wrote to Mrs. Bruce, thanking her, but saying that being sold from one owner to another seemed too much like slavery; that such a great obligation could not be easily cancelled; and that I preferred to go to my brother in California.

Without my knowledge, Mrs. Bruce employed a gentleman in New York to enter into negotiations with Mr. Dodge. He proposed to pay three hundred dollars down, if Mr. Dodge would sell me, and enter into obligations to relinquish all claim to me or my children forever after. He who called himself my master said he scorned so small an offer for such a valuable servant. The gentleman replied, "You can do as you choose, sir. If you reject this offer you will never get any thing; for the woman has friends who will convey her and her children out of the country."

Mr. Dodge concluded that "half a loaf was better than no bread," and he agreed to the proffered terms. By the next mail I received this brief letter from Mrs. Bruce: "I am rejoiced to tell you that the money for your freedom has been paid to Mr. Dodge. Come home to-morrow. I long to see you and my sweet babe."

My brain reeled as I read these lines. A gentleman near me said, "It's true; I have seen the bill of sale." "The bill of sale!" Those words struck me like a blow. So I was *sold* at last! A human being *sold* in the free city of New York! The bill of sale is on record, and future generations will learn from it that women were articles of traffic in New York, late in the nineteenth century of the Christian religion. It may hereafter prove a useful document to antiquaries,[45] who are seeking to measure the progress of civilization in the United States. I well know the value of that bit of paper; but much as I love freedom, I do not like to look upon it. I am deeply grateful to the generous friend who procured it, but I despise the miscreant who demanded payment for what never rightfully belonged to him or his.

I had objected to having my freedom bought, yet I must confess that when it was done I felt as if a heavy load had been lifted from my weary shoulders. When I rode home in the cars I was no longer afraid to unveil my face and look at people as they passed. I should have been glad to have met Daniel Dodge himself; to have had him seen me and known me, that he might have mourned over the untoward circumstances which compelled him to sell me for three hundred dollars.

When I reached home, the arms of my benefactress were thrown

45 Those who study antique artifacts, especially texts.

round me, and our tears mingled. As soon as she could speak, she said, "O Linda, I'm so glad it's all over! You wrote to me as if you thought you were going to be transferred from one owner to another. But I did not buy you for your services. I should have done just the same, if you had been going to sail for California to-morrow. I should, at least, have the satisfaction of knowing that you left me a free woman."

My heart was exceedingly full. I remembered how my poor father had tried to buy me, when I was a small child, and how he had been disappointed. I hoped his spirit was rejoicing over me now. I remembered how my good old grandmother had laid up her earnings to purchase me in later years, and how often her plans had been frustrated. How that faithful, loving old heart would leap for joy, if she could look on me and my children now that we were free! My relatives had been foiled in all their efforts, but God had raised me up a friend among strangers, who had bestowed on me the precious, long-desired boon. Friend! It is a common word, often lightly used. Like other good and beautiful things, it may be tarnished by careless handling; but when I speak of Mrs. Bruce as my friend, the word is sacred.

My grandmother lived to rejoice in my freedom; but not long after, a letter came with a black seal. She had gone "where the wicked cease from troubling, and the weary are at rest."[46]

Time passed on, and a paper came to me from the south, containing an obituary notice of my uncle Phillip. It was the only case I ever knew of such an honor conferred upon a colored person. It was written by one of his friends, and contained these words: "Now that death has laid him low, they call him a good man and a useful citizen; but what are eulogies to the black man, when the world has faded from his vision? It does not require man's praise to obtain rest in God's kingdom." So they called a colored man a *citizen*! Strange words to be uttered in that region!

Reader, my story ends with freedom; not in the usual way, with marriage. I and my children are now free! We are as free from the power of slaveholders as are the white people of the north; and though that, according to my ideas, is not saying a great deal, it is a vast improvement in *my* condition. The dream of my life is not yet realized. I do not sit with my children in a home of my own. I still long for a hearthstone of my own, however humble. I wish it for my children's sake far more than for my own. But God so orders circumstances as to keep me with my friend Mrs.

46 Job 3:17.

Bruce. Love, duty, gratitude, also bind me to her side. It is a privilege to serve her who pities my oppressed people, and who has bestowed the inestimable boon of freedom on me and my children.

It has been painful to me, in many ways, to recall the dreary years I passed in bondage. I would gladly forget them if I could. Yet the retrospection is not altogether without solace; for with those gloomy recollections come tender memories of my good old grandmother, like light, fleecy clouds floating over a dark and troubled sea.

KIMBERLY GIBBS BURNETT

E. ARMISTEAD LEMON

Charles W. Chesnutt as a twenty-five-year-old teacher
at Fayetteville Colored Normal School
(Cleveland Public Library Special Collections Department, Cleveland, Ohio)

CHARLES WADDELL CHESNUTT was the first African American to receive critical recognition as a short story writer and novelist and was one of the most influential African American writers during the late nineteenth and early twentieth centuries. An aspiring writer from his early years in North Carolina, Chesnutt voiced his desire for literary recognition. He ultimately achieved this goal in the form of two collections of short stories and three novels, which he published between 1899 and 1905. Though his career as a full-time author was relatively short, he was rarely without pen in hand during his lifetime. His personal journals, letters, critical essays, and speeches all testify to his keen interest in the pre– and post–Civil War social and political situation of African Americans in the United States and the South in particular. In 1928, Chesnutt was awarded the Spingarn Medal from the National Association for the Advancement of Colored People for devoting his literary career to advocating the human rights of African Americans. Though his fiction waned in popularity upon his death, a revival of critical interest in Chesnutt in recent decades celebrates him as a pioneer in the African American short story tradition and one of North Carolina's literary lights.

Born on June 20, 1858, in Cleveland, Ohio, to Anna Maria Sampson and Andrew Jackson Chesnutt, both free African Americans of mixed-race heritage, Chesnutt returned with his parents to their hometown of Fayetteville, North Carolina, after the fall of the Confederacy. By his late teens he was advanced in his studies enough to be appointed assistant principal of the Fayetteville Colored Normal School (now Fayetteville State University). Chesnutt married Susan Perry in 1878 but was hesitant to settle his new family in a South that offered restricted social and economic opportunities for blacks. Although he was frustrated by the lack of intellectual companionship he found in the South, his personal experiences with southern folklore and racial prejudice would be a major influence on Chesnutt's writing throughout his life.

In 1884, Chesnutt moved his family to Cleveland, where he began a successful legal stenography business. In 1887, he passed the Ohio state bar and published his first work of fiction in the *Atlantic Monthly*. "The Goophered Grapevine," a dialect story written in the southern local-color tradition, was soon followed by the publication of two more stories in this vein, all incorporating instances of conjure, an African American form of witchcraft practiced during slavery times. When Chesnutt lobbied the prestigious Boston publishing firm Houghton Mifflin to publish a volume of his short stories, his editor, Walter Hines Page, suggested that his conjure tales might make a successful collection. Upon Chesnutt's rapid completion of additional conjure tales to round out the book, *The Conjure Woman* was published in 1899 to an approving national audience. Each tale revolves around a white northern couple settling on a plantation in the postwar South and their friend and employee Uncle Julius McAdoo, an ex-slave who spins tales about life on the plantation before the war. Julius's tales highlight the subversive ways by which blacks had learned to manipulate and even overturn the oppressive conditions of slavery and illustrate the storyteller's own ability to gain the upper hand over his often naive and uninitiated northern employers.

After the success of *The Conjure Woman*, Chesnutt eagerly pushed for the publication of another volume of stories. He hoped to gain acclaim as more than a local-color and dialect writer by using his growing popularity to confront contemporary racial issues. His second collection of short stories, *The Wife of His Youth and Other Stories of the Color Line*, published in December of 1899, prompted Chesnutt to close his stenography business to pursue a literary career full time. These stories signify a departure from *The Conjure Woman*, for Chesnutt drops dialect and conjure altogether, adopting a more serious tone as he explores the failure of Reconstruction and the lives of blacks who had migrated north in search of equality and economic opportunity. However, as Chesnutt depicts in such stories as "The Wife of His Youth" and "The Web of Circumstance," rather than a promised land in the North, African Americans often found racial prejudice awaiting them. This prejudice manifested itself many times within their own communities, as light-skinned blacks often considered themselves socially superior to dark-skinned blacks. Moreover, for those who remained in the South, as Chesnutt demonstrates in stories such as "The Sheriff's Children," the promises of Reconstruction and racial reconciliation were far from being realized, as whites and blacks struggled with the emotional and psychological repercussions of slavery.

Chesnutt also addressed pressing social concerns in his nonfictional works. In 1889, he published a provocative essay in the *Independent*, a national journal of public affairs, titled "What Is a White Man?" in which he offers a comparative study of the many conflicting definitions of the color line that existed on law books throughout the United States, ultimately exposing the hypocrisy of any attempt to make absolute determinations of whiteness.

In 1900, Chesnutt realized his dream of becoming a novelist when Houghton Mifflin published *The House Behind the Cedars*, which probes the emotional and ethical dilemmas of passing for white, as well as the social conflicts caused by the racial caste system. Chesnutt published his second and more ambitious novel, *The Marrow of Tradition* (1901), only a year later. Based on a white supremacist takeover of Wilmington, North Carolina, in 1898, this novel focuses on mixed-race families, corrupt southern politics, and mob violence in the post-Reconstruction South to investigate the legacy of southern racial prejudices. Though widely reviewed, *The Marrow of Tradition* did not achieve the popular success Chesnutt hoped for. By the time his third novel, *The Colonel's Dream*, appeared in 1905, Chesnutt's reputation as a prominent literary figure had begun to wane. He continued to write, though rarely reaching a national audience, while resuming his career as a full-time legal stenographer. Chesnutt died on November 15, 1932, at the age of seventy-four.

Today scholars continue to find Chesnutt's writing valuable for its perceptive analysis of social prejudice based on racial identity during the late nineteenth and early twentieth centuries. His influence manifests itself in the writing of later twentieth-century African American writers such as James Weldon Johnson and Nella Larsen, who confronted the issues of passing and the color line that Chesnutt first examined with compelling insight decades earlier.

Suggested Readings

Andrews, William L. *The Literary Career of Charles W. Chesnutt*. Baton Rouge: Louisiana State University Press, 1980. [A foundational study of the development of Chesnutt's literary career.]

Brodhead, Richard H., ed. *The Journals of Charles W. Chesnutt*. Durham: Duke University Press, 1993. [An annotated edition of the author's personal journals written between 1874 and 1882.]

Chesnutt, Charles W. *Charles W. Chesnutt: Stories, Novels and Essays*. Edited by Werner Sollors. New York: The Library of America, 2002. [The most complete one-volume collection of Chesnutt's most important fictional and nonfictional works.]

——. *Conjure Tales and Stories of the Color Line*. Edited by William L. Andrews. New York: Penguin Books, 2000. [A handy edition of Chesnutt's best short fiction.]

Chesnutt, Helen M. *Charles Waddell Chesnutt: Pioneer of the Color Line*. Chapel Hill: University Press of North Carolina, 1989. [Written by his oldest daughter, this biography is a tribute to Chesnutt's life and literary career.]

Keller, Frances Richardson. *An American Crusade: The Life of Charles Waddell Chesnutt*. Provo, Utah: Brigham Young University Press, 1978. [The most recent critical biography of Charles W. Chesnutt.]

McElrath, Joseph R., et al, eds. *Charles W. Chesnutt: Essays and Speeches*. Stanford, Calif.: Stanford University Press, 1999.

———, ed. *Critical Essays on Charles W. Chesnutt*. New York: G. K. Hall and Co., 1999.

McWilliams, Dean. *Charles W. Chesnutt and the Fictions of Race*. Athens and London: University of Georgia Press, 2002. [A study of the language variations within Chesnutt's fiction and nonfiction as a means of situating him within the modernist literary tradition.]

Sundquist, Eric J. *To Wake the Nations: Race in the Making of American Literature*. Cambridge: Harvard University Press, 1993. [Includes a compelling estimate of Chesnutt's contribution to American literature concerning the color line.]

Note on the Text

"Po' Sandy" was first published in the *Atlantic Monthly* in May 1888 and later included in *The Conjure Woman* (Boston: Houghton Mifflin, 1899). The text of "Po' Sandy" selected for this volume reprints the version of "Po' Sandy" in *The Conjure Woman*. "The Sheriff's Children" was originally published in the New York *Independent* on November 7, 1889, and later reprinted in Chesnutt's second short story collection, *The Wife of His Youth and Other Stories of the Color Line* (Boston: Houghton Mifflin, 1899). The text of "The Sheriff's Children" selected for this volume reprints the version in *The Wife of His Youth*. The text of "What Is a White Man?" is reprinted from its original publication in the New York *Independent* of May 30, 1889. The selected entries from Chesnutt's journals that appear in this anthology have been excerpted from Brodhead, ed., *Journals of Charles W. Chesnutt*.

The Howard School in Fayetteville,
where Charles Chesnutt attended as a child
*(Cleveland Public Library Special Collections Department,
Cleveland, Ohio)*

Charles W. Chesnutt as a forty-year-old author
(North Carolina Collection, Wilson Library,
University of North Carolina at Chapel Hill)

PO' SANDY

On the northeast corner of my vineyard in central North Carolina, and fronting on the Lumberton plank-road,[1] there stood a small frame house, of the simplest construction. It was built of pine lumber, and contained but one room, to which one window gave light and one door admission. Its weather-beaten sides revealed a virgin innocence of paint. Against one end of the house, and occupying half its width, there stood a huge brick chimney: the crumbling mortar had left large cracks between the bricks; the bricks themselves had begun to scale off in large flakes, leaving the chimney sprinkled with unsightly blotches. These evidences of decay were but partially concealed by a creeping vine, which extended its slender branches hither and thither in an ambitious but futile attempt to cover the whole chimney. The wooden shutter, which had once protected the unglazed window, had fallen from its hinges, and lay rotting in the rank grass and jimson-weeds beneath. This building, I learned when I bought the place, had been used as a schoolhouse for several years prior to the breaking out of the war, since which time it had remained unoccupied, save when some stray cow or vagrant hog had sought shelter within its walls from the chill rains and nipping winds of winter.

One day my wife requested me to build her a new kitchen. The house erected by us, when we first came to live upon the vineyard, contained a very conveniently arranged kitchen; but for some occult reason my wife wanted a kitchen in the back yard, apart from the dwelling-house, after the usual Southern fashion. Of course I had to build it.

To save expense, I decided to tear down the old schoolhouse, and use the lumber, which was in a good state of preservation, in the construction of the new kitchen. Before demolishing the old house, however, I made an estimate of the amount of material contained in it, and found that I would have to buy several hundred feet of lumber additional, in order to build the new kitchen according to my wife's plan.

One morning old Julius McAdoo, our colored coachman, harnessed the gray mare to the rockaway, and drove my wife and me over to the sawmill from which I meant to order the new lumber. We drove down the long lane which led from our house to the plank-road; following the

---

1 Plank-road: a road constructed of boards.

plank-road for about a mile, we turned into a road running through the forest and across the swamp to the sawmill beyond. Our carriage jolted over the half-rotted corduroy road which traversed the swamp, and then climbed the long hill leading to the sawmill. When we reached the mill, the foreman had gone over to a neighboring farmhouse, probably to smoke or gossip, and we were compelled to await his return before we could transact our business. We remained seated in the carriage, a few rods from the mill, and watched the leisurely movements of the mill-hands. We had not waited long before a huge pine log was placed in position, the machinery of the mill was set in motion, and the circular saw began to eat its way through the log, with a loud whir which resounded throughout the vicinity of the mill. The sound rose and fell in a sort of rhythmic cadence, which, heard from where we sat, was not unpleasing, and not loud enough to prevent conversation. When the saw started on its second journey through the log, Julius observed, in a lugubrious tone, and with a perceptible shudder:—

"Ugh! but dat des do cuddle my blood!"

"What's the matter, Uncle Julius?" inquired my wife, who is of a very sympathetic turn of mind. "Does the noise affect your nerves?"

"No, Mis' Annie," replied the old man, with emotion, "I ain' narvous; but dat saw, a-cuttin' en grindin' thoo dat stick er timber, en moanin', en groanin,' en sweekin', kyars[2] my 'memb'ance back ter ole times, en' min's me er po' Sandy." The pathetic intonation with which he lengthened out the "po' Sandy" touched a responsive chord in our own hearts.

"And who was poor Sandy?" asked my wife, who takes a deep interest in the stories of plantation life which she hears from the lips of the older colored people. Some of these stories are quaintly humorous; others wildly extravagant, revealing the Oriental cast of the negro's imagination; while others, poured freely into the sympathetic ear of a Northern-bred woman, disclose many a tragic incident of the darker side of slavery.

"Sandy," said Julius in reply to my wife's question, "was a nigger w'at useter b'long ter ole Mars Marrabo McSwayne. Mars Marrabo's place wuz on de yuther side'n de swamp, right nex' ter yo place. Sandy wuz a monst'us good nigger, en could do so many things erbout a plantation, en alluz 'ten' ter his wuk so well, dat w'en Mars Marrabo's chilluns growed up en married off, dey all un 'em wanted dey daddy fer ter gin 'em[3] Sandy fer a weddin' present. But Mars Marrabo knowed de res' wouldn' be satisfied ef he gin Sandy ter a'er one[4] un 'em; so w'en dey wuz all done

2 Kyars: carries.   4 A'er one: either one, any one.
3 Gin 'em: give them.

married, he fix it by 'lowin' one er his chilluns ter take Sandy fer a mont'
er so, en den ernudder for a mont' er so, en so on dat erway tel dey had
all had 'im de same lenk er time; en den dey would all take him roun'
ag'in, 'cep'n' oncet[5] in a w'ile w'en Mars Marrabo would len' 'im ter some
er his yuther kinfolks 'roun' de country, w'en dey wuz short er han's; tel
bimeby[6] it got so Sandy didn' hardly knowed whar he wuz gwine[7] ter stay
fum one week's een' ter de yuther.

"One time w'en Sandy wuz lent out ez yushal, a spekilater[8] come erlong wid a lot er niggers, en Mars Marrabo swap' Sandy's wife off fer a
noo 'oman. W'en Sandy come back, Mars Marrabo gin 'im a dollar, en
'lowed he wuz monst'us sorry fer ter break up de fambly, but de spekilater
had gin 'im big boot,[9] en times wuz hard en money skase,[10] en so he wuz
bleedst[11] ter make de trade. Sandy tuk on some 'bout losin' his wife, but
he soon seed dey want no use cryin' ober spilt merlasses; en bein' ez he
lacked de looks er de noo 'oman, he tuk up wid her atter she'd be'n on de
plantation a mont' er so.

"Sandy en his noo wife got on mighty well tergedder, en de niggers all
'mence' ter talk about how lovin' dey wuz. W'en Tenie wuz tuk sick oncet,
Sandy useter set up all night wid 'er, en den go ter wuk in de mawnin' des
lack he had his reg'lar sleep; en Tenie would 'a' done anythin' in de worl'
for her Sandy.

"Sandy en Tenie hadn' be'n libbin' tergedder fer mo' d'n two mont's
befo' Mars Marrabo's old uncle, w'at libbed down in Robeson County,[12]
sent up ter fin' out ef Mars Marrabo couldn' len' 'im er hire 'im a good
han' fer a mont' er so. Sandy's marster wuz one er dese yer easy-gwine
folks w'at wanter please eve'ybody, en he says yas, he could len' 'im Sandy.
En Mars Marrabo tol' Sandy fer ter git ready ter go down ter Robeson
nex' day, fer ter stay a mont' er so.

"It wuz monst'us hard on Sandy fer ter take 'im 'way fum Tenie. It
wuz so fur down ter Robeson dat he didn' hab no chance er comin' back
ter see her tel de time wuz up; he wouldn' 'a' minc comin' ten er fifteen
mile at night ter see Tenie, but Mars Marrabo's uncle's plantation wuz
mo' d'n forty mile off. Sandy wuz mighty sad en cas' down atter w'at
Mars Marrabo tol' 'im, en he says ter Tenie, sezee:—

5 'Cep'n' oncet: except once.
6 Bimeby: by and by.
7 Gwine: going.
8 Spekilator: speculator.
9 Boot: money.
10 Skase: scarce.

11 Bleedst: obliged.
12 Robeson County: The county seat
first founded in 1787, located in
the southeastern section of North
Carolina.

"'I'm gittin' monst'us ti'ed er dish yer gwine roun' so much. Here I is lent ter Mars Jeems dis mont', en I got ter do so-en-so; en ter Mars Archie de nex' mont', en I got ter do so-en-so; den I got ter go ter Miss Jinnie's: en hit's Sandy dis en Sandy dat, en Sandy yer en Sandy dere, tel it 'pears ter me I ain' got no home, ner no marster, ner no mistiss, ner no nuffin. I can't eben keep a wife: my yuther ole 'oman wuz sol' away widout my gittin' a chance fer ter tell her good-by; en now I got ter go off en leab you, Tenie, en I dunno whe'r I'm eber gwine ter see you ag'in er no I wisht I wuz a tree, er a stump, er a rock, er sump'n w'at could stay on de plantation fer a w'ile.'

"Atter Sandy got thoo talkin', Tenie didn' say naer word, but des sot dere[13] by de fier, studyin' en studyin'. Bimeby she up'n' says:—

"'Sandy, is I eber tol' you I wuz a cunjuh 'oman?'[14]

"Co'se Sandy hadn' nebber dremp' er nuffin lack dat, en he made a great 'miration[15] w'en he hear w'at Tenie say. Bimeby Tenie went on:—

"'I ain' goophered nobody, ner done no cunjuh wuk, fer fifteen year er mo'; en w'en I got religion I made up my mine I wouldn' wuk no mo' goopher.[16] But dey is some things I doan b'lieve it's no sin fer ter do; en ef you doan wanter be sent roun' fum pillar ter pos', en ef you doan wanter go down ter Robeson, I kin fix things so you won't haf ter. Ef you'll des say de word, I kin turn you ter w'ateber you wanter be, en you kin stay right whar you wanter, ez long ez you mineter.'[17]

"Sandy say he dean keer; he's willin' fer ter do anythin' fer ter stay close ter Tenie. Den Tenie ax 'im ef he doan wanter be turnt inter a rabbit.

"Sandy say, 'No, de dogs mought git atter me.'

"'Shill I turn you ter a wolf?' sez Tenie.

"'No, eve'ybody's skeered er a wolf, en I doan want nobody ter be skeered er me.'

"'Shill I turn you ter a mawkin'bird?'

"'No, a hawk mought ketch me. I wanter be turnt inter sump'n w'at'll stay in one place.'

"'I kin turn you ter a tree,' sez Tenie. 'You won't hate no mouf ner years, but I kin turn you back oncet in a w'ile, so you kin git sump'n ter eat, en hear w'at's gwine on.'

"Well, Sandy say dat'll do. En so Tenie tuk 'im down by de aidge er

13 Des sot dere: just sat there.
14 Cunjuh 'oman: a practitioner of African American witchcraft or hoodoo.
15 Great 'miration: excitement, to-do.

16 Goopher: a magic spell of African origin.
17 Mineter: mind to.

de swamp, not fur fum de quarters, en turnt 'im inter a big pine-tree, en sot[18] 'im out 'mongs' some yuther trees. En de nex' mawnin', ez some er de fiel' han's wuz gwine long dere, dey seed a tree w'at dey didn' 'member er habbin' seed befo'; it wuz monst'us quare,[19] en dey wuz bleedst ter 'low dat dey hadn' 'membered right, er e'se one er de saplin's had be'n growin' monst'us fas'.

"W'en Mars Marrabo 'skiver' dat Sandy wuz gone, he 'lowed Sandy had runned away. He got de dogs out, but de last place dey could track Sandy ter wuz de foot er dat pine-tree. En dere de dogs stood en barked, en bayed, en pawed at de tree, en tried ter climb up on it; en w'en dey wuz tuk roun' thoo de swamp ter look fer de scent, dey broke loose en made fer dat tree ag'in. It wuz de beatenis' thing de w'ite folks eber hearn of, en Mars Marrabo 'lowed dat Sandy must 'a' clim' up on de tree en jump' off on a mule er sump'n, en rid fur ernuff fer ter spile[20] de scent. Mars Marrabo wanted ter 'cuse some er de yuther niggers er heppin' Sandy off, but dey all 'nied it ter de las'; en eve'ybody knowed Tenie sot too much sto' by Sandy fer ter he'p 'im run away whar she couldn' nebber see 'im no mo'.

"W'en Sandy had be'n gone long ernuff fer folks ter think he done got clean away, Tenie useter go down ter de woods at night en turn 'im back, en den dey'd slip up ter de cabin en set by de fire en talk. But dey ha' ter be monst'us keerful, er e'se somebody would 'a' seed 'em, en dat would 'a' spile' de whole thing; so Tenie alluz turns Sandy back in de mawnin' early, befo' anybody wuz a-stirrin'.

"But Sandy didn' git erlong widout his trials en tribberlations. One day a woodpecker come erlong en 'mence' ter peck at de tree; en de nex' time Sandy wuz turns back he had a little roun' hole in his arm, des lack a sharp stick be'n stuck in it. Atter dat Tenie sot a sparrer-hawk fer ter watch de tree; en w'en de woodpecker come erlong nex' mawnin' fer ter finish his nes', he got gobble' up mos'' fo' he stuck his bill in de bark.

"Nudder time, Mars Marrabo sent a nigger out in de woods fer ter chop tuppentime boxes.[21] De man chop a box in dish yer tree, en hack' de bark up two er th'ee feet, fer ter let de tuppentime run. De nex' time Sandy wuz turnt back he had a big skyar on his lef' leg, des lack it be'n skunt;[22] en it tuk Tenie nigh 'bout all night fer ter fix a mixtry ter kyo[23] it up. Atter dat, Tenie sot a hawnet for ter watch de tree; en w'en de nigger

18 Sot: set.
19 Quare: queer, strange.
20 Spile: spoil.

21 Tuppentime boxes: cavities dug into trees to collect sap.
22 Skunt: skinned.
23 Kyo: cure.

come back ag'in fer ter cut ernudder box on de yuther side'n de tree, de hawnet stung 'im so hard dat de ax slip en cut his foot nigh 'bout off.

"W'en Tenie see so many things happenin' ter de tree, she 'cluded she'd ha' ter turn Sandy ter sump'n e'se; en atter studyin' de matter ober, en talkin' wid Sandy one ebenin', she made up her mine fer ter fix up a goopher mixtry w'at would turn herse'f en Sandy ter foxes, er sump'n, so dey could run away en go some'rs whar dey could be free en lib lack w'ite folks.

"But dey ain' no tellin' w'at's gwine ter happen in dis worl'. Tenie had got de night sot fer her en Sandy ter run away, w'en dat ve'y day one er Mars Marrabo's sons rid up ter de big house in his buggy, en say his wife wuz monst'us sick, en he want his mammy ter len' 'im a 'oman fer ter nuss his wife. Tenie's mistiss say sen' Tenie; she wuz a good nuss. Young mars wuz in a tarrible hurry fer ter git back home. Tenie wuz washin' at de big house dat day, en her mistiss say she should go right 'long wid her young marster. Tenie tried ter make some 'scuse fer ter git away en hide 'tel night, w'en she would have eve'ything fix' up fer her en Sandy; she say she wanter go ter her cabin fer ter git her bonnet. Her mistiss say it doan matter 'bout de bonnet; her head-hankcher wuz good ernuff. Den Tenie say she wanter git her bes' frock; her mistiss say no, she doan need no mo' frock, en w'en dat one got dirty she could git a clean one whar she wuz gwine. So Tenie had ter git in de buggy en go 'long wid young Mars Dunkin ter his plantation, w'ich wuz mo' d'n twenty mile away; en dey wa'n't no chance er her seein' Sandy no mo' 'tel she come back home. De po' gal felt monst'us bad 'bout de way things wuz gwine on, en she knowed Sandy mus' be a wond'rin' why she didn' come en turn 'im back no mo'.

"W'iles Tenie wuz away nussin' young Mars Dunkin's wife, Mars Marrabo tuk a notion fer ter buil' 'im a noo kitchen; en bein' ez he had lots er timber on his place, he begun ter look 'roun' fer a tree ter hab de lumber sawed out'n. En I dunno how it come to be so, but he happen fer ter hit on de ve'y tree w'at Sandy wuz turns inter. Tenie wuz gone, en dey wa'n't nobody ner nuffin fer ter watch de tree.

"De two men w'at cut de tree down say dey nebber had sech a time wid a tree befo': dey axes would glansh off, en didn' 'pear ter make no progress thoo de wood; en of all de creakin', en shakin', en wobblin' you eber see, dat tree done it w'en it commence' ter fall. It wuz de beatenis' thing!

"W'en dey got de tree all trim' up, dey chain it up ter a timber waggin, en start fer de sawmill. But dey had a hard time gittin' de log dere:

fus' dey got stuck in de mud w'en dey wuz gwine crosst de swamp, en it wuz two er th'ee hours befo' dey could git out. W'en dey start' on ag'in, de chain kep' a-comin' loose, en dey had ter keep a-stoppin' en a-stoppin' fer ter hitch de log up ag'in. W'en dey commence' ter climb de hill ter de sawmill, de log broke loose, en roll down de hill en in 'mongs' de trees, en hit tuk nigh 'bout half a day mo' ter git it haul' up ter de sawmill.

"De nex' mawnin' atter de day de tree wuz haul' ter de sawmill, Tenie come home. W'en she got back ter her cabin, de fus' thing she done wuz ter run down ter de woods en see how Sandy wuz gittin' on. W'en she seed de stump standin' dere, wid de sap runnin' out'n it, en de limbs layin' scattered roun', she nigh 'bout went out'n her min'. She run ter her cabin, en got her goopher mixtry, en den follered de track er de timber waggin ter de sawmill. She knowed Sandy couldn' lib mo' d'n a minute er so ef she turns him back, fer he wuz all chop' up so he 'd 'a' be'n bleedst ter die. But she wanted ter turn 'im back long ernuff fer ter 'splain ter 'im dat she hadn' went off a-purpose, en lef' 'im ter be chop' down en sawed up. She didn' want Sandy ter die wid no hard feelin's to'ds her.

"De han's at de sawmill had des got de big log on de kerridge, en wuz startin' up de saw, w'en dey seed a 'oman runnin' up de hill, all out er bref, cryin' en gwine on des lack she wuz plumb 'stracted. It wuz Tenie; she come right inter de mill, en th'owed herse'f on de log, right in front er de saw, a-hollerin' en cryin' ter her Sandy ter fergib her, en not ter think hard er her, fer it wa'n't no fault er hern. Den Tenie 'membered de tree didn' hab no years, en she wuz gittin' ready fer ter wuk her goopher mixtry so ez ter turn Sandy back, w'en de mill-hands kotch holt[24] er her en tied her arms wid a rope, en fasten' her to one er de posts in de sawmill; en den dey started de saw up ag'in, en cut de log up inter bo'ds en scantlin's[25] right befo' her eyes. But it wuz mighty hard wuk; fer of all de sweekin', en moanin', en groanin', dat log done it w'iles de saw wuz a-cuttin' thoo it. De saw wuz one er dese yer ole-timey, up-en-down saws, en hit tuk longer dem days ter saw a log 'en it do now. Dey greased de saw, but dat didn' stop de fuss; hit kep' right on, tel fin'ly dey got de log all sawed up.

"W'en de oberseah w'at run de sawmill come fum breakfas', de han's up en tell him 'bout de crazy 'oman—ez dey s'posed she wuz—w'at had come runnin' in de sawmill, a-hollerin' en gwine on, en tried ter th'ow herse'f befo' de saw. En de oberseah sent two er th'ee er de han's fer ter take Tenie back ter her marster's plantation.

24 Kotch holt: caught hold.
25 Scantlin's: a timber beam of small cross-section, especially one less than five inches square.

"Tenie 'peared ter be out'n her min' fer a long time, en her marster ha' ter lock her up in de smoke-'ouse 'tel she got ober her spells. Mars Marrabo wuz monst'us mad, en hit would 'a' made yo' flesh crawl fer ter hear him cuss, 'caze he say de spekilater w'at he got Tenie fum had fooled 'im by wukkin' a crazy 'oman off on him. W'iles Tenie wuz lock up in de smoke-'ouse, Mars Marrabo tuk 'n' haul de lumber fum de sawmill, en put up his noo kitchen.

"W'en Tenie got quiet' down, so she could be 'lowed ter go 'roun' de plantation, she up'n 'tole her marster all erbout Sandy en de pine-tree; en w'en Mars Marrabo hearn it, he 'lowed she wuz de wuss 'stracted nigger he eber hearn of. He didn' know w'at ter do wid Tenie: fus' he thought he'd put her in de po'house; but fin'ly, seein' ez she didn' do no harm ter nobody ner nuffin, but des went 'roun' moanin', en groanin', en shakin' her head, he 'cluded ter let her stay on de plantation en nuss de little nigger chilluns w'en dey mammies wuz ter wuk in de cotton-fiel'.

"De noo kitchen Mars Marrabo buil' wuz n' much use, fer it hadn' be'n put up long befo' de niggers 'mence' ter notice quare things erbout it. Dey could hear sump'n moanin' en groanin' 'bout de kitchen in de night-time, en w'en de win' would blow dey could hear sump'n a-hollerin' en sweekin' lack it wuz in great pain en sufferin'. En it got so atter a w'ile dat it wuz all Mars Marrabo's wife could do ter git a 'oman ter stay in de kitchen in de daytime long ernuff ter do de cookin'; en dey wa'n't naer[26] nigger on de plantation w'at wouldn' rudder take forty dan[27] ter go 'bout dat kitchen after dark,—dat is, 'cep'n' Tenie; she didn' 'pear ter min' de ha'nts.[28] She useter slip 'roun' at night, en set on de kitchen steps, en lean up agin de do'jamb, en run on ter herse'f wid some kine er foolishness w'at nobody couldn' make out; for Mars Marrabo had th'eaten' ter sen' her off'n de plantation ef she say anythin ter any er de yuther niggers 'bout de pine-tree. But somehow er 'rudder de niggers foun' out all erbout it, en dey all knowed de kitchen wuz ha'nted by Sandy's sperrit. En bimeby hit got so Mars Marrabo's wife herse'f wuz skeered ter go out in de yard after dark.

"W'en it come ter dat, Mars Marrabo tuk en to' de kitchen down, en use' de lumber fer ter buil' dat ole school'ouse w'at you er talkie' 'bout pullin' down. De school'ouse wuz n' use' 'cep'n' in de daytime, en on dark nights folks gwine long de road would hear quare soun's en see quare things. Po' ole Tenie useter go down dere at night, en wander 'roun' de

---

26 Naer: narry; not one.

27 Take forty dan: take forty lashes or strikes as from a whip than.

28 Ha'nts: haunts or ghosts.

school'ouse; en de niggers all 'lowed she went fer ter talk wid Sandy's sperrit. En one winter mawnin', w'en one er de boys went ter school early fer ter start de fire, w'at should he fin' but po' ole Tenie, layin' on de flo', stiff, en col', en dead. Dere didn' 'pear ter be nuffin pertickler de matter wid her,—she had des grieve' herse'f ter def fer her Sandy. Mars Marrabo did'n shed no tears. He thought Tenie wuz crazy, en dey wa'n't no tellin' w'at she mought do nex'; en dey ain' much room in dis worl' fer crazy w'ite folks, let 'lone a crazy nigger.

"Hit wa'n't long atter dat befo' Mars Marrabo sol' a piece er his track er lan' ter Mars Dugal' McAdoo,—*my* ole marster,—en dat's how de ole school'ouse happen to be on yo' place. W'en de wah broke out, de school stop', en de ole school'ouse be'n stannin' empty ever sence,—dat is, 'cep'n' fer de ha'nts. En folks sez dat de ole school'ouse, er any yuther house w'at got any er dat lumber in it w'at wuz sawed out'n de tree w'at Sandy wuz turnt inter, is gwine ter be ha'nted tel de las' piece er plank is rotted en crumble' inter dus'."

Annie had listened to this gruesome narrative with strained attention.

"What a system it was," she exclaimed, when Julius had finished, "under which such things were possible!"

"What things?" I asked, in amazement. "Are you seriously considering the possibility of a man's being turned into a tree?"

"Oh, no," she replied quickly, "not that;" and then she murmured absently, and with a dim look in her fine eyes, "Poor Tenie!"

We ordered the lumber, and returned home. That night, after we had gone to bed, and my wife had to all appearances been sound asleep for half an hour, she startled me out of an incipient doze by exclaiming suddenly,—

"John, I don't believe I want my new kitchen built out of the lumber in that old schoolhouse."

"You wouldn't for a moment allow yourself," I replied, with some asperity, "to be influenced by that absurdly impossible yarn which Julius was spinning to-day?"

"I know the story is absurd," she replied dreamily, "and I am not so silly as to believe it. But I don't think I should ever be able to take any pleasure in that kitchen if it were built out of that lumber. Besides, I think the kitchen would look better and last longer if the lumber were all new."

Of course she had her way. I bought the new lumber, though not without grumbling. A week or two later I was called away from home on business. On my return, after an absence of several days, my wife remarked to me,—

"John, there has been a split in the Sandy Run Colored Baptist Church, on the temperance question. About half the members have come out from the main body, and set up for themselves. Uncle Julius is one of the seceders, and he came to me yesterday and asked if they might not hold their meetings in the old schoolhouse for the present."

"I hope you didn't let the old rascal have it," I returned, with some warmth. I had just received a bill for the new lumber I had bought.

"Well," she replied, "I couldn't refuse him the use of the house for so good a purpose."

"And I'll venture to say," I continued, "that you subscribed something toward the support of the new church?"

She did not attempt to deny it.

"What are they going to do about the ghost?" I asked, somewhat curious to know how Julius would get around this obstacle.

"Oh," replied Annie, "Uncle Julius says that ghosts never disturb religious worship, but that if Sandy's spirit *should* happen to stray into meeting by mistake, no doubt the preaching would do it good."

THE SHERIFF'S CHILDREN

Branson County, North Carolina,[29] is in a sequestered district of one of the staidest and most conservative States of the Union. Society in Branson County is almost primitive in its simplicity. Most of the white people own the farms they till, and even before the war there were no very wealthy families to force their neighbors, by comparison, into the category of "poor whites."

To Branson County, as to most rural communities in the South, the war is the one historical event that overshadows all others. It is the era from which all local chronicles are dated,—births, deaths, marriages, storms, freshets.[30] No description of the life of any Southern community would be perfect that failed to emphasize the all pervading influence of the great conflict.

Yet the fierce tide of war that had rushed through the cities and along the great highways of the country had comparatively speaking but slightly disturbed the sluggish current of life in this region, remote from railroads and navigable streams. To the north in Virginia, to the west in Tennessee, and all along the seaboard the war had raged; but the thunder of its cannon had not disturbed the echoes of Branson County, where the loudest sounds heard were the crack of some hunter's rifle, the baying of some deep-mouthed hound, or the yodel of some tuneful negro on his way through the pine forest. To the east, Sherman's army had passed on its march to the sea; but no straggling band of "bummers"[31] had penetrated the confines of Branson County. The war, it is true, had robbed the county of the flower of its young manhood; but the burden of taxation, the doubt and uncertainty of the conflict, and the sting of ultimate defeat, had been borne by the people with an apathy that robbed misfortune of half its sharpness.

The nearest approach to town life afforded by Branson County is found in the little village of Troy, the county seat, a hamlet with a population of four or five hundred.

Ten years make little difference in the appearance of these remote

29 Branson County, North Carolina: founded in 1849, near the North Carolina and Virginia border.

30 Freshets: a flood or river caused by heavy rain.

31 Bummers: renegades.

Southern towns. If a railroad is built through one of them, it infuses some enterprise; the social corpse is galvanized by the fresh blood of civilization that pulses along the farthest ramifications of our great system of commercial highways. At the period of which I write, no railroad had come to Troy. If a traveler, accustomed to the bustling life of cities, could have ridden through Troy on a summer day, he might easily have fancied himself in a deserted village. Around him he would have seen weather-beaten houses, innocent of paint, the shingled roofs in many instances covered with a rich growth of moss. Here and there he would have met a razor-backed hog lazily rooting his way along the principal thoroughfare; and more than once be would probably have had to disturb the slumbers of some yellow dog, dozing away the hours in the ardent sunshine, and reluctantly yielding up his place in the middle of the dusty road.

On Saturdays the village presented a somewhat livelier appearance, and the shade trees around the court house square and along Front Street served as hitching-posts for a goodly number of horses and mules and stunted oxen, belonging to the farmer-folk who had come in to trade at the two or three local stores.

A murder was a rare event in Branson County. Every well-informed citizen could tell the number of homicides committed in the county for fifty years back, and whether the slayer, in any given instance, had escaped either by flight or acquittal, or had suffered the penalty of the law. So, when it became known in Troy early one Friday morning in summer, about ten years after the war, that old Captain Walker, who had served in Mexico under Scott, and had left an arm on the field of Gettysburg, had been foully murdered during the night, there was intense excitement in the village. Business was practically suspended, and the citizens gathered in little groups to discuss the murder, and speculate upon the identity of the murderer. It transpired from testimony at the coroner's inquest, held during the morning, that a strange mulatto had been seen going in the direction of Captain Walker's house the night before, and had been met going away from Troy early Friday morning, by a farmer on his way to town. Other circumstances seemed to connect the stranger with the crime. The sheriff organized a posse to search for him, and early in the evening, when most of the citizens of Troy were at supper, the suspected man was brought in and lodged in the county jail.

By the following morning the news of the capture had spread to the farthest limits of the county. A much larger number of people than usual came to town that Saturday,—bearded men in straw hats and blue home-spun shirts, and butternut trousers of great amplitude of material and vagueness of outline; women in homespun frocks and slat-bonnets,[32] with faces as expressionless as the dreary sandhills which gave them a meagre sustenance.

The murder was almost the sole topic of conversation. A steady stream of curious observers visited the house of mourning, and gazed upon the rugged face of the old veteran, now stiff and cold in death; and more than one eye dropped a tear at the remembrance of the cheery smile, and the joke—sometimes superannuated, generally feeble, but always good-natured—with which the captain had been wont[33] to greet his acquaintances. There was a growing sentiment of anger among these stern men, toward the murderer who had thus cut down their friend, and a strong feeling that ordinary justice was too slight a punishment for such a crime.

Toward noon there was an informal gathering of citizens in Dan Tyson's store.

"I hear it 'lowed that Square Kyahtah's too sick ter hol' co'te this evenin'," said one, "an' that the purlim'nary hearin' 'll haf ter go over 'tel nex' week."

A look of disappointment went round the crowd.

"Hit's the durndes', meanes' murder ever committed in this caounty," said another, with moody emphasis.

"I s'pose the nigger 'lowed the Cap'n had some greenbacks," observed a third speaker.

"The Cap'n," said another, with an air of superior information, "has left two bairls of Confedrit money, which he 'spected 'ud be good some day er nuther."

This statement gave rise to a discussion of the speculative value of Confederate money; but in a little while the conversation returned to the murder.

"Hangin' air too good fer the murderer," said one; "he oughter be burnt, stidier bein' hung."

There was an impressive pause at this point, during which a jug of moonlight whiskey went the round of the crowd.

"Well," said a round-shouldered farmer, who, in spite of his peaceable expression and faded gray eye, was known to have been one of the most daring followers of a rebel guerrilla chieftain, "what air yer gwine ter do about it? Ef you fellers air gwine ter set down an' let a wuthless nigger

32 Slat-bonnet: bonnet named after the wooden "slats" used to stiffen its brim.

33 Wont: accustomed.

kill the bes' white man in Branson, an' not say nuthin' ner do nuthin', *I'll* move outen the caounty."

This speech gave tone and direction to the rest of the conversation. Whether the fear of losing the round-shouldered farmer operated to bring about the result or not is immaterial to this narrative; but, at all events, the crowd decided to lynch the negro. They agreed that this was the least that could be done to avenge the death of their murdered friend, and that it was a becoming way in which to honor his memory. They had some vague notions of the majesty of the law and the rights of the citizen, but in the passion of the moment these sunk into oblivion; a white man had been killed by a negro.

"The Cap'n was an ole sodger," said one of his friends solemnly. "He 'll sleep better when he knows that a co'te-martial has be'n hilt an' jestice done."

By agreement the lynchers were to meet at Tyson's store at five o'clock in the afternoon, and proceed thence to the jail, which was situated down the Lumberton Dirt Road (as the old turnpike antedating the plank-road was called), about half a mile south of the court-house. When the preliminaries of the lynching had been arranged, and a committee appointed to manage the affair, the crowd dispersed, some to go to their dinners, and some to secure recruits for the lynching party.

It was twenty minutes to five o'clock, when an excited negro, panting and perspiring, rushed up to the back door of Sheriff Campbell's dwelling, which stood at a little distance from the jail and somewhat farther than the latter building from the court-house. A turbaned colored woman came to the door in response to the negro's knock.

"Hoddy, Sis' Nance."

"Hoddy, Brer Sam."

"Is de shurff in," inquired the negro.

"Yas, Brer Sam, he's eatin' his dinner," was the answer.

"Will yer ax 'im ter step ter de do' a minute, Sis' Nance?"

The woman went into the dining-room, and a moment later the sheriff came to the door. He was a tall, muscular man, of a ruddier complexion than is usual among Southerners. A pair of keen, deep-set gray eyes looked out from under bushy eyebrows, and about his mouth was a masterful expression, which a full beard, once sandy in color, but now profusely sprinkled with gray, could not entirely conceal. The day was hot; the sheriff had discarded his coat and vest, and had his white shirt open at the throat.

"What do you want, Sam?" he inquired of the negro, who stood hat in hand, wiping the moisture from his face with a ragged shirt-sleeve.

"Shurff, dey gwine ter hang de pris'ner w'at's lock' up in de jail. Dey 're comin' dis a-way now. I wuz layin' down on a sack er corn down at de sto', behine a pile er flourbairls, w'en I hearn Doc' Cain en Kunnel Wright talkin' erbout it. I slip' outen de back do', en run here as fas' as I could. I hearn you say down ter de sto' once't dat you would n't let nobody take a pris'ner 'way fum you widout walkin' over yo' dead body, en I thought I'd let you know 'fo' dey come, so yer could pertec' de pris'ner."

The sheriff listened calmly, but his face grew firmer, and a determined gleam lit up his gray eyes. His frame grew more erect, and he unconsciously assumed the attitude of a soldier who momentarily expects to meet the enemy face to face.

"Much obliged, Sam," he answered. "I'll protect the prisoner. Who's coming?"

"I dunno who-all *is* comin'," replied the negro. "Dere's Mistah Mc-Swayne, en Doc' Cain, en Maje' McDonal', en Kunnel Wright, en a heap er yuthers. I wuz so skeered I done furgot mo'd'n half un em. I spec' dey mus' be mos' here by dis time, so I'll git outen de way, fer I don' want nobody fer ter think I wuz mix' up in dis business." The negro glanced nervously down the road toward the town, and made a movement as if to go away.

"Won't you have some dinner first?" asked the sheriff.

The negro looked longingly in at the open door, and sniffed the appetizing odor of boiled pork and collards.

"I ain't got no time fer ter tarry, Shurff," he said, "but Sis' Nance mought gin me sump'n I could kyar in my han' en eat on de way."

A moment later Nancy brought him a huge sandwich of split corn-pone,[34] with a thick slice of fat bacon inserted between the halves, and a couple of baked yams. The negro hastily replaced his ragged hat on his head, dropped the yams in the pocket of his capacious trousers, and, taking the sandwich in his hand, hurried across the road and disappeared in the woods beyond.

The sheriff reëntered the house, and put on his coat and hat. He then took down a double-barreled shotgun and loaded it with buckshot. Filling the chambers of a revolver with fresh cartridges, he slipped it into the pocket of the sack-coat which he wore.

34 Corn-pone: cornbread cooked in a special cast-iron skillet.

A comely young woman in a calico dress watched these proceedings with anxious surprise.

"Where are you going, father?" she asked. She had not heard the conversation with the negro.

"I am goin' over to the jail," responded the sheriff. "There's a mob comin' this way to lynch the nigger we've got locked up. But they won't do it," he added, with emphasis.

"Oh, father! don't go!" pleaded the girl, clinging to his arm; "they'll shoot you if you don't give him up."

"You never mind me, Polly," said her father reassuringly, as he gently unclasped her hands from his arm. "I'll take care of myself and the prisoner, too. There ain't a man in Branson County that would shoot me. Besides, I have faced fire too often to be scared away from my duty. You keep close in the house," he continued, "and if any one disturbs you just use the old horse-pistol in the top bureau drawer. It's a little old-fashioned, but it did good work a few years ago."

The young girl shuddered at this sanguinary allusion, but made no further objection to her father's departure.

The sheriff of Branson was a man far above the average of the community in wealth, education, and social position. His had been one of the few families in the county that before the war had owned large estates and numerous slaves. He had graduated at the State University at Chapel Hill, and had kept up some acquaintance with current literature and advanced thought. He had traveled some in his youth, and was looked up to in the county as an authority on all subjects connected with the outer world. At first an ardent supporter of the Union, he had opposed the secession movement in his native State as long as opposition availed to stem the tide of public opinion. Yielding at last to the force of circumstances, he had entered the Confederate service rather late in the war, and served with distinction through several campaigns, rising in time to the rank of colonel. After the war he had taken the oath of allegiance, and had been chosen by the people as the most available candidate for the office of sheriff, to which he had been elected without opposition. He had filled the office for several terms, and was universally popular with his constituents.

Colonel or Sheriff Campbell, as he was indifferently called, as the military or civil title happened to be most important in the opinion of the person addressing him, had a high sense of the responsibility attaching to his office. He had sworn to do his duty faithfully, and he knew what his duty was, as sheriff, perhaps more clearly than he had apprehended it in other passages of his life. It was, therefore, with no uncertainty in regard to his course that he prepared his weapons and went over to the jail. He had no fears for Polly's safety.

The sheriff had just locked the heavy front door of the jail behind him when a half dozen horsemen, followed by a crowd of men on foot, came round a bend in the road and drew near the jail. They halted in front of the picket fence that surrounded the building, while several of the committee of arrangements rode on a few rods farther to the sheriff's house. One of them dismounted and rapped on the door with his riding-whip.

"Is the sheriff at home?" he inquired.

"No, he has just gone out," replied Polly, who had come to the door.

"We want the jail keys," he continued.

"They are not here," said Polly. "The sheriff has them himself." Then she added, with assumed indifference, "He is at the jail now."

The man turned away, and Polly went into the front room, from which she peered anxiously between the slats of the green blinds of a window that looked toward the jail. Meanwhile the messenger returned to his companions and announced his discovery. It looked as though the sheriff had learned of their design and was preparing to resist it.

One of them stepped forward and rapped on the jail door.

"Well, what is it?" said the sheriff, from within.

"We want to talk to you, Sheriff," replied the spokesman.

There was a little wicket in the door; this the sheriff opened, and answered through it.

"All right, boys, talk away. You are all strangers to me, and I don't know what business you can have." The sheriff did not think it necessary to recognize anybody in particular on such an occasion; the question of identity sometimes comes up in the investigation of these extra-judicial executions.

"We're a committee of citizens and we want to get into the jail."

"What for? It ain't much trouble to get into jail. Most people want to keep out."

The mob was in no humor to appreciate a joke, and the sheriff's witticism fell dead upon an unresponsive audience.

"We want to have a talk with the nigger that killed Cap'n Walker."

"You can talk to that nigger in the courthouse, when he's brought out for trial. Court will be in session here next week. I know what you fellows want, but you can't get my prisoner to-day. Do you want to take the bread out of a poor man's mouth? I get seventy-five cents a day for keeping this prisoner, and he's the only one in jail. I can't have my family suffer just to please you fellows."

One or two young men in the crowd laughed at the idea of Sheriff Campbell's suffering for want of seventy-five cents a day; but they were frowned into silence by those who stood near them.

"Ef yer don't let us in," cried a voice, "we'll bu's' the do' open."

"Bust away," answered the sheriff, raising his voice so that all could hear. "But I give you fair warning. The first man that tries it will be filled with buckshot. I'm sheriff of this county; I know my duty, and I mean to do it."

"What's the use of kicking, Sheriff?" argued one of the leaders of the mob. "The nigger is sure to hang anyhow; he richly deserves it; and we 've got to do something to teach the niggers their places, or white people won't be able to live in the county."

"There 's no use talking, boys," responded the sheriff. "I'm a white man outside, but in this jail I'm sheriff; and if this nigger's to be hung in this county, I propose to do the hanging. So you fellows might as well right-about-face, and march back to Troy. You've had a pleasant trip, and the exercise will be good for you. You know *me*. I've got powder and ball, and I've faced fire before now, with nothing between me and the enemy, and I don't mean to surrender this jail while I'm able to shoot." Having thus announced his determination, the sheriff closed and fastened the wicket, and looked around for the best position from which to defend the building.

The crowd drew off a little, and the leaders conversed together in low tones.

The Branson County jail was a small, two-story brick building, strongly constructed, with no attempt at architectural ornamentation. Each story was divided into two large cells by a passage running from front to rear. A grated iron door gave entrance from the passage to each of the four cells. The jail seldom had many prisoners in it, and the lower windows had been boarded up. When the sheriff had closed the wicket, he ascended the steep wooden stairs to the upper floor. There was no window at the front of the upper passage, and the most available position from which to watch the movements of the crowd below was the front window of the cell occupied by the solitary prisoner.

The sheriff unlocked the door and entered the cell. The prisoner was crouched in a corner, his yellow face, blanched with terror, looking ghastly in the semi-darkness of the room. A cold perspiration had gathered on his forehead, and his teeth were chattering with affright.

"For God's sake, Sheriff," he murmured hoarsely, "don't let 'em lynch me; I did n't kill the old man."

The sheriff glanced at the cowering wretch with a look of mingled contempt and loathing.

"Get up," he said sharply. "You will probably be hung sooner or later, but it shall not be to-day, if I can help it. I'll unlock your fetters, and if I can't hold the jail, you'll have to make the best fight you can. If I'm shot, I'll consider my responsibility at an end."

There were iron fetters on the prisoner's ankles, and handcuffs on his wrists. These the sheriff unlocked, and they fell clanking to the floor.

"Keep back from the window," said the sheriff. "They might shoot if they saw you."

The sheriff drew toward the window a pine bench which formed a part of the scanty furniture of the cell, and laid his revolver upon it. Then he took his gun in hand, and took his stand at the side of the window where he could with least exposure of himself watch the movements of the crowd below.

The lynchers had not anticipated any determined resistance. Of course they had looked for a formal protest, and perhaps a sufficient show of opposition to excuse the sheriff in the eye of any stickler for legal formalities. They had not however come prepared to fight a battle, and no one of them seemed willing to lead an attack upon the jail. The leaders of the party conferred together with a good deal of animated gesticulation, which was visible to the sheriff from his outlook, though the distance was too great for him to hear what was said. At length one of them broke away from the group, and rode back to the main body of the lynchers, who were restlessly awaiting orders.

"Well, boys," said the messenger, "we'll have to let it go for the present. The sheriff says he'll shoot, and he's got the drop on us this time. There ain't any of us that want to follow Cap'n Walker jest yet. Besides, the sheriff is a good fellow, and we don't want to hurt 'im. But," he added, as if to reassure the crowd, which began to show signs of disappointment, "the nigger might as well say his prayers, for he ain't got long to live."

There was a murmur of dissent from the mob, and several voices insisted that an attack be made on the jail. But pacific counsels finally prevailed, and the mob sullenly withdrew.

The sheriff stood at the window until they had disappeared around the bend in the road. He did not relax his watchfulness when the last one was out of sight. Their withdrawal might be a mere feint, to be followed by a further attempt. So closely, indeed, was his attention drawn to the outside, that he neither saw nor heard the prisoner creep stealthily across the floor, reach out his hand and secure the revolver which lay on the bench behind the sheriff, and creep as noiselessly back to his place in the corner of the room.

A moment after the last of the lynching party had disappeared there was a shot fired from the woods across the road; a bullet whistled by the window and buried itself in the wooden casing a few inches from where the sheriff was standing. Quick as thought, with the instinct born of a semi-guerrilla army experience, he raised his gun and fired twice at the point from which a faint puff of smoke showed the hostile bullet to have been sent. He stood a moment watching, and then rested his gun against the window, and reached behind him mechanically for the other weapon. It was not on the bench. As the sheriff realized this fact, he turned his head and looked into the muzzle of the revolver.

"Stay where you are, Sheriff," said the prisoner, his eyes glistening, his face almost ruddy with excitement.

The sheriff mentally cursed his own carelessness for allowing him to be caught in such a predicament. He had not expected anything of the kind. He had relied on the negro's cowardice and subordination in the presence of an armed white man as a matter of course. The sheriff was a brave man, but realized that the prisoner had him at an immense disadvantage. The two men stood thus for a moment, fighting a harmless duel with their eyes.

"Well, what do you mean to do?" asked the sheriff with apparent calmness.

"To get away, of course," said the prisoner, in a tone which caused the sheriff to look at him more closely, and with an involuntary feeling of apprehension; if the man was not mad, he was in a state of mind akin to madness, and quite as dangerous. The sheriff felt that he must speak the prisoner fair, and watch for a chance to turn the tables on him. The keen-eyed, desperate man before him was a different being altogether from the groveling wretch who had begged so piteously for life a few minutes before.

At length the sheriff spoke:—

"Is this your gratitude to me for saving your life at the risk of my own? If I had not done so, you would now be swinging from the limb of some neighboring tree."

"True," said the prisoner, "you saved my life, but for how long? When you came in, you said Court would sit next week. When the crowd went away they said I had not long to live. It is merely a choice of two ropes."

"While there's life there's hope," replied the sheriff. He uttered this commonplace mechanically, while his brain was busy in trying to think out some way of escape. "If you are innocent you can prove it."

The mulatto kept his eye upon the sheriff. "I didn't kill the old man," he replied; "but I shall never be able to clear myself. I was at his house at nine o'clock. I stole from it the coat that was on my back when I was taken. I would be convicted, even with a fair trial, unless the real murderer were discovered beforehand."

The sheriff knew this only too well. While he was thinking what argument next to use, the prisoner continued:—

"Throw me the keys—no, unlock the door."

The sheriff stood a moment irresolute. The mulatto's eye glittered ominously. The sheriff crossed the room and unlocked the door leading into the passage.

"Now go down and unlock the outside door."

The heart of the sheriff leaped within him. Perhaps he might make a dash for liberty, and gain the outside. He descended the narrow stairs, the prisoner keeping close behind him.

The sheriff inserted the huge iron key into the lock. The rusty bolt yielded slowly. It still remained for him to pull the door open.

"Stop!" thundered the mulatto, who seemed to divine the sheriff's purpose. "Move a muscle, and I'll blow your brains out."

The sheriff obeyed; he realized that his chance had not yet come.

"Now keep on that side of the passage, and go back upstairs."

Keeping the sheriff under cover of the revolver, the mulatto followed him up the stairs. The sheriff expected the prisoner to lock him into the cell and make his own escape. He had about come to the conclusion that the best thing he could do under the circumstances was to submit quietly, and take his chances of recapturing the prisoner after the alarm had been given. The sheriff had faced death more than once upon the battlefield. A few minutes before, well armed, and with a brick wall between him and them he had dared a hundred men to fight; but he felt instinctively that the desperate man confronting him was not to be trifled with, and he was too prudent a man to risk his life against such heavy odds. He had Polly to look after, and there was a limit beyond which devotion to duty would be quixotic and even foolish.

"I want to get away," said the prisoner, "and I don't want to be captured; for if I am I know I will be hung on the spot. I am afraid," he added somewhat reflectively, "that in order to save myself I shall have to kill you."

"Good God!" exclaimed the sheriff in involuntary terror; "you would not kill the man to whom you owe your own life."

"You speak more truly than you know," replied the mulatto. "I indeed owe my life to you."

The sheriff started. He was capable of surprise, even in that moment of extreme peril. "Who are you?" he asked in amazement.

"Tom, Cicely's son," returned the other. He had closed the door and stood talking to the sheriff through the grated opening. "Don't you remember Cicely—Cicely whom you sold, with her child, to the speculator on his way to Alabama?"

The sheriff did remember. He had been sorry for it many a time since. It had been the old story of debts, mortgages, and bad crops. He had quarreled with the mother. The price offered for her and her child had been unusually large, and he had yielded to the combination of anger and pecuniary stress.

"Good God!" he gasped, "you would not murder your own father?"

"My father?" replied the mulatto. "It were well enough for me to claim the relationship, but it comes with poor grace from you to ask anything by reason of it. What father's duty have you ever performed for me? Did you give me your name, or even your protection? Other white men gave their colored sons freedom and money, and sent them to the free States. *You* sold *me* to the rice swamps."

"I at least gave you the life you cling to," murmured the sheriff.

"Life?" said the prisoner, with a sarcastic laugh. "What kind of a life? You gave me your own blood, your own features,—no man need look at us together twice to see that,—and you gave me a black mother. Poor wretch! She died under the lash, because she had enough womanhood to call her soul her own. You gave me a white man's spirit, and you made me a slave, and crushed it out."

"But you are free now," said the sheriff. He had not doubted, could not doubt, the mulatto's word. He knew whose passions coursed beneath that swarthy skin and burned in the black eyes opposite his own. He saw in this mulatto what he himself might have become had not the safeguards of parental restraint and public opinion been thrown around him.

"Free to do what?" replied the mulatto. "Free in name, but despised and scorned and set aside by the people to whose race I belong far more than to my mother's."

"There are schools," said the sheriff. "You have been to school." He had noticed that the mulatto spoke more eloquently and used better language than most Branson County people.

"I have been to school, and dreamed when I went that it would work some marvelous change in my condition. But what did I learn? I learned to feel that no degree of learning or wisdom will change the color of my skin and that I shall always wear what in my own country is a badge of degradation. When I think about it seriously I do not care particularly for such a life. It is the animal in me, not the man, that flees the gallows. I owe you nothing," he went on, "and expect nothing of you; and it would be no more than justice if I should avenge upon you my mother's wrongs and my own. But still I hate to shoot you; I have never yet taken human life—for I did *not* kill the old captain. Will you promise to give no alarm and make no attempt to capture me until morning, if I do not shoot?"

So absorbed were the two men in their colloquy and their own tumultuous thoughts that neither of them had heard the door below move upon its hinges. Neither of them had heard a light step come stealthily up the stairs, nor seen a slender form creep along the darkening passage toward the mulatto.

The sheriff hesitated. The struggle between his love of life and his sense of duty was a terrific one. It may seem strange that a man who could sell his own child into slavery should hesitate at such a moment, when his life was trembling in the balance. But the baleful influence of human slavery poisoned the very fountains of life, and created new standards of right. The sheriff was conscientious; his conscience had merely been warped by his environment. Let no one ask what his answer would have been; he was spared the necessity of a decision.

"Stop," said the mulatto, "you need not promise. I could not trust you if you did. It is your life for mine; there is but one safe way for me; you must die."

He raised his arm to fire, when there was a flash—a report from the passage behind him. His arm fell heavily at his side, and the pistol dropped at his feet.

The sheriff recovered first from his surprise, and throwing open the door secured the fallen weapon. Then seizing the prisoner he thrust him into the cell and locked the door upon him; after which he turned to Polly, who leaned half-fainting against the wall, her hands clasped over her heart.

"Oh, father, I was just in time!" she cried hysterically, and, wildly sobbing, threw herself into her father's arms.

"I watched until they all went away," she said. "I heard the shot from the woods and I saw you shoot. Then when you did not come out I feared something had happened, that perhaps you had been wounded. I got out the other pistol and ran over here. When I found the door open, I knew something was wrong, and when I heard voices I crept up stairs, and reached the top just in time to hear him say he would kill you. Oh, it was a narrow escape!"

When she had grown somewhat calmer, the sheriff left her standing there and went back into the cell. The prisoner's arm was bleeding from a flesh wound. His bravado had given place to a stony apathy. There was no sign in his face of fear or disappointment or feeling of any kind. The sheriff sent Polly to the house for cloth, and bound up the prisoner's wound with a rude skill acquired during his army life.

"I'll have a doctor come and dress the wound in the morning," he said to the prisoner. "It will do very well until then, if you will keep quiet. If the doctor asks you how the wound was caused, you can say that you were struck by the bullet fired from the woods. It would do you no good to have known that you were shot while attempting to escape."

The prisoner uttered no word of thanks or apology, but sat in sullen silence. When the wounded arm had been bandaged, Polly and her father returned to the house.

The sheriff was in an unusually thoughtful mood that evening. He put salt in his coffee at supper, and poured vinegar over his pancakes. To many of Polly's questions he returned random answers. When he had gone to bed he lay awake for several hours.

In the silent watches of the night, when he was alone with God, there came into his mind a flood of unaccustomed thoughts. An hour or two before, standing face to face with death, he had experienced a sensation similar to that which drowning men are said to feel—a kind of clarifying of the moral faculty, in which the veil of the flesh, with its obscuring passions and prejudices, is pushed aside for a moment, and all the acts of one's life stand out, in the clear light of truth, in their correct proportions and relations,—a state of mind in which one sees himself as God may be supposed to see him. In the reaction following his rescue, this feeling had given place for a time to far different emotions. But now, in the silence of midnight, something of this clearness of spirit returned to the sheriff. He saw that he had owed some duty to this son of his,—that neither law nor custom could destroy a responsibility inherent in the nature of mankind. He could not thus, in the eyes of God at least, shake off the consequences of his sin. Had he never sinned, this wayward spirit would never have come back from the vanished past to haunt him. As these thoughts came, his anger against the mulatto died away, and in its place there sprang up a great pity. The hand of parental authority might have restrained the passions he had seen burning in the prisoner's eyes when the desperate man spoke the words which had seemed to doom his father to death. The sheriff felt that he might have saved this fiery spirit from the slough of slavery; that he might have sent him to the free North, and given him there, or in some other land, an opportunity to turn to usefulness and honorable pursuits the talents that had run to crime, perhaps to madness; he might, still less, have given this son of his the poor simulacrum of liberty which men of his caste could possess in a slave-holding community; or least of all, but still something, he might have kept the boy on the plantation, where the burdens of slavery would have fallen lightly upon him.

The sheriff recalled his own youth. He had inherited an honored name to keep untarnished; he had had a future to make; the picture of a fair young bride had beckoned him on to happiness. The poor wretch now stretched upon a pallet of straw between the brick walls of the jail had had none of these things,—no name, no father, no mother—in the true meaning of motherhood,—and until the past few years no possible future, and then one vague and shadowy in its outline, and dependent for form and substance upon the slow solution of a problem in which there were many unknown quantities.

From what he might have done to what he might yet do was an easy transition for the awakened conscience of the sheriff. It occurred to him, purely as a hypothesis, that he might permit his prisoner to escape; but his oath of office, his duty as sheriff, stood in the way of such a course, and the sheriff dismissed the idea from his mind. He could, however, investigate the circumstances of the murder, and move Heaven and earth to discover the real criminal, for he no longer doubted the prisoner's innocence; he could employ counsel for the accused, and perhaps influence public opinion in his favor. An acquittal once secured, some plan could be devised by which the sheriff might in some degree atone for his crime against this son of his—against society—against God.

When the sheriff had reached this conclusion he fell into an unquiet slumber, from which he awoke late the next morning.

He went over to the jail before breakfast and found the prisoner lying on his pallet, his face turned to the wall; he did not move when the sheriff rattled the door.

"Good-morning," said the latter, in a tone intended to waken the prisoner.

There was no response. The sheriff looked more keenly at the recumbent figure; there was an unnatural rigidity about its attitude.

He hastily unlocked the door and, entering the cell, bent over the prostrate form. There was no sound of breathing; he turned the body over—it was cold and stiff. The prisoner had torn the bandage from his wound and bled to death during the night. He had evidently been dead several hours.

CHARLES W. CHESNUTT

❖

WHAT IS A WHITE MAN?

The fiat having gone forth from the wise men of the South that the "all-pervading, all-conquering Anglo-Saxon race" must continue forever to exercise exclusive control and direction of the government of this so-called Republic, it becomes important to every citizen who values his birthright to know who are included in this grandiloquent term. It is of course perfectly obvious that the writer or speaker who used this expression—perhaps Mr. Grady[35] of Georgia—did not say what he meant. It is not probable that he meant to exclude from full citizenship the Celts and Teutons and Gauls and Slavs who make up so large a proportion of our population; he hardly meant to exclude the Jews, for even the most ardent fireeater would hardly venture to advocate the disfranchisement of the thrifty race whose mortgages cover so large a portion of Southern soil. What the eloquent gentleman really meant by this high-sounding phrase was simply the white race; and the substance of the argument of that school of Southern writers to which he belongs, is simply that for the good of the country the Negro should have no voice in directing the government or public policy of the Southern States or of the nation.

But it is evident that where the intermingling of the races has made such progress as it has in this country, the line which separates the races must in many instances have been practically obliterated. And there has arisen in the United States a very large class of the population who are certainly not Negroes in an ethnological sense, and whose children will be no nearer Negroes than themselves. In view, therefore, of the very positive ground taken by the white leaders of the South, where most of these people reside, it becomes in the highest degree important to them to know what race they belong to. It ought to be also a matter of serious concern to the Southern white people; for if their zeal for good government is so great that they contemplate the practical overthrow of the Constitution and laws of the United States to secure it, they ought at least to be sure that no man entitled to it by their own argument, is robbed of a right so precious as that of free citizenship; the "all-pervading, all conquering Anglo-Saxon" ought to set as high a value on American citizenship as the

35 Mr. Grady of Georgia: Henry W. Grady (1850–89), editor of the *Atlanta Constitution*, largely responsible for the perpetuation of the myth of the New South.

all-conquering Roman placed upon the franchise of his State two thousand years ago. This discussion would of course be of little interest to the genuine Negro, who is entirely outside of the charmed circle, and must content himself with the acquisition of wealth, the pursuit of learning and such other privileges as his "best friends" may find it consistent with the welfare of the nation to allow him; but to every other good citizen the inquiry ought to be a momentous one. What is a white man?

In spite of the virulence and universality of race prejudice in the United States, the human intellect long ago revolted at the manifest absurdity of classifying men fifteen-sixteenths white as black men; and hence there grew up a number of laws in different states of the Union defining the limit which separated the white and colored races, which was, when these laws took their rise and is now to a large extent, the line which separated freedom and opportunity from slavery or hopeless degradation. Some of these laws are of legislative origin; others are judge-made laws, brought out by the exigencies of special cases which came before the courts for determination. Some day they will, perhaps, become mere curiosities of jurisprudence; the "black laws" will be bracketed with the "blue laws,"[36] and will be at best but landmarks by which to measure the progress of the nation. But to-day these laws are in active operation, and they are, therefore, worthy of attention; for every good citizen ought to know the law, and, if possible, to respect it; and if not worthy of respect, it should be changed by the authority which enacted it. Whether any of the laws referred to here have been in any manner changed by very recent legislation the writer cannot say, but they are certainly embodied in the latest editions of the revised statutes of the states referred to.

The colored people were divided, in most of the Southern States, into two classes, designated by law as Negroes and mulattoes respectively. The term Negro was used in its ethnological sense, and needed no definition; but the term "mulatto" was held by legislative enactment to embrace all persons of color not Negroes. The words "quadroon" and "mestizo" are employed in some of the law books, tho not defined; but the term "octoroon," as indicating a person having one-eighth of Negro blood, is not used at all, so far as the writer has been able to observe.

The states vary slightly in regard to what constitutes a mulatto or person of color, and as to what proportion of white blood should be sufficient to remove the disability of color. As a general rule, less than one-fourth of

36 Blue laws: laws regulating public and private behavior on Sundays in the Puritan colonies of New England. Although a number of these laws remain on state law books, many states no longer enforce them.

Negro blood left the individual white—in theory; race questions being, however, regulated very differently in practice. In Missouri, by the code of 1855, still in operation, so far as not inconsistent with the Federal Constitution and laws, "any person other than a Negro, any one of whose grandmothers or grandfathers is or shall have been a Negro, tho all of his or her progenitors except those descended from the Negro may have been white persons, shall be deemed a mulatto." Thus the color-line is drawn at one-fourth of Negro blood, and persons with only one-eighth are white.

By the Mississippi code of 1880, the color-line is drawn at one-fourth of Negro blood, all persons having less being theoretically white.

Under the code noir[37] of Louisiana, the descendant of a white and a quadroon is white, thus drawing the line at one-eighth of Negro blood. The code of 1876 abolished all distinctions of color; as to whether they have been re-enacted since the Republican Party went out of power in that state the writer is not informed.

Jumping to the extreme North, persons are white within the meaning of the Constitution of Michigan who have less than one-fourth of Negro blood.

In Ohio the rule, as established by numerous decisions of the Supreme Court, was that a preponderance of white blood constituted a person a white man in the eye of the law, and entitled him to the exercise of all the civil rights of a white man. By a retrogressive step the color-line was extended in 1861 in the case of marriage, which by statute was forbidden between a person of pure white blood and one having a visible admixture of African blood. But by act of legislature, passed in the spring of 1887, all laws establishing or permitting distinctions of color were repealed. In many parts of the state these laws were always ignored, and they would doubtless have been repealed long ago but for the sentiment of the southern counties, separated only by the width of the Ohio River from a former slave-holding state.[38] There was a bill introduced in the legislature during the last session to reenact the "black laws," but it was hopelessly defeated; the member who introduced it evidently mistook his latitude; he ought to be a member of the Georgia legislature.

But the state which, for several reasons, one might expect to have the strictest laws in regard to the relations of the races, has really the loosest.

37 Code noir: The Code Noir of Louisiana, made at Versailles in March of 1724, limited the rights of blacks in the New World and declared them the personal property of their white owners.

38 Kentucky.

Two extracts from decisions of the Supreme Court of South Carolina will make clear the law of that state in regard to the color-line.[39]

"The definition of the term mulatto, as understood in this state, seems to be vague, signifying generally a person of mixed white or European and Negro parentage, in whatever proportions the blood of the two races may be mingled in the individual. But it is not invariably applicable to every admixture of African blood with the European, nor is one having all the features of a white to be ranked with the degraded class designated by the laws of this state as persons of color, because of some remote taint of the Negro race. The line of distinction, however, is not ascertained by any rule of law. . . . Juries would probably be justified in holding a person to be white in whom the admixture of African blood did not exceed the proportion of one-eighth. But it is in all cases a question for the jury, to be determined by them upon the evidence of features and complexion afforded by inspection, the evidence of reputation as to parentage, and the evidence of the rank and station in society occupied by the party. The only rule which can be laid down by the courts is that where there is a distinct and visible admixture of Negro blood, the individual is to be denominated a mulatto or person of color."

In a later case the court held: "The question whether persons are colored or white, where color or feature are doubtful, is for the jury to decide by reputation, by reception into society, and by their exercise of the privileges of the white man, as well as by admixture of blood."

It is an interesting question why such should have been, and should still be, for that matter, the law of South Carolina, and why there should exist in that state a condition of public opinion which would accept such a law. Perhaps it may be attributed to the fact that the colored population of South Carolina always outnumbered the white population, and the eagerness of the latter to recruit their ranks was sufficient to overcome in some measure their prejudice against the Negro blood. It is certainly true that the color-line is, in practice as in law, more loosely drawn in South Carolina than in any other Southern State, and that no inconsiderable element of the population of that state consists of these legal white persons, who were either born in the state, or, attracted thither by this feature of the laws, have come in from surrounding states, and, forsaking home and kindred, have taken their social position as white people. A reasonable

39 Definition of the term mulatto from *State v. Davis*, S.C. 2 Bailey 558 (1831).

CHARLES W. CHESNUTT

degree of reticence in regard to one's antecedents is, however, usual in such cases.

Before the War the color-line, as fixed by law, regulated in theory the civil and political status of persons of color. What that status was, was expressed in the Dred Scott decision.[40] But since the War, or rather since the enfranchisement of the colored people, these laws have been mainly confined—in theory, be it always remembered—to the regulation of the intercourse of the races in schools and in the marriage relation. The extension of the color-line to places of public entertainment and resort, to inns and public highways, is in most states entirely a matter of custom. A colored man can sue in the courts of any Southern State for the violation of his common-law rights, and recover damages of say fifty cents without costs. A colored minister who sued a Baltimore steamboat company a few weeks ago for refusing him first-class accommodation, he having paid first-class fare, did not even meet with that measure of success; the learned judge, a Federal judge by the way, held that the plaintiff's rights had been invaded, and that he had suffered humiliation at the hands of the defendant company, but that "the humiliation was not sufficient to entitle him to damages." And the learned judge dismissed the action without costs to either party.

Having thus ascertained what constitutes a white man, the good citizen may be curious to know what steps have been taken to preserve the purity of the white race. Nature, by some unaccountable oversight having to some extent neglected a matter so important to the future prosperity and progress of mankind. The marriage laws referred to here are in active operation, and cases under them are by no means infrequent. Indeed, instead of being behind the age, the marriage laws in the Southern States are in advance of public opinion; for very rarely will a Southern community stop to figure on the pedigree of the contracting parties to a marriage where one is white and the other is known to have any strain of Negro blood.

In Virginia, under the title "Offenses against Morality," the law provides that "any white person who shall intermarry with a Negro shall be confined in jail not more than one year and fined not exceeding one hundred dollars." In a marginal note on the statute-book, attention is called to the fact that "a similar penalty is not imposed on the Negro"—a

40 In *Dred Scott v. Sandford* (1857) the U.S. Supreme Court ruled that Congress could not prohibit slavery in federal Midwest territories and that free blacks were not U.S. citizens.

stretch of magnanimity to which the laws of other states are strangers. A person who performs the ceremony of marriage in such a case is fined two hundred dollars, one-half of which goes to the informer.

In Maryland, a minister who performs the ceremony of marriage between a Negro and a white person is liable to a fine of one hundred dollars.

In Mississippi, code of 1880, it is provided that "the marriage of a white person to a Negro or mulatto or person who shall have one-fourth or more of Negro blood, shall be unlawful"; and as this prohibition does not seem sufficiently emphatic, it is further declared to be "incestuous and void," and is punished by the same penalty prescribed for marriage within the forbidden degrees of consanguinity.

But it is Georgia, the *alma genetrix*[41] of the chain-gang, which merits the questionable distinction of having the harshest set of color laws. By the law of Georgia the term "person of color" is defined to mean "all such as have an admixture of Negro blood, and the term 'Negro,' includes mulattoes." This definition is perhaps restricted somewhat by another provision, by which "all Negroes, mestizoes, and their descendants, having one-eighth of Negro or mulatto blood in their veins, shall be known in this State as persons of color." A colored minister is permitted to perform the ceremony of marriage between colored persons only, tho white ministers are not forbidden to join persons of color in wedlock. It is further provided that "the marriage relation between white persons and persons of African descent is forever prohibited, and such marriages shall be null and void." This is a very sweeping provision; it will be noticed that the term "persons of color," previously defined, is not employed, the expression "persons of African descent" being used instead. A court which was so inclined would find no difficulty in extending this provision of the law to the remotest strain of African blood. The marriage relation is forever prohibited. Forever is a long time. There is a colored woman in Georgia said to be worth $300,000—an immense fortune in the poverty stricken South. With a few hundred such women in that state, possessing a fair degree of good looks, the color-line would shrivel up like a scroll in the heat of competition for their hands in marriage. The penalty for the violation of the law against intermarriage is the same sought to be imposed by

41 *Alma genetrix*: fostering progenitor.

CHARLES W. CHESNUTT

the defunct Glenn Bill[42] for violation of its provisions; i.e., a fine not to exceed one thousand dollars, and imprisonment not to exceed six months, or twelve months in the chain-gang.

Whatever the wisdom or justice of these laws, there is one objection to them which is not given sufficient prominence in the consideration of the subject, even where it is discussed at all; they make mixed blood a *prima-facie*[43] proof of illegitimacy. It is a fact that at present, in the United States, a colored man or woman whose complexion is white or nearly white is presumed, in the absence of any knowledge of his or her antecedents, to be the offspring of a union not sanctified by law. And by a curious but not uncommon process, such persons are not held in the same low estimation as white people in the same position. The sins of their fathers are not visited upon the children, in that regard at least; and their mothers' lapses from virtue are regarded either as misfortunes or as faults excusable under the circumstances.[44] But in spite of all this, illegitimacy is not a desirable distinction, and is likely to become less so, as these people of mixed blood advance in wealth and social standing. This presumption of illegitimacy was once, perhaps, true of the majority of such persons; but the times have changed. More than half of the colored people of the United States are of mixed blood; they marry and are given in marriage, and they beget children of complexions similar to their own.[45] Whether or not, therefore, laws which stamp these children as illegitimate, and which by indirection establish a lower standard of morality for a large part of the population than the remaining part is judged by, are wise laws; and whether or not the purity of the white race could not be as well preserved by the exercise of virtue, and the operation of those natural laws which are so often quoted by Southern writers as the justification of all sorts of Southern "policies"—are questions which the good citizen may at least turn over in his mind occasionally, pending the settlement of other complications which have grown out of the presence of the Negro on this continent.

42 Glenn Bill: Introduced into the lower house of the Georgia State Legislature in 1887, this bill would have mandated school segregation in Georgia, but it never passed the state senate.

43 *Prima-facie*: a legal presumption of fact, literally "at first sight."

44 Exodus 20:5: "Thou shalt not bow down thyself to them, nor serve them: for I the LORD thy God am a jealous God, visiting the iniquity of the fathers upon the children unto the third and fourth generation of them that hate me."

45 Matthew 22:30: "For in the resurrection they neither marry, nor are given in marriage, but are as the angels of God in heaven."

❖

From THE JOURNALS OF CHARLES W. CHESNUTT

March 16, 1880

Judge Tourgee has sold the "Fool's Errand," I understand, for $20,000.[46] I suppose he had already received a large royalty on the sale of the first few editions. The work has gained an astonishing degree of popularity, and is to be translated into the French.

Now, Judge Tourgee's book is about the south,—the manners, customs, modes of thought, etc., which are prevalent in this section of the country. Judge Tourgee is a Northern man, who has lived at the South since the war, until recently. He knows a great deal about the politics, history, and laws of the South. He is a close observer of men and things, and has exercised this faculty of observation upon the character of the Southern people. Nearly all his stories are more or less about colored people, and this very feature is one source of their popularity. There is something romantic, to the Northern mind, about the southern negro, as commonplace and vulgar as he seems to us who come in contact with him every day. And there is a romantic side to the history of this people. Men are always more ready to extend their sympathy to those at a distance, than to the suffering ones in their midst. And the north, their eyes not blinded by the dirt and the hazy moral and social atmosphere which surrounds the average negro in the south, their interest not blunted by familiarity with the state of affairs in the south, or prejudiced by a love of "our institutions"—sees the south as it is; or is ever eager for something which will show it in a correct light. They see in the Colored people a race, but recently emancipated from a cruel bondage; struggling for education, for a higher social and moral life, against wealth, intelligence, and race prejudice, which are all united to keep them down. And they hear the cry of the oppressed and struggling ones, and extend a hand to help them; they lend a willing ear to all that is spoken or written concerning their character, habits, etc. And if judge Tourgee, with his necessarily limited intercourse with colored people, and with his limited stay in the South, can write such interesting descriptions, such vivid pictures of Southern life and character as to make himself rich and famous, why could not

46 Albion W. Tourgée (1838–1905), Union army officer who served as a judge during Reconstruction in North Carolina; author of the novel *A Fool's Errand* (1879).

a colored man, who has lived among colored people all his life; who is familiar with their habits, their ruling passions, their prejudices; their whole moral and social condition; their public and private ambitions; their religious tendencies and habits;—why could not a colored man who knew all this, and who, besides, had possessed such opportunities for observation and conversation with the better class of white men in the south as to understand their modes of thinking; who was familiar with the political history of the country, and especially with all the phases of the slavery question;—why could not such a man, if he possessed the same ability, write a far better book about the South than Judge Tourgee or Mrs. Stowe[47] has written? Answer who can! But the man is yet to make his appearance; and if I can't be the man I shall be the first to rejoice at his *debut* and give God speed! to his work.

I intend to record my impressions of men and things, and such incidents or conversations which take place within my knowledge, with a view to future use in literary work. I shall not record stale negro minstrel jokes, or worn out newspaper squibs[48] on the "man and brother." I shall leave the realm of fiction, where most of this stuff is manufactured, and come down to hard facts. There are many things about the Colored people which are peculiar, to some extent, to them, and which are interesting to any thoughtful observer, and would be doubly interesting to people who know little about them.

❖ ❖ ❖

May 29, 1880

I think I must write a book. I am almost afraid to undertake a book so early and with so little experience in composition. But it has been my cherished dream, and I feel an influence that I cannot resist calling me to the task. Besides, I do not know but I am as well prepared as some other successful writers. A fair knowledge of the classics, a speaking acquaintance with the modern languages, an intimate friendship with literature, etc.; seven years experience in the school room, two years of married life, and a habit of studying character have I think, left me not entirely unprepared to write even a book. Fifteen years of life in the South, in one of the most eventful eras of its history; among a people whose life is rich in the elements of romance; under conditions calculated to stir one's soul to the very depths;—I think there is here a fund of experience, a supply of

47 Harriet Beecher Stowe (1811–96), author of the novel *Uncle Tom's Cabin* (1852).

48 A short witty news story.

material, which a skillful pers[on] could work up with tremendous effect. Besides, If I do write, I shall write for a purpose, a high, holy purpose, and this will inspire me to greater effort. The object of my writings would be not so much the elevation of the colored people as the elevation of the whites,—for I consider the unjust spirit of caste which is so insidious as to pervade a whole nation, and so powerful as to subject a whole race and all connected with it to scorn and social ostracism—I consider this a barrier to the moral progress of the American people; and I would be one of the first to head a determined, organized crusade against it. Not a fierce indiscriminate onslaught; not an appeal to force, for this is something that force can but slightly affect; but a moral revolution which must be brought about in a different manner. The Abolition[ist]s stirred up public opinion in behalf of the slave, by appealing in trumpet tones to those principles of justice and humanity which were only lying dormant in the northern heart. The iron hand of power set the slave free from personal bondage, and by admitting him to all the rights of citizenship—the ballot, education—is fast freeing him from the greater bondage of ignorance. But the subtle almost indefinable feeling of repulsion toward the negro, which is common to most Americans—and easily enough accounted for—, cannot be stormed and taken by assault; the garrison will not capitulate: so their position must be mined, and we will find ourselves in their midst before they think it.

This work is of a twofold character. The negro's part is to prepare himself for social recognition and equality; and it is the province of literature to open the way for him to get it—to accustom the public mind to the idea; and while amusing them to lead them on imperceptibly, unconsciously step by step to the desired state of feeling. If I can do anything to further this work, and can see any likelihood of obtaining success in it, I would gladly devote my life to the work.

❖ ❖ ❖

Saturday, March 26, 1881
I have just finished Thackeray's[49] "Vanity Fair", his first great novel. He had written much previous to its appearance, but with "Vanity Fair["] he made himself a reputation.

Every time I read a good novel, I want to write one. It is the dream of my life-to be an author! It is not so much the *monstrari digito*,[50] though

49 William Makepeace Thackeray (1811–63), author of the novel *Vanity Fair* (1848).

50 To be noted as a famous person. Literally translated, "to point out with the finger."

that has something to do with my aspirations. It is not altogether the money. It is a mixture of motives. I want fame; I want money; I want to raise my children in a different rank of life from that I sprang from. In my present vocation, I would never accumulate a competency, with all the economy and prudence, and parsimony in the world. In law or medicine, I would be compelled to wait half a life-time to accomplish anything. But literature pays—the successful. There is a fascination about this calling that draws a scribbler irresistibly toward his doom. He knows that the chance of success is hardly one out of a hundred; but he is foolish enough to believe, or sanguine enough to hope, that he will be the successful one.

I am confident that I can succeed, in some degree, at any rate. It is the only thing I can do without capital, under my present circumstances, except teach. My three month vacation is before me after the lapse of another three, and I shall strike for an entering wedge in the literary world, which I can drive in further afterwards. "Where there's a will etc", and there is certainly a will in this case.

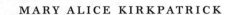

MARY ALICE KIRKPATRICK

Anna Julia Cooper

(Scurlock Studio Records, Archives Center, National Museum of American History,
Behring Center, Smithsonian Institution, Washington, D.C.)

A LIFELONG EDUCATOR, scholar, and social activist, Anna Julia Haywood Cooper worked tirelessly to promote equal rights and higher education for African Americans. She was born August 10, 1858, in Raleigh, North Carolina. Her mother, Hannah Stanley, was enslaved to her white father, George Washington Haywood. From 1868 to 1877, young Annie Haywood attended St. Augustine's Normal and Collegiate Institute (now St. Augustine's College) on a scholarship, working as a student tutor. On June 21, 1877, following her graduation, she married George A. C. Cooper, an instructor of Greek at St. Augustine's who was later ordained as an Episcopal clergyman. The couple worked as schoolteachers at St. Augustine's. After her husband's death in 1879, Anna remained on the faculty an additional two years. Widowed at twenty-one, Cooper never remarried. Nevertheless, she fostered two orphaned children and became guardian of her brother Andrew's five grandchildren in 1915.

Enrolling at Oberlin College (located in Oberlin, Ohio) in 1881, Cooper began her quest for advanced education. Earning an A.B. in 1884, she intended to resume teaching at her Raleigh alma mater. However, a disagreement over her position resulted in her yearlong employment at Wilberforce College in Ohio. The following year, Cooper accepted a faculty position at St. Augustine's, offering courses in mathematics, Latin, and Greek. Largely based on the strength of her teaching, Oberlin College conferred a master's degree on her in 1887.

In September of the same year, Cooper moved to Washington, D.C., taking a position at the renowned M Street School (later Dunbar High School), where she eventually served as principal (1902–6). During her occasionally tumultuous tenure as principal, Cooper became the center of a debate over black educational priorities between espousers of Booker T. Washington's industrial education model and proponents (including W. E. B. Du Bois) of a college preparatory model. Resisting pressure to adopt an industrial program, Cooper advocated a rigorous classical curriculum to prepare students to pursue degrees at prestigious universities such as Harvard, Brown, and Yale. Because of this controversy, Cooper's contract was not renewed in 1906. Obliged to teach briefly at Lincoln Institute in Jefferson City, Missouri, Cooper returned to the M Street School in 1910.

Cooper's vocal participation in a vibrant African American intellectual community exemplified the integral role that she believed black women should play in shaping and sustaining such communities. She was a leading spokeswoman at both the 1893 World's Congress of Representative Women and the 1900 Pan-African Congress while maintaining her active role in the Black Woman's Club movement. Cooper's intellectual journey, from her early days at St. Augustine's and Oberlin to three years of doctoral studies at Columbia University (1914–17), reached fruition in 1925, when she received her Ph.D. from the University of Paris (Sorbonne). After her retirement, she assumed the presidency of Frelinghuysen University in Washington, D.C., in 1930. Cooper died in Washington on February 27, 1964.

Cooper's most famous book, *A Voice from the South by a Black Woman from the South* (1892), is one of the first black feminist texts. A collection of speeches and essays, *A Voice from the South* is divided into two parts characterized by two distinct voices: individual and collective. Drawing from personal experiences and hypothetical examples, Cooper convincingly shows how race, gender, and caste prejudices hampered black Americans, particularly black women, after Emancipation and Reconstruction. Promoting black women's status through education, Cooper extended her argument to other people of color. Unafraid to criticize black men's sexism, as well as white feminists' racism, Cooper championed the black woman, whose unique voice and moral vision she both nurtured and embodied.

In her prologue to *A Voice from the South*, "Our Raison d'Être," Cooper introduces her narrator, the Black Woman from the South, whose muted voice must be heard. The remainder of the book emphasizes the responsibility of this heretofore-ignored Black Woman to speak her mind plainly. Cooper insists in "The Higher Education of Women," the book's second essay, that every deserving woman should have equal access to higher education, "so that she may fitly and intelligently stamp her force on the forces of her day." In this essay, Cooper also demonstrates her academic proficiency, effortlessly engaging with ancient and contemporary scholars. More problematic are her attempts to speak for a black female majority that remained largely uneducated. Critics have also questioned her attempts to reconcile her feminism to lingering ideals of domesticity prescribed for women. Throughout *A Voice from the South*, Cooper's sometimes biting sarcasm and her willingness to reveal herself through personal anecdotes allow readers to glimpse her remarkable drive, personal ambition, and fiery personality, qualities that distinguished this highly respected African American intellectual and social leader.

Suggested Readings

Baker-Fletcher, Karen. *A Singing Something: Womanist Reflections on Anna Julia Cooper*. New York: Crossroad, 1994.

Carby, Hazel. *Reconstructing Womanhood: The Emergence of the Afro-American Woman Novelist*. New York: Oxford University Press, 1987.

Gabel, Leona C. *From Slavery to the Sorbonne and Beyond: The Life and Writings of Anna J. Cooper*. Northampton, Mass.: Smith College History Department, 1982.

Giddings, Paula. *When and Where I Enter: The Impact of Black Women on Race and Sex in America*. New York: W. Morrow, 1984.

Hutchinson, Louise Daniel. *Anna J. Cooper: A Voice from the South*. Washington, D.C.: Smithsonian Institution Press, 1981.

Johnson, Karen Ann. *Uplifting the Women and the Race: The Lives, Educational Philosophies and Social Activism of Anna Julia Cooper and Nannie Helen Burroughs*. New York: Garland Publishing, 2000.

Lemert, Charles, and Esme Bahn, eds. *The Voice of Anna Julia Cooper*. New York: Rowman and Littlefield, 1998.

Washington, Mary Helen. Introduction to *A Voice from the South*, by Anna Julia Cooper. 1892. New York: Oxford University Press, 1988.

Note on the Text

The texts of "Our Raison d'Être" and "The Higher Education of Women" are reprinted in full from Cooper's *A Voice from the South* (Xenia, Ohio: the Author, 1892), pp. i–iii, 48–79.

The campus of St. Augustine's Preparatory School
when Anna Julia Cooper was on the faculty
*(North Carolina Department of Cultural Resources,
Office of Archives and History, Raleigh)*

❖

From A VOICE FROM THE SOUTH

Our Raison d'Être

In the clash and clatter of our American Conflict, it has been said that the South remains Silent. Like the Sphinx[1] she inspires vociferous disputation, but herself takes little part in the noisy controversy. One muffled strain in the Silent South, a jarring chord and a vague and uncomprehended cadenza has been and still is the Negro. And of that muffled chord, the one mute and voiceless note has been the sadly expectant Black Woman,

> An infant crying in the night,
> An infant crying for the light;
> And with *no language — but a cry.*[2]

The colored man's inheritance and apportionment is still the sombre crux, the perplexing *cul de sac*[3] of the nation, — the dumb skeleton in the closet provoking ceaseless harangues, indeed, but little understood and seldom consulted. Attorneys for the plaintiff and attorneys for the defendant, with bungling *gaucherie*[4] have analyzed and dissected, theorized and synthesized with sublime ignorance or pathetic misapprehension of counsel from the black client. One important witness has not yet been heard from. The summing up of the evidence deposed, and the charge to the jury have been made — but no word from the Black Woman.

It is because I believe the American people to be conscientiously committed to a fair trial and ungarbled evidence, and because I feel it essential to a perfect understanding and an equitable verdict that truth from *each* standpoint be presented at the bar, — that this little Voice, has been added to the already full chorus. The "other side" has not been represented by one who "lives there." And not many can more sensibly realize and more accurately tell the weight and the fret of the "long dull pain" than the open-eyed but hitherto voiceless Black Woman of America.

1 Sphinx, monster in Greek mythology possessing a woman's face, a lion's body, and a bird's wings, who would devour any man who could not answer her riddle.

2 From section 54 of the poem *In Memoriam A. H. H.* (1850) by Alfred Lord Tennyson (1809–92).

3 Dead end.

4 Clumsiness.

The feverish agitation, the perfervid energy, the busy objectivity of the more turbulent life of our men serves, it may be, at once to cloud or color their vision somewhat, and as well to relieve the smart and deaden the pain for them. Their voice is in consequence not always temperate and calm, and at the same time radically corrective and sanatory. At any rate, as our Caucasian barristers are not to blame if they cannot *quite* put themselves in the dark man's place, neither should the dark man be wholly expected fully and adequately to reproduce the exact Voice of the Black Woman.

Delicately sensitive at every pore to social atmospheric conditions, her calorimeter may well be studied in the interest of accuracy and fairness in diagnosing what is often conceded to be a "puzzling" case. If these broken utterances can in any way help to a clearer vision and a truer pulse-beat in studying our Nation's Problem, this Voice by a Black Woman of the South will not have been raised in vain.

TAWAWA CHIMNEY CORNER,[5]

SEPT. 17, 1892.

The Higher Education of Women

In the very first year of our century, the year 1801, there appeared in Paris, a book by Silvain Marechal,[6] entitled "Shall Woman Learn the Alphabet." The book proposes a law prohibiting the alphabet to women, and quotes authorities weighty and various, to prove that the woman who knows the alphabet has already lost part of her womanliness. The author declares that woman can use the alphabet only as Moliére[7] predicted they would, in spelling out the verb *amo*[8] that they have no occasion to peruse Ovid's[9] *Ars Amoris*, since that is already the ground and limit of their intuitive furnishing; that Madame Guion[10] would have been far more ador-

5 A community near Wilberforce, Ohio.

6 Pierre-Sylvain Maréchal (1750–1803), French poet and radical socialist. For her essay, Cooper also draws on an essay titled "Ought Women to Learn the Alphabet?" by Thomas Wentworth Higginson (1823–1911), editor, abolitionist, and advocate of women's rights, who first published his essay in the *Atlantic Monthly* in February 1859.

7 Molière (1622–73), pen name of Jean-Baptiste Poquelin, a French comic playwright.

8 I love (Latin).

9 Ovid (43 B.C.E.–C.E. 17 or 18), Roman poet whose *Ars amatoria* (*The Art of Love*) explores the arts of seduction and intrigue.

10 Jeanne-Marie de la Motte, known as Madame Guyon (1648–1717), French poet and mystic whose writings were condemned by the Catholic Church.

able had she remained a beautiful ignoramus as nature made her; that Ruth, Naomi, the Spartan woman, the Amazons, Penelope, Andromache, Lucretia, Joan of Arc, Petrarch's Laura, the daughters of Charlemagne,[11] could not spell their names; while Sappho, Aspasia, Madame de Maintenon, and Madame de Staël[12] could read altogether too well for their good; finally, that if women were once permitted to read Sophocles[13] and work with logarithms, or to nibble at any side of the apple of knowledge, there would be an end forever to their sewing on buttons and embroidering slippers.

Please remember this book was published at the *beginning* of the Nineteenth Century. At the end of its first third, (in the year 1833) one solitary college in America decided to admit women within its sacred precincts, and organized what was called a "Ladies' Course" as well as the regular B.A. or Gentlemen's course.

It was felt to be an experiment—a rather dangerous experiment—and was adopted with fear and trembling by the good fathers, who looked as if they had been caught secretly mixing explosive compounds and

11 These daughters of the Frankish king Charlemagne, or Charles the Great (742–814), later crowned emperor of the West by Pope Leo III (in 800), were discouraged from marrying and forced to enter monasteries following their father's death. Ruth, Moabite widow in the Old Testament book of Ruth, remained dutiful to her Hebrew mother-in-law, Naomi, and later married Boaz, her redeemer. Spartan women, unlike their Athenian counterparts, were permitted to own, inherit, and dispose of property and also may have been taught to read and write. The ancient Amazons were a legendary race of warrior women. Penelope, faithful wife of Odysseus in Homer's epic poem, the *Odyssey* (c. 725 B.C.E.); Andromache, loyal wife of the Trojan hero Hector; and Lucretia (c. 510 B.C.E.), virtuous Roman wife of Collatinus, were all exemplars of married womanhood in classical lore. Joan of Arc (1412–31), French peasant heroine who led French troops

to victory over the English but was later tried for sorcery and burned at the stake. Petrarch (1304–84), Italian poet and scholar whose beloved Laura was the celebrated subject of much of his poetry.

12 Madame de Staël (1766–1817), born Anne Louise Germaine Necker, French novelist and early champion of women's rights. Sappho (c. 610–580 B.C.E.), Greek lyric poet and native of Lesbos who helped educate young women in music, poetry, and the arts. Aspasia (c. 445 B.C.E.), Milesian-born mistress of the famed Athenian statesman Pericles, whose home was a center of literary and philosophical society. Madame de Maintenon (1636–1719), formerly Françoise d'Aubigné, second wife of King Louis XIV, who created and ran a secular school for girls at St. Cyr.

13 Sophocles (c. 496–406 B.C.E.), Greek tragic dramatist best known for his plays *Oedipus Rex*, *Oedpius at Colonus*, *Antigone*, and the *Electra*.

were guiltily expecting every moment to see the foundations under them shaken and rent and their fair superstructure shattered into fragments.

But the girls came, and there was no upheaval. They performed their tasks modestly and intelligently. Once in a while one or two, were found choosing the gentleman's course. Still no collapse; and the dear, careful, scrupulous, frightened old professors were just getting their hearts out of their throats and preparing to draw one good free breath, when they found they would have to change the names of those courses; for there were as many ladies in the gentlemen's course as in the ladies', and a distinctively Ladies' Course, inferior in scope and aim to the regular classical course, did not and could not exist.

Other colleges gradually fell into line, and to-day there are one hundred and ninety-eight colleges for women, and two hundred and seven coeducational colleges and universities in the United States alone offering the degree of B.A. to women, and sending out yearly into the arteries of this nation a warm, rich flood of strong, brave, active, energetic, well-equipped, thoughtful women—women quick to see and eager to help the needs of this needy world—women who can think as well as feel, and who feel none the less because they think—women who are none the less tender and true for the parchment scroll they bear in their hands—women who have given a, deeper, richer, nobler and grander meaning to the word "womanly" than any one-sided masculine definition could ever have suggested or inspired—women whom the world has long waited for in pain and anguish till there should be at last added to its forces and allowed to permeate its thought the complement of that masculine influence which has dominated it for fourteen centuries.

Since the idea of order and subordination succumbed to barbarian brawn and brutality in the fifth century, the civilized world has been like a child brought up by his father. It has needed the great mother heart to teach it to be pitiful, to love mercy, to succor the weak and care for the lowly.

Whence came this apotheosis of greed and cruelty? Whence this sneaking admiration we all have for bullies and prize-fighters? Whence the self-congratulation of "dominant" races, as if "dominant" meant "righteous" and carried with it a title to inherit the earth? Whence the scorn of so-called weak or unwarlike races and individuals, and the very comfortable assurance that it is their manifest destiny to be wiped out as vermin before this advancing civilization? As if the possession of the Christian graces of meekness, non-resistance and forgiveness, were incompatible with a civilization professedly based on Christianity, the religion of love! Just listen to this little bit of Barbarian brag: "As for Far Orientals, they are not of those who will survive. Artistic attractive people that they are, their civilization is like their own tree flowers, beautiful blossoms destined never to bear fruit. If these people continue in their old course, their earthly career is closed. Just as surely as morning passes into afternoon, so surely are these races of the Far East, if unchanged, destined to disappear before the advancing nations of the West. Vanish, they will, off the face of the earth, and leave our planet the eventual possession of the dwellers where the day declines. Unless their newly imported ideas really take root, it is from this whole world that Japanese and Koreans, as well as Chinese, will inevitably be excluded. Their Nirvana[14] is already being realized; already, it has wrapped Far Eastern Asia in its winding sheet."—*Soul of the Far East—P. Lowell.*[15]

Delightful reflection for "the dwellers where day declines." A spectacle to make the gods laugh, truly, to see the scion of an upstart race by one sweep of his generalizing pen consigning to annihilation one-third the inhabitants of the globe—a people whose civilization was hoary headed before the parent elements that begot his race had advanced beyond nebulosity.

How like Longfellow's Iagoo,[16] we Westerners are, to be sure! In the few hundred years, we have had to strut across our allotted territory and bask in the afternoon sun, we imagine we have exhausted the possibilities of humanity. Verily, we are the people, and after us there is none other. Our God is power; strength, our standard of excellence, inherited from barbarian ancestors through a long line of male progenitors, the Law Salic[17] permitting no feminine modifications.

Says one, "The Chinaman is not popular with us, and we do not like the Negro. It is not that the eyes of the one are set bias, and the other is dark-skinned; but the Chinaman, the Negro is weak—*and Anglo Saxons don't like weakness.*"

The world of thought under the predominant man-influence, unmollified and unrestrained by its complementary force, would become like Daniel's fourth beast: "dreadful and terrible, and *strong* exceedingly;" "it

---

14 Absence of pain and desire. In Buddhism, release from the cycle of death and reincarnation.
15 Percival Lowell (1855–1916), American astronomer and author of *The Soul of the Far East* (1888).
16 Henry Wadsworth Longfellow (1807–82), American poet in whose "Song of Hiawatha" Iagoo is called "the great boaster" and "the marvelous storyteller."
17 A code of Germanic law written under Clovis (476–511) for the Salic Franks.

had great iron teeth; it devoured and brake in pieces, and stamped the residue with the feet of it;"[18] and the most independent of us find ourselves ready at times to fall down and worship this incarnation of power.

Mrs. Mary A. Livermore,[19] a woman whom I can mention only to admire, came near shaking my faith a few weeks ago in my theory of the thinking woman's mission to put in the tender and sympathetic chord in nature's grand symphony, and counteract, or better, harmonize the diapason of more strength and might.

She was dwelling on the Anglo-Saxon genius for power and his contempt for weakness, and described a scene in San Francisco which she had witnessed.

The incorrigible animal known as the American small-boy, had pounced upon a simple, unoffending Chinaman, who was taking home his work, and had emptied the beautifully laundried contents of his basket into the ditch. "And," said she, "when that great man stood there and blubbered before that crowd of lawless urchins, to any one of whom he might have taught a lesson with his two fists, *I didn't much care*."

This is said like a man! It grates harshly. It smacks of the worship of the beast. It is contempt for weakness, and taken out of its setting it seems to contradict my theory. It either shows that one of the highest exponents of the Higher Education can be at times untrue to the instincts I have ascribed to the thinking woman and to the contribution she is to add to the civilized world, or else the influence she wields upon our civilization may be potent without being necessarily and always direct and conscious. The latter is the case. Her voice may strike a false note, but her whole being is musical with the vibrations of human suffering. Her tongue may parrot over the cold conceits that some man has taught her, but her heart is aglow with sympathy and loving kindness, and she cannot be true to her real self without giving out these elements into the forces of the world.

No one is in any danger of imagining Mark Antony[20] "a plain blunt man," nor Cassius[21] a sincere one—whatever the speeches they may make.

As individuals, we are constantly and inevitably, whether we are con-

18 From Daniel 7:7.
19 Mrs. Mary A. Livermore (1820–1905), American suffragist, lecturer, and founding editor of the *Agitator* (1868), a feminist newspaper.
20 Mark Antony (c. 82–30 B.C.E.), Roman politician, soldier, and orator. In Shakespeare's *Julius Caesar* (act 3, scene 2, line 218) he describes himself as "a plain blunt man."
21 Cassius, or Gaius Cassius Longinus (?–42 B.C.), Roman general and politician who was a leader in the conspiracy to assassinate Julius Caesar.

scious of it or not, giving out our real selves into our several little worlds, inexorably adding our own true ray to the flood of starlight, quite independently of our professions and our masquerading; and so in the world of thought, the influence of thinking woman far transcends her feeble declamation and may seem at times even opposed to it.

A visitor in Oberlin once said to the lady principal, "Have you no rabble in Oberlin? How is it I see no police here, and yet the streets are as quiet and orderly as if there were an officer of the law standing on every corner." Mrs. Johnston[22] replied, "Oh, yes; there are vicious persons in Oberlin just as in other towns—*but our girls are our police.*"

With from five to ten hundred pure-minded young women threading the streets of the village every evening unattended, vice must slink away, like frost before the rising sun and yet I venture to say there was not one in a hundred of those girls who would not have run from a street brawl as she would from a mouse, and who would not have declared she could never stand the sight of blood and pistols.

There is, then, a real and special influence of woman. An influence subtle and often involuntary, an influence so intimately interwoven in, so intricately interpenetrated by the masculine influence of the time that it is often difficult to extricate the delicate meshes and analyze and identify the closely clinging fibers. And yet, without this influence—so long as woman sat with bandaged eyes and manacled hands, fast bound in the clamps of ignorance and inaction, the world of thought moved in its orbit like the revolutions of the moon; with one face (the man's face) always out, so that the spectator could not distinguish whether it was disc or sphere.

Now I claim that it is the prevalence of the Higher Education among women, the making it a common everyday affair for women to reason and think and express their thought, the training and stimulus which enable and encourage women to administer to the world the bread it needs as well as the sugar it cries for; in short it is the transmitting the potential forces of her soul into dynamic factors that has given symmetry and completeness to the world's agencies. So only could it be consummated that Mercy, the lesson she teaches, and Truth, the task man has set himself, should meet together: that righteousness, or *rightness*, man's ideal,—and *peace*, its necessary 'other half,' should kiss each other.

We must thank the general enlightenment and independence of woman

22 Mrs. Adelia A. Field Johnston (1837–1910), principal (1870–94) and dean (1894–1900) of the Women's Department at Oberlin College in Ohio.

(which we may now regard as a *fait accompli*[23]) that both these forces are now at work in the world, and it is fair to demand from them for the twentieth century a higher type of civilization than any attained in the nineteenth. Religion, science, art, economics, have all needed the feminine flavor; and literature, the expression of what is permanent and best in all of these, may be gauged at any time to measure the strength of the feminine ingredient. You will not find theology consigning infants to lakes of unquenchable fire long after women have had a chance to grasp, master, and wield its dogmas. You will not find science annihilating personality from the government of the Universe and making of God an ungovernable, unintelligible, blind, often destructive physical force; you will not find jurisprudence formulating as an axiom the absurdity that man and wife are one, and that one the man—that the married woman may not hold or bequeath her own property save as subject to her husband's direction; you will not find political economists declaring that the only possible adjustment between laborers and capitalists is that of selfishness and rapacity—that each must get all he can and keep all that he gets, while the world cries *laissez faire*[24] and the lawyers explain, "it is the beautiful working of the law of supply and demand;" in fine, you will not find the law of love shut out from the affairs of men after the feminine half of the world's truth is completed.

Nay, put your ear now close to the pulse of the time. What is the key-note of the literature of these days? What is the banner cry of all the activities of the last half decade? What is the dominant seventh which is to add richness and tone to the final cadences of this century and lead by a grand modulation into the triumphant harmonies of the next? Is it not compassion for the poor and unfortunate, and, as Bellamy has expressed it, "indignant outcry against the failure of the social machinery as it is, to ameliorate the miseries of men!"[25] Even Christianity is being brought to the bar of humanity and tried by the standard of its ability to alleviate the world's suffering and lighten and brighten its woe. What else can be the meaning of Matthew Arnold's[26] saddening protest, "We cannot do without Christianity," cried he, "and we cannot endure it as it is."

23 An accomplished, presumably irreversible deed or fact (French).
24 Allow to do (French). Also the doctrine of governmental noninterference with business affairs.
25 From the utopian novel *Looking Backward, 2000–1887* (1888) by Edward Bellamy (1850–98), American writer and reformer.
26 Matthew Arnold (1822–88), English poet and critic who encouraged the public, particularly the middle classes, to pursue education and culture.

When went there by an age, when so much time and thought, so much money and labor were given to God's poor and God's invalids, the lowly and unlovely, the sinning as well as the suffering—homes for inebriates and homes for lunatics, shelter for the aged and shelter for babes, hospitals for the sick, props and braces for the falling, reformatory prisons and prison reformatories, all show that a "mothering" influence from some source is leavening the nation.

Now please understand me. I do not ask you to admit that these benefactions and virtues are the exclusive possession of women, or even that women are their chief and only advocates. It may be a man who formulates and makes them vocal. It may be, and often is, a man who weeps over the wrongs and struggles for the amelioration: but that man has imbibed those impulses from a mother rather than from a father and is simply materializing and giving back to the world in tangible form the ideal love and tenderness, devotion and care that have cherished and nourished the helpless period of his own existence.

All I claim is that there is a feminine as well as a masculine side to truth; that these are related not as inferior and superior, not as better and worse, not as weaker and stronger, but as complements—complements in one necessary and symmetric whole. That as the man is more noble in reason, so the woman is more quick in sympathy. That as he is indefatigable in pursuit of abstract truth, so is she in caring for the interests by the way—striving tenderly and lovingly that not one of the least of these 'little ones' should perish. That while we not unfrequently see women who reason, we say, with the coolness and precision of a man, and men as considerate of helplessness as a woman, still there is a general consensus of mankind that the one trait is essentially masculine and the other as peculiarly feminine. That both are needed to be worked into the training of children, in order that our boys may supplement their virility by tenderness and sensibility, and our girls may round out their gentleness by strength and self-reliance. That, as both are alike necessary in giving symmetry to the individual, so a nation or a race will degenerate into mere emotionalism on the one hand, or bullyism on the other, if dominated by either exclusively; lastly, and most emphatically, that the feminine factor can have its proper effect only through woman's development and education so that she may fitly and intelligently stamp her force on the forces of her day, and add her modicum to the riches of the world's thought.

> "For woman's cause is man's: they rise or sink
> Together, dwarfed or godlike, bond or free:

For she that out of Lethe scales with man
The shining steps of nature, shares with man
His nights, his days, moves with him to one goal.
If she be small, slight-natured, miserable,
How shall men grow?
* * * Let, her make herself her own
To give or keep, to live and learn and be
All that not harms distinctive womanhood.
For woman is not undeveloped man
But diverse: could we make her as the man
Sweet love were slain; his dearest bond is this,
Not like to like, but like in difference.
Yet in the long years liker must they grow;
The man be more of woman, she of man;
He gain in sweetness and in moral height,
Nor lose the wrestling thews that throw the world;
She mental breadth, nor fail in childward care,
Nor lose the childlike in the larger mind;
Till at the last she set herself to man,
Like perfect music unto noble words."[27]

Now you will argue, perhaps, and rightly, that higher education for women is not a modern idea, and that, if that is the means of setting free and invigorating the long desired feminine force in the world, it has already had a trial and should, in the past, have produced some of these glowing effects. Sappho, the bright, sweet singer of Lesbos, "the violet-crowned, pure, sweetly smiling Sappho" as Alcaeus[28] calls her, chanted her lyrics and poured forth her soul nearly six centuries before Christ, in notes as full and free, as passionate and eloquent as did ever Archilochus or Anacreon.[29]

Aspasia, that earliest queen of the drawing-room, a century later ministered to the intellectual entertainment of Socrates[30] and the leading wits and philosophers of her time. Indeed, to her is attributed, by the best

27 From canto 7 of *The Princess* (1847) by Alfred Lord Tennyson (1809–92).
28 Alcaeus (c. 625 B.C.E.), Greek lyric poet and contemporary of Sappho.
29 Anacreon (born c. 575–570 B.C.E.), Greek lyric poet from Teos (in Ionia); Archilochus (c. 650 B.C.E), Greek iambic and elegiac poet from Paros.
30 Socrates (470?–399 B.C.E.), Athenian philosopher and teacher.

critics, the authorship of one of the most noted speeches ever delivered by Pericles.[31]

Later on, during the Renaissance period, women were professors in mathematics, physics, metaphysics, and the classic languages in Bologna, Pavia, Padua, and Brescia.[32] Olympia Fulvia Morata,[33] of Ferrara, a most interesting character, whose magnificent library was destroyed in 1553 in the invasion of Schweinfurt by Albert of Brandenburg, had acquired a most extensive education. It is said that this wonderful girl gave lectures on classical subjects in her sixteenth year, and had even before that written several very remarkable Greek and Latin poems, and what is also to the point, she married a professor at Heidelberg, and became a *help-meet for him.*

It is true then that the higher education for women—in fact, the highest that the world has ever witnessed—belongs to the past; but we must remember that it was possible, down to the middle of our own century, only to a select few; and that the fashions and traditions of the times were before that all against it. There were not only no stimuli to encourage women to make the most of their powers and to welcome their development as a helpful agency in the progress of civilization, but their little aspirations, when they had any, were chilled and snubbed in embryo, and any attempt at thought was received as a monstrous usurpation of man's prerogative.

Lessing[34] declared that "the woman who thinks is like the man who puts on rouge—ridiculous;" and Voltaire[35] in his coarse, flippant way used to say, "Ideas are like beards—women and boys have none." Dr. Maginn remarked, "We like to hear a few words of sense from a woman sometimes, as we do from a parrot—they are so unexpected!" and even the pious Fenelon[36] taught that virgin delicacy is almost as incompatible with learning as with vice.

31 Pericles (c. 500–429 B.C.E.), Athenian statesman who dominated Athens from 460 B.C.E. until his death.

32 Bologna, Pavia, Padua, and Brescia, leading Italian cultural centers during the Italian Renaissance.

33 Olympia Fulvia Morata (1526–55), Italian classical scholar raised in the court of Ferrara (Italy) who, following her marriage to Andreas Grunthler, moved with her husband to Schweinfurt, Germany, where she continued writing. When the city was later destroyed, most of Morata's written work was lost.

34 Gotthold Ephraim Lessing (1729–81), German aesthetician, dramatist, and critic.

35 Voltaire (1694–1778), pen name of François-Marie Arouet, a French philosopher and satirist.

36 François de Salignac de La Mothe-Fénelon (1651–1715), French Catholic theologian.

That the average woman retired before these shafts of wit and ridicule and even gloried in her ignorance is not surprising. The Abbe Choisi, it is said, praised the Duchesse de Fontanges[37] as being pretty as an angel and silly as a goose, and all the young ladies of the court strove to make up in folly what they lacked in charms. The ideal of the day was that "women must be pretty, dress prettily, flirt prettily, and not be too well informed;" that it was the *summum bonum*[38] of her earthly hopes to have, as Thackeray[39] puts it, "all the fellows battling to dance with her;" that she had no God-given destiny, no soul with unquenchable longings and inexhaustible possibilities—no work of her own to do and give to the world—no absolute and inherent value, no duty to self, transcending all pleasure-giving that may be demanded of a mere toy; but that her value was purely a relative one and to be estimated as are the fine arts—by the pleasure they give. "Woman, wine and song," as "the world's best gifts to man," were linked together in praise with as little thought of the first saying, "What doest thou," as that the wine and the song should declare, "We must be about our Father's business."[40]

Men believed, or pretended to believe, that the great law of self development was obligatory on their half of the human family only; that while it was the chief end of man to glorify God and put his five talents to the exchangers, gaining thereby other five, it was, or ought to be, the sole end of woman to glorify man and wrap her one decently away in a napkin, retiring into "Hezekiah Smith's lady during her natural life and Hezekiah Smith's relict on her tombstone;" that higher education was incompatible with the shape of the female cerebrum, and that even if it could be acquired it must inevitably unsex woman destroying the lisping, clinging, tenderly helpless, and beautifully dependent creatures whom men would so heroically think for and so gallantly fight for, and giving in their stead a formidable race of blue stockings with corkscrew ringlets and other sinister propensities.

But these are eighteenth century ideas.

We have seen how the pendulum has swung across our present cen-

37 Duchesse de Fontanges, or Marie-Angelique de Scoraille (1661–81), a favorite mistress of Louis XIV in 1679–80; according to James Boswell's *Life of Samuel Johnson* (1791), Abbe Choisi was part of an embassy from Louis XIV to the king of Siam.

38 The greatest or the supreme good (Latin).

39 From chapter 12 of the satiric novel *Vanity Fair* (1848) by William Makepeace Thackeray (1811–63).

40 In Luke 2:49 Jesus says, "I must be about my Father's business."

tury. The men of our time have asked with Emerson,[41] "that woman only show us how she can best be served;" and woman has replied: the chance of the seedling and of the animalcule is all I ask—the chance for growth and self development, the permission to be true to the aspirations of my soul without incurring the blight of your censure and ridicule.

"Audetque viris concurrere virgo."[42]

In soul-culture woman at last dares to contend with men, and we may cite Grant Allen (who certainly cannot be suspected of advocating the unsexing of woman) as an example of the broadening effect of this contest on the ideas at least of the men of the day. He says, in his *Plain Words on the Woman Question*,[43] recently published:

"The position of woman was not [in the past a] position which could bear the test of nineteenth-century scrutiny. Their education was inadequate, their social status was humiliating, their political power was nil, their practical and personal grievances were innumerable; above all, their relations to the family—to their husbands, their children, their friends, their property—was simply insupportable."

And again: "As a body we 'Advanced men' are, I think, prepared to reconsider, and to reconsider fundamentally, without prejudice or misconception, the entire question of the relation between the sexes. We are ready to make any modifications in those relations which will satisfy the woman's just aspiration for personal independence, for intellectual and moral development, for physical culture, for political activity, and for a voice in the arrangement of her own affairs, both domestic and national."

Now this is magnanimous enough, surely; and quite a step from eighteenth century preaching, is it not? The higher education of Woman has certainly developed the men;—let us see what it has done for the women.

Matthew Arnold during his last visit to America in '82 or '83, lectured before a certain co-educational college in the West. After the lecture he remarked, with some surprise, to a lady professor, that the young women in his audience, he noticed, "paid as close attention as the men, *all the*

41 Ralph Waldo Emerson (1803–82), American poet, essayist, and philosopher.

42 From Virgil's *Aeneid*, book 1. "*Audetque viris concurrere virgo*" (Latin) may be roughly translated, "A female warrior, a maiden who dared to join in battle with men." The reference is to the warrior-princess Penthesilea, whom Aeneas sees portrayed on the decorated walls of a temple in Carthage.

43 This essay by Grant Allen (1848–99), Canadian writer, appeared in the December 1889 *Fortnightly Review*.

way through." This led, of course, to a spirited discussion of the higher education for women, during which he said to his enthusiastic interlocutor, eyeing her philosophically through his English eyeglass: "But—eh—don't you think it—eh—spoils their *chawnces*, you know!"

Now, as to the result to women, this is the most serious argument ever used against the higher education. If it interferes with marriage, classical training has a grave objection to weigh and answer.

For I agree with Mr. Allen at least on this one point, that there must be marrying and giving in marriage even till the end of time.

I grant you that intellectual development, with the self-reliance and capacity for earning a livelihood which it gives, renders woman less dependent on the marriage relation for physical support (which, by the way, does not always accompany it). Neither is she compelled to look to sexual love as the one sensation capable of giving tone and relish, movement and vim to the life she leads. Her horison is extended. Her sympathies are broadened and deepened and multiplied. She is in closer touch with nature. Not a bud that opens, not a dew drop, not a ray of light, not a cloud-burst or a thunderbolt, but adds to the expansiveness and zest of her soul. And if the sun of an absorbing passion be gone down, still 'tis night that brings the stars. She has remaining the mellow, less obtrusive, but none the less enchanting and inspiring light of friendship, and into its charmed circle she may gather the best the world has known. She can commune with Socrates about the *daimon*[44] he knew and to which she too can bear witness; she can revel in the majesty of Dante, the sweetness of Virgil, the simplicity of Homer, the strength of Milton.[45] She can listen to the pulsing heart throbs of passionate Sappho's encaged soul, as she beats her bruised wings against her prison bars and struggles to flutter out into Heaven's æther, and the fires of her own soul cry back as she listens. "Yes; Sappho, I know it all; I know it all." Here, at last, can be communion without suspicion; friendship, without misunderstanding; love without jealousy.

We must admit then that Byron's[46] picture, whether a thing of beauty or not, has faded from the canvas of to-day.

44 A person's attendant spirit.
45 John Milton (1608–74), English poet and author of the epic *Paradise Lost* (1667). Dante Alighieri (1265–1321), Italian poet best known for *Commedia* (*The Divine Comedy*). Virgil (70–19 B.C.E.), Publius Vergilius Maro, Latin poet and author of the *Eclogues*, the *Georgics*, and the *Aeneid*. Homer (mid-eighth century B.C.E.), Greek epic poet credited with writing the *Iliad* (c. 750 B.C.E.) and the *Odyssey* (c. 725 B.C.E.).
46 George Gordon Byron, or Lord Byron (1788–1824), English Romantic poet.

"Man's love," he wrote, "is of man's life a thing apart,
'Tis woman's whole existence.
Man may range the court, camp, church, the vessel and the mart,
Sword, gown, gain, glory offer in exchange.
Pride, fame, ambition, to fill up his heart—
And few there are whom these cannot estrange.
Men have all these resources, we *but one*—
To love again and be again undone."[47]

This may have been true when written. *It is not true to-day.* The old, subjective, stagnant, indolent and wretched life for woman has gone. She has as many resources as men, as many activities beckon her on. As large possibilities swell and inspire her heart.

Now, then, does it destroy or diminish her capacity for loving?

Her standards have undoubtedly gone up. The necessity of speculating in 'chawnces' has probably shifted. The question is not now with the woman "How shall I so cramp, stunt, simplify and nullify myself as to make me eligible to the honor of being swallowed up into some little man?" but the problem, I trow,[48] now rests with the man as to how he can so develop his God-given powers as to reach the ideal of a generation of women who demand the noblest, grandest, and best achievements of which he is capable; and this surely is the only fair and natural adjustment of the chances. Nature never meant that the ideals and standards of the world should be dwarfing and minimizing ones, and the men should thank us for requiring of them the richest fruits which they can grow. If it makes them work, all the better for them.

As to the adaptability of the educated woman to the marriage relation, I shall simply quote from that excellent symposium of learned women that appeared recently under Mrs. Armstrong's signature in answer to the "Plain Words" of Mr. Allen, already referred to. "Admitting no longer any question as to their intellectual equality with the men whom they meet, with the simplicity of conscious strength, they take their place beside the men who challenge them, and fearlessly face the result of their actions. They deny that their education in any way unfits them for the duty of wifehood and maternity or primarily renders these conditions any less attractive to them than to the domestic type of woman. On the contrary, they hold that their knowledge of physiology makes them better mothers and housekeepers; their knowledge of chemistry makes them

47 From canto 1.194 of Byron's *Don Juan* (1819).

48 Believe.

better cooks; while from their training in other natural sciences and in mathematics, they obtain an accuracy and fair-mindedness which is of great value to them in dealing with their children or employees."

So much for their willingness. Now the apple may be good for food and pleasant to the eyes, and a fruit to be desired to make one wise. Nay, it may even assure you that it has no aversion whatever to being tasted. Still, if you do not like the flavor all these recommendations are nothing. Is the intellectual woman *desirable* in the matrimonial market?

This I cannot answer. I confess my ignorance. I am no judge of such things. I have been told that strong-minded women could be, when they thought it worth their while, quite endurable, and, judging from the number of female names I find in college catalogues among the alumnae with double patronymics, I surmise that quite a number of men are willing to put up with them.

Now I would that my task ended here. Having shown that a great want of the world in the past has been a feminine force; that that force can have its full effect only through the untrammelled development of woman; that such development, while it gives her to the world and to civilization, does not necessarily remove her from the home and fireside; finally, that while past centuries have witnessed sporadic instances of this higher growth, still it was reserved for the latter half of the nineteenth century to render it common and general enough to be effective; I might close with a glowing prediction of what the twentieth century may expect from this heritage of twin forces—the masculine battered and toil-worn as a grim veteran after centuries of warfare, but still strong, active, and vigorous, ready to help with his hard-won experience the young recruit rejoicing in her newly found freedom, who so confidently places her hand in his with mutual pledges to redeem the ages.

> "And so the twain upon the skirts of Time,
> Sit side by side, full-summed in all their powers,
> Dispensing harvest, sowing the To-be,
> Self-reverent each and reverencing each."[49]

Fain would I follow them, but duty is nearer home. The high ground of generalities is alluring but my pen is devoted to a special cause: and with a view to further enlightenment on the achievements of the century for THE HIGHER EDUCATION OF COLORED WOMEN, I wrote a few days ago to the colleges which admit women and asked how many colored

49 From canto 7 of *The Princess* (1847) by Tennyson (1809–92).

women had completed the B.A. course in each during its entire history. These are the figures returned: Fisk leads the way with twelve; Oberlin next with five; Wilberforce, four; Ann Arbor and Wellesley three each, Livingstone two, Atlanta one, Howard,[50] as yet, none.

I then asked the principal of the Washington High School[51] how many out of a large number of female graduates from his school had chosen to go forward and take a collegiate course. He replied that but one had ever done so, and she was then in Cornell.[52]

Others ask questions too, sometimes, and I was asked a few years ago by a white friend, "How is it that the men of your race seem to outstrip the women in mental attainment?" "Oh," I said, "so far as it is true, the men, I suppose, from the life they lead, gain more by contact; and so far as it is only apparent, I think the women are more quiet. They don't feel called to mount a barrel and harangue by the hour every time they imagine they have produced an idea."

But I am sure there is another reason which I did not at that time see fit to give. The atmosphere, the standards, the requirements of our little world do not afford any special stimulus to female development.

It seems hardly a gracious thing to say, but it strikes me as true, that while our men seem thoroughly abreast of the times on almost every other subject, when they strike the woman question they drop back into sixteenth century logic. They leave nothing to be desired generally in regard to gallantry and chivalry, but they actually do not seem sometimes to have outgrown that old contemporary of chivalry—the idea that women may stand on pedestals or live in doll houses, (if they happen to have them) but they must not furrow their brows with thought or attempt to help men tug at the great questions of the world. I fear the majority of

50 Fisk University (established in 1866), founded in Nashville, Tennessee. Oberlin College (1833), Cooper's own alma mater in Oberlin, Ohio. Wilberforce University (1856), located in Wilberforce, Ohio. Ann Arbor (1817), presumably the University of Michigan, which moved from Detroit to Ann Arbor in 1837 and began admitting women in 1870. Livingstone College (1879) in Salisbury, North Carolina (formerly the Zion Wesley Institute of Concord, North Carolina). Atlanta University (1865), founded by the Freedmen's

Bureau in Atlanta, Georgia. Howard University (1867), located in Washington, D.C.

51 Most likely a reference to the M Street School (later Dunbar High School) in Washington, D.C., which was founded in 1870 as the Colored Preparatory High School and was the first public high school for African Americans.

52 Graduated from Scientific Course, June 1890, the first colored woman to graduate from Cornell. [Cooper's note]

colored men do not yet think it worth while that women aspire to higher education. Not many will subscribe to the "advanced" ideas of Grant Allen already quoted. The three R's, a little music and a good deal of dancing, a first rate dress-maker and a bottle of magnolia balm, are quite enough generally to render charming any woman possessed of tact and the capacity for worshipping masculinity.

My readers will pardon my illustrating my point and also giving a reason for the fear that is in me, by a little bit of personal experience. When a child I was put into a school near home that professed to be normal and collegiate, i.e. to prepare teachers for colored youth, furnish candidates for the ministry, and offer collegiate training for those who should be ready for it. Well, I found after a while that I had a good deal of time on my hands. I had devoured what was put before me, and, like Oliver Twist,[53] was looking around to ask for more. I constantly felt (as I suppose many an ambitious girl has felt) a thumping from within unanswered by any beckoning from without. Class after class was organized for these ministerial candidates (many of them men who had been preaching before I was born). Into every one of these classes I was expected to go, with the sole intent, I thought at the time, of enabling the dear old principal, as he looked from the vacant countenances of his sleepy old class over to where I sat, to get off his solitary pun—his never-failing pleasantry, especially in hot weather—which was, as he called out "Any one!" to the effect that "*any* one" then meant "*Annie* one."

Finally a Greek class was to be formed. My inspiring preceptor informed me that Greek had never been taught in the school, but that he was going to form a class *for the candidates for the ministry*, and if I liked I might join it. I replied—humbly I hope, as became a female of the human species—that I would like very much to study Greek, and that I was thankful for the opportunity, and so it went on. A boy, however meager his equipment and shallow his pretentions, had only to declare a floating intention to study theology and he could get all the support, encouragement and stimulus he needed, be absolved from work and invested beforehand with all the dignity of his far away office. While a self-supporting girl had to struggle on by teaching in the summer and working after school hours to keep up with her board bills, and actually to fight her way against positive discouragements to the higher education; till one such girl one day flared out and told the principal "the only

53 The orphaned title character of *Oliver Twist*, a novel by the English writer Charles Dickens (1812–70).

mission opening before a girl in his school was to marry one of those candidates." He said he didn't know but it was. And when at last that same girl announced her desire and intention to go to college it was received with about the same incredulity and dismay as if a brass button on one of those candidate's coats had propounded a new method for squaring the circle or trisecting the arc.

Now this is not fancy. It is a simple unvarnished photograph, and what I believe was not in those days exceptional in colored schools, and I ask the men and women who are teachers and co-workers for the highest interests of the race, that they give the girls a chance! We might as well expect to grow trees from leaves as hope to build up a civilization or a manhood without taking into consideration our women and the home life made by them, which must be the root and ground of the whole matter. Let us insist then on special encouragement for the education of our women and special care in their training. Let our girls feel that we expect something more of them than that they merely look pretty and appear well in society. Teach them that there is a race with special needs which they and only they can help; that the world needs and is already asking for their trained, efficient forces. Finally, if there is an ambitious girl with pluck and brain to take the higher education, encourage her to make the most of it. Let there be the same flourish of trumpets and clapping of hands as when a boy announces his determination to enter the lists; and then, as you know that she is physically the weaker of the two, don't stand from under and leave her to buffet the waves alone. Let her know that your heart is following her, that your hand, though she sees it not, is ready to support her. To be plain, I mean let money be raised and scholarships be founded in our colleges and universities for self-supporting, worthy young women, to offset and balance the aid that can always be found for boys who will take theology.

The earnest well trained Christian young woman, as a teacher, as a home-maker, as wife, mother, or silent influence even, is as potent a missionary agency among our people as is the theologian; and I claim that at the present stage of our development in the South she is even more important and necessary.

Let us then, here and now, recognize this force and resolve to make the most of it—not the boys less, but the girls more.

JEEHYUN LIM

David Bryant Fulton

(from the frontispiece to Fulton's Eagle Clippings, *in the North Carolina Collection,*
Wilson Library, University of North Carolina, Chapel Hill)

THROUGH FICTION, JOURNALISM, and autobiographical writing, David Bryant Fulton determined from the outset of his largely self-published literary career to be a vigorous, uncompromising defender of black America. Writing at the turn of the century, an era deemed "the nadir" of African American social and political fortunes by the historian Rayford Logan, Fulton adopted the combative pen name Jack Thorne to reinforce his literary vocation as an unabashed polemicist whose dedication to racial pride and advocacy of black solidarity place him in the line of black nationalists headed by David Walker. Fulton championed African Americans who often went unnoticed in contemporary writing, particularly black women and the black working class, which may help to explain why he achieved little more than local fame.

Fulton was born in Fayetteville, North Carolina, to Lavinia Robinson Fulton and Benjamin Fulton, both ex-slaves from North Carolina. In 1867, the family moved to Wilmington, where Fulton attended first the Williston School and later the Gregory Normal Institute. In 1883, he married a longtime friend, Virginia Moore, from Wilmington. Fulton worked at Banneker Hose Reel Company for approximately four years as a foreman before moving to Brooklyn, New York, in 1887. Recounting the process of his relocation to Brooklyn, Fulton's "A Dock Laborer" typifies the experience of the numerous southern migrants who moved North in the latter decades of the nineteenth century. A year after his arrival in New York, Fulton went to work for the Pullman Palace Car Company as a porter.

Fulton launched his writing career by chronicling his experience as a railroad porter in sketches published by the *Record*, the first newspaper owned by an African American in Wilmington, North Carolina. These sketches were later collected into a small book, *Recollections of a Sleeping Car Porter* (1892), that Fulton published himself. Though Fulton was an expatriate from his native state, his ties to the South are evident in *Recollections*, which offers an extended travelogue through the Southeast from the standpoint of a black porter, and in his self-published miscellany of newspaper articles, *Eagle Clippings* (1907). Fulton's interests as an amateur North Carolina ethnologist inform his poem "De Coonah Man" (1913), which fondly recalls the John Kooner, or Jonkonnu, festivals on Christmas Day in Wilmington, a half century after Harriet Jacobs portrayed the same events in Edenton in *Incidents in the Life of a Slave Girl*.

In addition to his job with the Pullman Company, Fulton also worked for Sears Roebuck, a music publishing house, and the central branch of the Brooklyn YMCA. He was a leader in the Negro Society for Historical Research, cofounded in 1911 by John Edward Bruce, the noted African American journalist, and Arthur Schomburg, one of the most influential bibliophiles in African American letters.

Fulton's best-known work, *Hanover; or, The Persecution of the Lowly. A Story of the Wilmington Massacre*, was published in 1899, one year after the violent insurgence that brought about the establishment of a white supremacist government in Wilmington. Part exposé and part fiction, *Hanover* illustrates, in Fulton's own words, his efforts to present "a truthful statement of the causes" of the Wilmington massacre of November 1898. His indefatigable defense of black rights and his persistent efforts to rectify racial prejudices come to the fore in *Eagle Clippings*. "Race Unification: How It May Be Accomplished," published in the *African Times and Orient Review* in 1913, shows how Fulton envisioned an autonomous black community and race pride as requisites for advancement and harmonious relationships to whites.

Fulton's pioneering feminism is evidenced in his efforts to admit black women to the meetings of the Society for the Sons of North Carolina, a social organization he founded in Brooklyn in 1895. *A Plea for Social Justice for the Negro Woman*, published by the Negro Society for Historical Research in 1912, expresses Fulton's commitment to African American women's rights. Invited to address the annual convention of the New York Colored Women's Clubs in July 1923, he presented the poem "Mother of Mine; Ode to the Negro Woman."

In his dedication copy of *Hanover* to Arthur Schomburg, Fulton wrote, "This little volume Hanover is the outpouring of a heart full of love for the people of my race." These words serve as an apt epitaph to Fulton's entire literary career.

Suggested Readings

Fulton, David Bryant [Jack Thorne]. *Hanover; or, The Persecution of the Lowly. A Story of the Wilmington Massacre.* 1899. 2nd ed. New York: Arno Press, 1969. Also available in electronic form through Documenting the American South, an electronic database sponsored by The Academic Affairs Library at the University of North Carolina at Chapel Hill, <http://docsouth.unc.edu/nc/thorne/menu.html>.

———. *Eagle Clippings.* Brooklyn, N.Y.: Self-published, 1907. Also available in electronic form through Documenting the American South, an electronic database sponsored by The Academic Affairs Library at the University of North Carolina at Chapel Hill, <http://docsouth.unc.edu/nc/thorne/menu.html>.

Gleason, William. "Voices at the Nadir: Charles Chesnutt and David Bryant Fulton." *American Literary Realism* 24, no. 3 (Spring 1992): 22–41.

Gunning, Sandra. *Race, Rape, and Lynching: The Red Record of American Literature, 1890–1912.* New York: Oxford University Press, 1996.

Prather, H. Leon. *We Have Taken a City: Wilmington Racial Massacre and Coup of 1898.* Rutherford: Fairleigh Dickinson University Press, 1984. [The most conscientious study of the Wilmington massacre.]

Yarborough, Richard. "Violence, Manhood, and Black Heroism: The Wilmington Riot in Two Turn-of-the-Century African American Novels." In *Democracy Betrayed*, edited by David S. Cecelski and Timothy B. Tyson, 225–51. Chapel Hill: University of North Carolina Press, 1998. [Discusses *Hanover* and Chesnutt's *The Marrow of Tradition*.]

Note on the Text

The text of "A Dock Laborer" is taken from *Eagle Clippings*, published by Fulton himself in Brooklyn, New York, in 1907. The text of "De Coonah Man" is reprinted from the *African Times and Orient Review* 2 (November–December 1913): 234. The poem appends Fulton's essay "Race Unification; How It May Be Accomplished," pp. 233–34, in the same issue of the *African Times and Orient Review*. "A Plea for Social Justice for the Negro Woman" was published in a series of "occasional papers" by the Negro Society for Historical Research in 1912 in Yonkers, New York. Fulton was the librarian of the Negro Society for Historical Research, whose president was John E. Bruce and whose secretary-treasurer was Arthur A. Schomburg. The text of "A Plea for Social Justice for the Negro Woman" is reprinted from a microfilm copy in the Arthur Schomburg Collection of the New York Public Library.

❖

A DOCK LABORER

*Experiences of One Man Who Came to the Metropolis in
The Late Eighties, Looking for Honest Employment.*

(From *The Brooklyn Citizen.*[1])

From the time of my arrival in New York in '87, and entering the employ
of the Pullman Palace Car Co.,[2] in '88, up to Dec., 1905, I had been able
to give a pretty accurate account of my time—nine years in the Palace
car service, four years in a large music house in New York City, two
years at odd jobs, and at the close of the year 1905 I had about wound
up four years in the employ of the Central Branch of The Young Men's
Christian Association of Brooklyn, feeling that a change of atmosphere
would perhaps conduce toward the strengthening of my faith in the ef-
ficacy of Christian religion[3] which contact with "Scribes"[4] had somewhat
weakened. The uninitiated, perusing the columns of the great New York
dailies with their innumerable "Help Wanted" advertisements, would
readily conclude that the seeking of employment in the great Metropolis
need be no irksome task to any one. But the major portion of these want
ads, are mere will-o'-the-wisps,[5] put there apparently to tantalize and to
throw into the abyss of despair honest seekers after the tangible. Such
announcements as "Wanted—Cooks, waiters, chambermaids, coachmen,
butlers, hall-boys, bellmen, laundresses," etc., etc., are invariably the
fabrications of unscrupulous employment agents, who spread their nets
to catch the unwary, whose money they greedily pocket and hurry them
off to fill positions which, to their knowledge, are already filled through
other agencies. Experience had taught me that in seeking work in New
York, both of these mediums were to be eschewed. My first position,
which cost me just half of my fortune, was a place way out in Fordham,
where I was engaged to drive a horse and milk the cow. In less than a

1 A daily newspaper published in
Brooklyn, New York, from 1886 to
1947.
2 Founded by George Pullman in
1867, the Pullman Palace Car Company featured its founder's specially
designed sleeping cars for railroads.

3 Fulton's mother was one of the
founders of the First Congregational
Church in Wilmington.
4 In the New Testament, a scholar of
Jewish law who scoffs at Christ's
teachings.
5 Delusions.

week I had broken the shaft of the man's buggy, was dismissed, and with my belongings was on my way back to the shrewd son of Abraham,[6] who had followed me to the door on the day of my departure from his office, rubbing his clammy hands and whining: "Eef th' blace dus nod suit you, vhy cum back an' I gif you a nudder." But when he saw me approaching the office a second time he met me at the door and, holding up his hands in feigned horror, swore by the beard of the prophet that he had fulfilled his contract and would do no more. If he did not see greenness[7] in my face, he took the chance at bluffing me out of three dollars, and succeeded. This well-remembered experience turned me into other channels in search of work this time. Accepting the agency of a Health and Accident Insurance Company, at the end of a month of canvassing I had on my book the names of a host of sympathetic friends who, although well provided for in that line, were, on account of their great love for me, ready to invest in more insurance. One very dear friend to whom I thought I had convincingly set forth the advantages and inducements my company offered, and why a woman of her environments and temperament would profit by taking out a policy therein, and who had, in turn, eloquently acquiesced and expressed her desire and determination to subscribe, had at the conclusion of two weeks, the time appointed for the issuing of the policy, prepared such an eloquent speech in support of a demurrer, that, after listening in amazement to it, I threw aside my insurance outfit in disgust, purchased hook and overalls and sought employment among the dock laborers.

It was in 1892 that the Ward Steamship Company of New York terminated a series of strikes among its dock laborers and stevedores,[8] entailing great financial loss, by substituting Negro labor for Irish and Italian. The Irishman is the very embodiment of discontent, the instigator of nearly all the troubles in the labor field, the inaugurator of political upheavals and race clashings. Ever ready to strike for higher wages and shorter hours, the Irishman would burn his own dwelling from over his head if he thought that thereby he might do injury to an unyielding employer. The Ward Steamship Company, financially embarrassed by frequent revolutions in its labor department, and at the mercy of labor unions had yielded step by step until the longshoreman's[9] pay had advanced from thirty to forty-five cents an hour. But the demand for fifty cents was the straw that broke the camel's back. The Italians who, with difficulty sup-

6 A Jew.
7 Naïveté.

8 A person who is in charge of loading and unloading ships at ports.
9 Stevedore.

planted the Irish and went into the holds of the ships to work for twenty-five cents per hour, were not sufficiently bulky nor experienced to insure independence of the lusty son of Erin,[10] and the Negro, who, previous to this time, had only been allowed to step in here and there along the water front, was called in to take charge of the work of loading and discharging the great ships of the Ward Steamship Company. The Negro workman, pushing out over the North and West, is confronted by more serious and exasperating obstacles than any other human creature. Securing work in big corporations only as a strike-breaker, he, in many instances, has only been retained until the white man chose to return to work. But the Ward Steamship Company had called to its rescue, men schooled in Yankee duplicity, who did not "turn to" until this very important matter was settled. But the scale of wages made by the Italian strike-breaker was not advanced in favor of the efficient black stevedore. And the twelve years of unprecedented prosperity, during which the company has had to double its carrying capacity by adding in its fleet several large and more commodious ships, an advance in wages from twenty-five cents an hour so far has never been offered these benefactors, who freed the company from the meshes of labor unions, brought order out of chaos and started them on the road to prosperity. It must not be conceded that because of its rough character, the work of the stevedore is a calling that does not require intelligence, cool-headedness and skill; for without coolness and thorough knowledge on the part of those appointed to direct it, the work of loading and unloading these great ships would be attended by far greater loss of life and limb than is now recorded. It was a cold morning in the month of February when I joined the anxious crowd of laborers at Pier 15, East River, Brooklyn side, waiting to be "shaped." To be shaped is to secure at the timekeeper's window a brass check with a number engraved upon it, which is written in his book opposite your name, and passing the foreman who engages you, you call out this number, which is jotted down in his book. On quitting work each man calls out his number to the timekeeper, and returning, reports both to timekeeper and foreman. "Push in," said a sympathetic fellow, noticing my embarrassment, "your chance may be as good as the oldest; no man has a cinch[11] here."

"Stand in line and take your turn," said another man, as he noticed me endeavoring to push my truck past the fellow in front of me. "The Irishman tries to make a job last as long as possible, while the Negro sings and runs himself out of work." My first day's work consisted of unloading

10 An Irishman.   11 Certainty.

DAVID BRYANT FULTON

fruit and pig lead;[12] and as I climbed the hill homeward at the conclusion of the day my limbs almost refused to support me. The following day, still sore and stiff from the previous day's toil, I reported again at Pier 15, and by sheer ambition trudged through another day of the hardest toil of my life. In discharging ships, foremen may employ as many as twenty men in their gangs, but they dwindle to sixteen when loading. Failing to get a "shape" on the third day, I wended my way back home to return in the evening to try my luck with the night gangs. To my mind, it requires more than ordinary courage on the part of a new and inexperienced hand to join a company of men going into a ship's hold to store freight, aided only by the light of lanterns. The gang in which I worked began in the ship's hold to be shifted to the docks, and from thence off shore to hoist freight from one of the many lighters[13] which flanked the great vessel. The angry, black waters, lashed into fury by the fierce cold winds, seemed anxiously waiting to swallow into its depths the timid wretch who, stumbling blindly over the many pitfalls, chanced to miss his footing. This, together with the oaths of the experienced and unsympathetic workmen, the ear-piercing calls of the gangwayman, the deafening roar of machinery so exasperated and confused me that I was tempted to climb back upon the dock and scamper off for home. But as the night grew old and the owl-like hoot of craft in the great harbor lessened, the lights in the distant towers went out one by one and the great bridge, no longer disturbed by moving cars and the tread of restless feet, stood there calm and tranquil in the glimmering shadows, I became more reconciled to my surroundings and the task became less irksome. Current stories of crime, of midnight assassinations, of suicides, give New York harbor at dead of night a weird and fantastic aspect. Yet in spite of all this it is a fascinating sight. I soon discovered that one man's chances were not, if green, as good as another old and experienced hand, and justly so. The mastery of stevedore work is as difficult a task as the mastery of algebra, it seems to me. It was perfectly natural for the foremen to cull out the men whom they knew could do creditable work. My first employer was Capt. John Simonds (colored), who was doubtless moved more by my willingness than my value as a workman, and though I got in now and then with Powell, with Rainey and with Butler, it seemed less difficult to shape with Simonds. For quite a month or more I beat about the decks, following the gangs from pier to pier and from sugar house to sugar house with varying

12 Crude lead cast in blocks.
13 Small barges that unload goods to or from cargo ships.

luck. One evening at Erie Basin, I joined the gang of a foreman whom they called "Buster Brown." "Buster Brown" was a wild, swearing Negro of the Guinea type,[14] with protruding forehead, staring eyes and heavy lips that could utter oaths and filthy epithets that would put a pirate to blush. Brown was the type of Negro indispensable to the overseer of the slave plantation, who wished to wring out the very last drop of blood from his chattels; who often as "drivers" strung up and lashed their own mothers. It is a type of native used by the British now plundering South Africa, to get the most out of the workers in the mines. This fellow kept the air lurid with oaths and vulgarity, buldozing the men, threatening them with his fist and with his gun, and in turn cringing like a cur when addressed by the white supervisor. I looked at this Negro both in pity and disgust and wondered what kind of a home it was over which he presided. Although the night was cold and men were constantly dropping out to warm up at a near-by saloon, I stuck to my post lest the impetuosity of this foreman tempt me to lay his thick head upon the dock and thereby lose a night's work. Fortunately, "Buster Brown" is not the prevailing type of stevedore; I found a sufficient number of sober, industrious and goodly disposed men engaged in work there to make it quite a pleasant place to be. There are many incidents during my employ there on the docks that I recall with pleasure, for I believe the Negro works with a lighter heart, and infuses more music and fun into labor than any other human being. Most of these men are from Virginia and the Carolinas, where music and laughter drive away the irksomeness of toil. No group of men was without its jester, who was often a Godsend to the discouraged and melancholy. I recall with a great deal of mirth the side-splitting jokes gotten off by "Squire Rigger" on "Sheep" and "Sheep's" witty retorts and sarcastic flings at "Rabbit," or Philip Hooper's droll, yet mirth-provoking tales of his adventures. Phil had traveled extensively and worked at nearly every imaginable calling in the labor world, and his retentive memory was never taxed for some interesting, instructive and yet amusing story.

14 A native of West Africa.

❖

DE COONAH MAN[15]

W'en Chrismus comes uh rollin' roun', ma h'art gits young agin,
    As down de misty way in tho't I run,
To times w'en toot'n' horns an' sich was not declarr'd uh sin,
    An' Chrismus was uh ginal[16] feast ob fun.
Hit want[17] uh day w'en people bent dey[18] hades in t'ankful prayah
    To Gawd de gibber ob de Blessed Chile;
We heah'd not ob de shepuds nor de anguls bright an' fayah,
    Nor ob de Virgin Mary, meek an' mile.

But dey dat santimonious trow solemnity away, an' say dat
    Chrismus comes but wunst uh yeah;
An' in de fun an' frolickin' de cripple, ol' an' gray,
    'Ud jine de young in scramblin' fuh uh sheah.[19]
Grandad was pious to de coe, but tho't hit not uh sin
    Fuh ebry man to hab his Chrismus dram;[20]
An' tho' he strove troout de yeah de sinnah fuh to win,
    De Chrismus jug sot waitin' in de jam.

Ol' Santi Claus was not so pop'lar, kase[21] he mighty slow—
    An' den so many chimleys he 'ud shun;
But we hilt no grudge agin him, fuh hit did'n' check de flow
    Ob Chrismus cheer, ob merriment an' fun.
Fuh mo'e welcome den[22] ol' Santi was de ragged coonah man,
    Uh dancin' an' uh caperin' about;
Makin' moshuns an' uh shufflin' jes to mek de chillan run,
    Whilst de older ones uh follerin' 'ud shout:—

15 The John Kooner, or Jonkonnu, festival originated from the West Coast of Africa and was first practiced during the slavery era predominantly in coastal communities in the southeastern United States. In North Carolina, there are records of the festival having been celebrated in Edenton, Hillsboro, and Wilmington.

16 Genial.
17 Wasn't.
18 Their.
19 Share.
20 A small drink of liquor.
21 Because.
22 Than.

"Show yo moshun, mister coonah, blow horn, blow!
Yaller gal go roun' de cornah, blow horn, blow!
Chrismus comes but wunst uh yeah, blow horn, blow!
Ebery niggah habs his sheah, blow horn, blow!"

Wondah whar is Whistlin' Henry, Chicken Bill, an' Uncle Guy,
    Red-eyed Quimbo, Cripple Dick and Rusty Joe?
Mos' ob dem hab crossed de ribber to dey home beyan de sky,
    Still—heahs dey shouts, dey singin' sorf an' low;
"Blow horn, blow—w'en yer comin' ober? blow horn, blow,
Ehly in de mawnin'; blow horn, blow! Blow horn, blow, blow-o-o-o!"

❖

A PLEA FOR SOCIAL JUSTICE

FOR THE NEGRO WOMAN

Occasional Paper
Issued by
Negro Society for Historical Research
Yonkers, N.Y.[23]

"I am black but comely, O ye daughters of Jerusalem,
as the tents of Kedar, as the curtains of Solomon."[24]

In beginning the discussion of this subject it is both fitting and comforting to revert to that period in the history of the world when the dominant races were sable races; and the black and swarthy skin was of course a mark of honor; when the women of whose beauty and charms the bards wrote in such extravagant eulogy were colored women, and the warriors and heroes whose praise the women chanted so justly, as is recorded in both sacred and profane history were swarthy and black. When we consider further the fact that Meroe[25] in northern Africa was the world's seat of learning when Athens[26] was a mere province; that in Egypt and Ethiopia there were art schools, literary societies, libraries, homes of culture and refinement twelve hundred years before the race of the writer of Solomon's Songs was evolved from the Semitic tribes of the desert,[27] we must conclude that the social position of the woman of color was more to be envied than despised. When we further consider the fact that the Jew who went down into Egypt[28] to dwell was not white, but an Asiatic, and that four hundred years of a yellow race's mingling and intermarrying with the blacks of Ethiopia and Egypt would not tend towards the lightening up of a people, we must conclude that the writer of Solomon's

23 Cofounded by journalist John Edward Bruce and bibliophile Arthur Schomburg in 1911, this organization published occasional papers by African American intellectuals.
24 Song of Solomon 1:5–6.
25 A city of ancient Nubia, now in Sudan, and the capital of the Cushite Dynasty from 530 B.C. to A.D. 350.
26 Capital of Greece, often regarded as the seed of Western civilization. Athens prospered most after the Persian wars (500–449 B.C.).
27 Solomon (c. 970–c. 930 B.C.), king of Israel and purported author of the Song of Solomon. The Semitic tribes are sometimes identified as the descendants of Shem, son of Noah.
28 Joseph, the son of Jacob. See Genesis 37:28.

Songs did not mean to have it understood that this Egyptian woman's reference to her complexion was an apology. Bishop Tanner[29] in his book "The Color of Solomon" says: "Solomon had a passion for women manifestly of darker hue than women of Israel of pure Israelitish blood, chief among whom (was) the daughter of Pharoah concerning whom we find it convenient to say: First, she was black according to her own words: but not indeed, as our white translators of the Bible give them.
According to those she is made to say;

'I am black but comely'

But what she really says is:

'I am black and comely,
O ye daughters of Jerusalem'—

"Quite as dark complexioned as was the daughter of Pharoah was that of other Hamitic[30] princesses of whom he (Solomon) became enamored, even the Queen of Sheba;[31] to say nothing of the Canaanitish[32] women, many of them Hittites,[33] with whom he filled his harem all of whom were of swarthy color."

Enough has been said along this line to awaken and stimulate pride in the fact that in discussing the woman of our race we are considering a woman of noble ancestry, worthy of our chivalry, our most strenuous efforts to protect, guard and encourage in her efforts to advance. For in spite of our inclination to evade the truth and seek some other way of settling a so-called "Perplexing Problem" we are to remain a distinct people in this country for many generations to come; and as a distinct people, apart from others, we must bear our part in the nation's progressive and onward movement; and this Negro woman is to be the mother of those men and women that must take their place in the ranks of this progressive army. Therefore it is our duty to begin the work of properly safeguarding the mother of our children. As was the case with other nations and races, quite a few of our African ancestors, having lost their power and prestige, retrograded, lapsed into barbarism; and for more than a thousand years Africa was and is still the prey of the plunderer and the slave catcher. And

29 Benjamin Tucker Tanner (1835–1923), author and eighteenth bishop of the African Methodist Episcopal Church.

30 Of the Hamites, people believed to have descended from Noah's son, Ham.

31 The legendary queen of ancient Abyssinia who, according to the Bible, visited Solomon after hearing of his famed wisdom.

32 Of Canaan, the "promised land" of the Jews in today's Palestine.

33 Ancient people who lived in Anatolia and Syria from c. 1800 B.C. to c. 1200 B.C.

of all the slave markets of the world America was the most lucrative; and to put a trifle more than three million Negroes in this country it cost the mother country millions human lives by murder, starvation and drowning. When we have advanced to that stage where the intrinsic worth of the purity of womanhood is known and appreciated we will then realize the degrading influences of American slavery. A nation cognizant of the worth of pure womanhood and boastful of the purity and chastity of its women denied it to the slave woman, and endeavored to crush out of her every innate, pure and ennobling attribute. She came to this country pure, and ignorant of the evils of civilization, to be taught to look upon sin as an honor. A nation boastful of its chivalry brazenly made one of the chief staples of its commerce the concubinage of its slave women. The Jews in Egypt[34] were slaves to the government only, and were employed upon government works; there was no extensive individual ownership as was the case in America. The Jew was therefore permitted to keep his household intact and cling to his religion and family traditions. The American master owned his slaves body and soul so to speak; and unrestrainedly led the pace in debauchery and seduction; and the ignorant, misguided black emulated his example. The close of this regime[35] found the Negro with nothing but his freedom in return for two centuries of degradation and unrequited toil. His upward strides have been wonderful along some lines; no other race has made such progress. He has reduced his illiteracy forty-five per cent and accumulated many millions in real, personal and church property. But, unfortunately, the building of the social structure has been slow and tedious. While the former master with sympathy for his ex-slave, would rent him land reasonably, lend him money, trust him with provisions and seed for his planting, and otherwise encourage him to get a foothold, on the other hand he thought nothing of enticing that Negro's wife, or robbing his daughter of her chastity. What he could no longer accomplish by force he now secured by appeals to ignorance, poverty and love of gaudy display. Then again, the Negro's eagerness for wealth spurred him on in its pursuit to the neglect of other equally important things. Plainly speaking, the essentials of race integrity and strength, virtue, honor and esteem were and are still secondary considerations to the bulk of the race. "Get Money! Get Homes!" is the popular cry. But what does that home amount to that cannot be defended; whose

34 The Egyptian exile of the enslaved Jews is recorded in Exodus.
35 Slavery was legally abolished in the United States in 1865, about six months after the collapse of the Confederate States of America.

sanctity can be invaded and despoiled by the lawless among the dominant race who refuse to concede to the Negro the right to guard and defend it. Many of the reports of lynchings for crime in the South are the result of the feeble yet brave efforts of some Negro man to defend the honor of wife or daughter by shooting to death some bold intruder into his home. The "Charlotte Observer"[36] a leading white southern organ in an editorial some time ago on the "Curse of the South" mentions an instance in South Carolina where a crippled Negro with but one arm and a deformed foot killed one of the two armed white men in the act of entering his home to attack his daughter. Although one of the men exonerated the Negro upon the witness stand by confessing his evil designs in entering or seeking to enter that house, this obscure hero was sentenced to imprisonment. Such actions on the part of a prejudiced jury should not deter the Negro in his efforts to protect his home; for such acts are more potent evidences of race advancement than the marvelous accumulation of wealth.

In the south (the north as well) after forty or more years removed from chattel slavery the Negro woman is still a slave, by law and public sentiment a debased, unworthy creature, it matters not what her character, aims or ambitions may be. Sanctioned by law and public sentiment, the Philistine mobocrat[37] protects (?) the woman of one race, and by the sanction of that same law and public sentiment entices, debauches and wrecks the woman and child of the other race and laughs at her from behind its strong (?) bulwark of defense. Right in those sections where race feeling runs highest, where black men are lynched, burned and flayed alive, this state of things obtains; the lyncher with his hands besmeared with blood seeks to consort with the wife, sweetheart or sister of his victim. When I was a boy in the south, the most popular Negro woman (among the whites) of my town was the courtesan,[38] the unchangeable believer in the inferiority of her own people; the woman who kept the house of ill-fame filled with the handsomest women and girls of her race for the exclusive pleasure of the white man; who spread her net to ensnare innocents and entice them into the clutches of the enemy. This harlot could enter any store and receive more attention than the wife of a Negro legislator; she could chat familiarly with the clerks and have her goods sent on "approval." In the city of Washington, D.C., there flourished for many years a house of ill-fame known as "Mahogany Hall." This questionable

36 A daily newspaper published in Charlotte, North Carolina, since 1886.
37 Someone who is guided by material-ism and swayed by the opinions of others.
38 A prostitute, usually with an upper-class clientele.

DAVID BRYANT FULTON

resort bid for the most beautiful and refined women of the Negro race. It required as much red tape[39] to become an inmate of this institute of prostitution as it did to get a lucrative government position; the applicant had to be vouched for by some Senator or Representative or other dignitary. These women were there for the exclusive pleasure of the men who make the nation's laws; the men who, in regulating and passing upon Interstate Commerce laws have sweepingly jim-crowed[40] all Negro women travellers upon railroads, placing them (good and bad) in the same category. Why this state of affairs? Why is not the manhood and the racial pride of the Negro man aroused? Why do such conditions the country over apparently meet the approval of the black man? The weak-kneed advance environment as an excuse for inaction; the Negro woman realizing the poverty and physical inability of man of her race to support, protect and defend her, naturally falls a victim to the flatteries of the other man; "as long as we have no money we can not control our women." This is the silliest rot ever advanced by a coward. There has been no woman among the degradingly environed, more hampered by poverty than the Jewish woman and there has been no man more helpless to defend the woman of his race than the Jew has been at times. He has stood helplessly by and gazed upon the humiliation of wife and daughter without the power to raise hand or voice in protest; yet through it all the Jewish woman's devotion to the man of her race is unsurpassed the world over.

PART II

The Negro in the North

No men of any race have the right to boast of education or wealth whose women are under the control and domination of the men of another race. No men deserve the respect of others who are not righteously jealous of their women; who willingly surrender them to the enemy and make excuses for their "weakness." Here in New York the Negro is almost exclusive landlord of the Harlem "Black Belt,"[41] and in less than a decade will own from 132nd street to the Harlem river and from Fifth to Ninth av-

39 Official procedures of bureaucratic regulation that are excessively complicated.
40 Racial segregation laws in the South after Reconstruction were referred to as Jim Crow laws.
41 The section of New York City in upper Manhattan that borders on the Harlem and East rivers. After African Americans first moved to Harlem in the early 1900s, this part of Manhattan rapidly became a center of black culture.

enues. Yet, in his own domain, under his own vine and fig tree, he stands and looks on unmoved while the white libertine from every other section of the city flocks there to consort with the women and girls of his race, a thing which if attempted by a Negro with the most obscure white street walker, in a white settlement, would precipitate a race riot. The white man looking for a good time at little cost seeks the "nigger wenches" in Harlem, or scours Hudson and Myrtle avenues in Brooklyn without as much as a word of protest from a single black man or boy. Why is this? To the average Negro it's a sop of "social equality"[42] or she's "gitt'n th' money." The apologist says further; "The Negro woman and girl unwilling to work takes to the streets and of course to the man who can furnish her with luxuries." Such an excuse might have some weight in the South where concubinage is still a custom; where white men are advised to sow their wild oats among the women of the race who have "no rights they are bound to respect;" where open adultery with the woman of our race does not affect his social standing. There the black mistress does receive considerable clandestine attention and in some instances lives in comparative ease and comfort. But here in the North it is different; there are too many white street walkers prowling about the streets looking for white men. To hotels, clubs and cafes frequented by men of means, the white prostitute has the free access and of course monopolizes the paying business. White men who frequent black communities are usually small-salaried clerks and laborers who have no more money to give to women than the Negro. The heart of a REAL MAN bleeds when he sees girls of tender age beautiful to look upon, buttonholing old, vermin-eaten white men upon the streets of our cities. To these ignorant creatures and their sympathizers this is "social equality" for they will turn and stare with amazement if rebuked by a man or woman of the race. No amount of money these women and girls can get will compensate for the risks to life and health from exposure in standing about the streets, upon stoops and in hallways and from loathsome diseases which send thousands of them into unmarked graves yearly. Visit their haunts and look at these bloated, poorly clad, poorly nourished creatures whose money is received from lecherous white men and is squandered by Negro loafers and be convinced that the woman working in service at twelve dollars a month is better off. That such a life for the Negro woman in the North is more lucrative than honest toil is a brazen untruth. This state of affairs will

42 Social interaction between whites and blacks decried by white racists as a prelude to intermarriage.

exist north and south as long as the Negro feels that the white man is entitled to the best he has, even the affections of the women of his race. In the south he charters the excursion train and advertises; "Special car for white folks" and gives the other man's wife the best car in the safest place on the train and gives his own wife a seat next to the engine and nearest danger. If the white man condescends to pay a visit to the Negro church that Negro's wife, mother, sister, sweetheart must surrender her seat if necessary, that the white god's wife, mother, sweetheart or sister may sit. If fear that the mind of our leading men is set too hopefully upon the—at present impracticable—yea impossible thing as a solution of the so-called "Race Problem" namely "Amalgamation," "Race Absorption" etc.[43] At the recent Race Congress held in London[44] where representatives of every race met to discuss and to devise means of closer union, it was left to the American Negro, in the person of one Prof. Finch of Wilberforce University to appear before that great body with a hand-licking and crawling proposition; "Race Blending," "Cross Breeding" as a means of "improving the stock," nothing more or less than an appeal to the vanity of white race and to the weakness of black women. Prof. Finch unwittingly proved that the American Negro was the only race that wished to be legislated or "cross breeded" off the earth for its own good. He mentions conditions in the Hawaiian and Tahiti Islands and the mulattoes in America as "superior in fertility, vitality and cultured worth to both of the parent stock" etc. Shall we the men of the Negro race in America continue to consent to the "improvement of the stock" as of old, at the expense of the chastity of our women? Not a single Negro man has been an instrument in the hands of God in the straightening of one hair or changing a single eye from brown to blue. He who deems intermarriage of races the surest solution of the race problem and that the accumulation of wealth on the part of the Negro will bring about the desired end "thinketh as the fool thinketh." Marriage is a contract made binding by love. Love is the greatest of the three Graces.[45] Love honors, protects, defends its object; Love is open, frank, loyal, true; it will not belittle, degrade nor defame. Let us not confound lust and criminal pas-

43 The idea that light-skinned African Americans should lose their racial identities by intermarrying with whites.

44 The Universal Race Congress of 1911. W. E. B. Du Bois and Franz Boas were among the 100 people

from fifty nations who attended the congress held at the University of London to oppose the eugenics movement.

45 In classical mythology, the goddesses of beauty, daughters of Zeus and Eurynome.

sion with this holy and most sacred of the three Graces. The white man does not love the black woman nor the mulatto woman, nor the octoroon woman[46], nor the quadroon woman.[47] He loves the white woman and the white woman only; for it is only the white woman whom he honors and protects. He is determined that the Negro man shall not encroach upon his domain and controls the situation by keeping the black man before her eyes in his most hideous aspect. In no white newspaper will you see the black man spoken of in any other but in a degrading, compromising manner; he is addicted to the "usual crime;"[48] he's a brute, a rapist, a menace to society. Every effort is put forward to keep alive her prejudice and fear. If in public places she essays to be civil to a colored man, enquiring, jealous eyes riveted upon her; and if she presumes to be independent in thought and action to the extent of recognizing the manliness of the Negro, she is immediately pounced upon by press and public. The white woman who braves the tirade of abuse that is sure to follow and clings to the man of our race, surely has sacrificed much. At the Alabama Conference which was convened at Montgomery in the spring of 1900 to discuss the "Negro Problem" John Temple Graves of Atlanta, Ga.,[49] speaking of assaults by Negroes upon white women said:

"Assemblages in the North frequently pass resolutions condemning lynching but never the crime for which it is the penalty." He advised the assembly or conference to appeal to the northern people to condemn in their resolutions not only lynchings, but also the unspeakable crime, deadlier than murder and more atrocious than assassination."

"Mr. Clinton R. Breckenridge of Arkansas[50] followed Mr. Graves, and spoke at length on the question of criminal assault upon white women. He approached the subject with much diffidence and many misgivings. When such a crime is perpetrated, it presents to the mind so many elements of horror that its calm and judicial contemplation becomes almost a matter of impossibility. The investigator who does not recognize the difference in the Anglo Saxon mind, at least that portion of it which resides in the South, and which must of necessity administer the remedy,

46 A person of one-eighth African American ancestry.
47 A person of one-fourth African American ancestry.
48 Rape of white women.
49 John Temple Graves (1856–1932), newspaper editor and public speaker. As the editor of newspapers in At-

lanta, Georgia, he was blamed for fueling racial animosity that exploded in the Atlanta riots of September 1906.
50 Clifton Rodes Breckenridge (1846–1932), cotton planter, diplomat, and congressman from Arkansas.

between assaults on white women by men of their own race, and those by men of a race deemed so inferior, that voluntary relations with it, if lawful would be considered the deepest degradation to which a white woman could descend."

Five hundred white women sat and listened to the whimperings of this special pleader, not one of who had the courage to stand up, and pointing her finger at him as Nathan of old,[51] and exclaim: "Thou art the man! Whose contemplation of illicit relations with the women of that race presents no horrors: Thou art the man! who for two hundred and fifty years reveled in the sin you now so loudly condemn." But it was a white man that spoke, and in defence of white women and white women only. Why should they say a word for the alien? Has the Negro woman remembered that in these wild shoutings for the protection of womanhood she is not considered; if she is to be protected, honored and safeguarded at all, it is to be done by the men of her own race; the other man seeks only her degradation. The Negro man must wake up to the full realization of his position in this country. If he is to hold his own and be counted among those who shall survive as "the fittest"[52] it is to be through the chastity and purity of the woman. To this end, he must lay more stress upon the acquisition of these requisites than upon face bleach and hair straightener. Appearance has nothing whatever to do with character; and if the woman cannot "improve" her "stock" honorably, let it go unimproved. We are the only people that love enemies; and to love them that hate us only begets justly merited contempt. "Love them that love you" is the maxim of races. The salvation of the Jew lay in his ability to hate enemies; and a race can have no worse enemy than he who seeks to degrade its women. That time is past when concubinage should be winked at and hailed as a benefaction. The love of that woman is surely unnatural that goes out to the man of a race that seeks her only under cover of darkness, to bask in her smiles, flatter her into sin; or in public places shun her as a viper, or among the women of the other race, hold her up to ridicule; who jim-crows her on trains and in places of amusement, publicly denounces her as being without honor, without virtue, points her out to men of her own race and boasts of his conquests. The average man likes to contemplate woman as a kind of goddess, a little above him; and there is no man, it matters not how low and depraved, but likes to boast of a pure mother, or

51 2 Samuel 12:7. Nathan the prophet was sent to chastise King David for causing the death of Uriah in order to take his wife, Bathsheba.

52 An allusion to the notion of "survival of the fittest" introduced into popular discourse by Charles Darwin's writings on evolution.

sister, or wife. If we would win our women from strange gods,[53] we must see that all that is beautiful, all that is desirable, all that is lovable [are] beneath and in the colored skin; and show her that attention and respect in public places and in the home that will encourage her to act her noblest and be her best. The woman should not be allowed to feel that beautiful skin and hair are more essential than purity of soul and character. Our greatest drawback in our struggles upward is our ignorance of our own history; to realize our own worth and possibilities.

53 See Genesis 35:2. "Put away the strange gods that are among you, and be clean."

　　　　DAVID BRYANT FULTON

TIMELINE

1669   British Lords Proprietors legalize and encourage Negro slavery in the charter of the new Carolina colony.

1712   Black population of North Carolina colony numbers approximately 800, mostly in the tobacco-planting eastern part of the state.

1715   North Carolina General Assembly enacts the state's first slave code, intended to define and regulate the slave population.

1720   South Carolina planters begin to settle the Lower Cape Fear region of the state, bringing with them rice culture and slaves.

1774   North Carolina bars the importation of slaves from other countries.

1776   Declaration of Independence published in Philadelphia. North Carolina passes a state constitution in which no provision is made to deny free blacks the right to vote. Quakers in North Carolina state public opposition to slaveholding.

1781   British surrender at Yorktown, Virginia, ends American Revolution.

1787   U.S. Constitution ratified, classifying a slave as three-fifths of a person for the sake of congressional apportionment.

1790   U.S. census indicates 31 percent of North Carolina families own slaves.

1791   Slave revolt in Saint-Domingue (now Haiti).

c. 1796   David Walker born in Wilmington, N.C.

c. 1797   George Moses Horton born in Northampton County, N.C.

1802   Slave insurrection rumors cause unrest in northeastern North Carolina.

1803   Lunsford Lane born in Raleigh, N.C.

1808   U.S. Congress outlaws the international slave trade.

1812   War of 1812.

1813   Harriet Ann Jacobs born in Edenton, N.C.

1815   Moses Roper born in Caswell County, N.C.

1829   George Moses Horton's *The Hope of Liberty* published in Raleigh. *David Walker's Appeal* published in Boston.

1830   North Carolina General Assembly prohibits teaching slaves to read or write. Death of David Walker in Boston.

1831	Nat Turner slave rebellion in Southampton County, Va.
1835	Revised North Carolina Constitution ends suffrage for free blacks.
1837	Moses Roper's *The Adventures and Escape of Moses Roper, from American Slavery* is published in London.
1838	U.S. government forcibly removes most Cherokee Indians from North Carolina to Indian Territory across the Mississippi River.
1839	Stephen Slade, a slave, discovers method of curing bright leaf tobacco.
1840	First public schools open in North Carolina.
1842	Lunsford Lane publishes *Narrative of Lunsford Lane* in Boston.
1845	*The Poetical Works of George M. Horton* is published in Hillsborough, N.C. *Narrative of the Life of Frederick Douglass, an American Slave* is published in Boston.
1846–48	War with Mexico.
1850–51	Raleigh *Register* and Wilmington *Daily Journal* become the state's first daily newspapers.
1857	Free suffrage amendment is adopted by North Carolina General Assembly.
1858	Charles Waddell Chesnutt born in Cleveland, Ohio. Anna Julia Cooper born in Raleigh, N.C.
1860	U.S. Census indicates 361,522 black residents of North Carolina, 36.5 percent of the state population; 30,463 free African Americans live in the state.
1861	North Carolina secedes from the Union. Harriet Jacobs's *Incidents in the Life of a Slave Girl* is published in Boston.
1863	David Bryant Fulton born in Fayetteville, N.C. Union army wins a decisive victory at the battle of Gettysburg in Pennsylvania.
1865	General William Tecumseh Sherman's army occupies Chapel Hill. President Abraham Lincoln assassinated. George Moses Horton's *Naked Genius* is published in Raleigh, N.C. North Carolina blacks convene in Raleigh to call for justice and equal rights.
1867	Congressional Reconstruction Act is passed. North Carolina becomes a part of the Second Military District.
1868	W. W. Holden, a Republican, elected governor. Revised state constitution establishes public schools for all. North Carolina readmitted to the Union.

1870	Proclaiming Alamance and Caswell counties in a state of insurrection, Governor Holden calls in federal troops.
1871	Holden impeached by Democrats in General Assembly and removed from office.
1874	R. J. Reynolds and Washington Duke build tobacco factories in Winston, N.C., and Durham, N.C.
1877	Zebulon B. Vance, a Democrat, becomes governor. Democrats regain control of state government. Federal troops are withdrawn from the South by order of President Rutherford B. Hayes. General Assembly establishes State Colored Normal School (now Fayetteville State University), the first teacher-training school for blacks in the South.
1882	African American James E. O'Hara of New Bern elected to U.S. House of Representatives from North Carolina's Second District.
1892	Anna Julia Cooper publishes *A Voice from the South* in Xenia, Ohio.
1894	Populists and Republicans fuse to gain control of state government.
1895	Booker T. Washington delivers his "Atlanta Exposition" speech in Atlanta.
1896	Daniel L. Russell, a Republican, is elected governor on the Fusion ticket, as 87 percent of eligible black voters go to the polls. African American George H. White of New Bern elected to Congress from the Second District (the last black person elected to Congress from the South until the 1960s). *Plessy v. Ferguson* U.S. Supreme Court decision confirms "separate but equal doctrine."
1897	Death of Harriet Jacobs in Washington, D.C.
1898	Red Shirt campaign enables Democrats to regain control of North Carolina legislature. Spanish-American War begins. African American John Merrick founds the North Carolina Mutual Insurance Company in Durham. White supremacists seize Wilmington, terrorizing the black population.
1899	Charles Chesnutt's *The Conjure Woman* published by Houghton Mifflin in Boston, which also publishes later in the year Chesnutt's *The Wife of His Youth and Other Stories of the Color Line*.
1900	Constitutional amendment is adopted in North Carolina providing for a literacy test and a grandfather clause,

effectively disfranchising black North Carolinians. Chesnutt's *The House Behind the Cedars* is published by Houghton Mifflin. David Bryant Fulton publishes *Hanover; or, The Persecution of the Lowly* in Philadelphia.

1901　Chesnutt's *The Marrow of Tradition* is published by Houghton Mifflin.

1907　David Bryant Fulton publishes *Eagle Clippings* in New York.

1909　National Association for the Advancement of Colored People founded in New York City.

1914　World War I begins in Europe.